Patterns of Fashion 1

Englishwomen's dresses & their construction c.1660-1860

WRITTEN AND ILLUSTRATED BY

JANET ARNOLD

CONTENTS

© Janet Arnold 1964, 1972

Republished with corrections 1972
Reprinted 1975
New Edition 1977 by
DRAMA BOOK SPECIALISTS/PUBLISHERS
New York
Library of Congress Catalog Card Number 76-189820
ISBN 0-910482-50-0

Reprinted 1978

Detailed list of drawings and patterns taken from original specimens

Acknowledgements and Introduction

I should like to thank the Directors, Curators and Assistants of the following Museums and Costume Collections for all their kindness and help while I was drawing the dresses and taking patterns.

The Gallery of English Costume, Platt Hall, Manchester.

Gloucester Museum.

The Laing Municipal Art Gallery and Museum, Newcastle-upon-Tyne.

The London Museum.

Northampton Museum.

The Salisbury, South Wilts and Blackmore Museum.

The Verney Collection, Claydon House, near Aylesbury (National Trust).

The Victoria and Albert Museum, London.

The Wade Collection, Snowshill Manor, near Broadway (National Trust).

My thanks are also due to the Trustees of the British Museum and the Victoria and Albert Museum Public Relations Department, for permission to print all the extracts and illustrations from the books in their care. I am very grateful to the staffs of these two Museum Libraries and the Bristol Reference Library for their assistance in tracing remote dressmaking terms, as well as their helpfulness at all times.

I am indebted to Miss Joan Godber, Bedford County Archivist, for providing a photograph of the letter from Christine Williamson, which was published in the Bedfordshire Historical Records Society's Publication, vol.xxxiv, 1954, edited by the late F. J. Manning; to Sidgwick and Jackson for permission to use extracts from *The Purefoy Letters*, edited by G. Eland in 1931; to Dr J. Henry for her assistance with the translation of *Le Tailleur Sincere*, *L'Art du Tailleur* and *L'Art de la Lingere*; to Miss Anne Buck, of the Gallery of English Costume, Platt Hall, for all her help and information about the wrapping gown at the Laing Municipal Art Gallery and Museum and allowing me to quote from her copy of *The Book of Trades;* to Miss Natalie Rothstein, of the Victoria and Albert Museum Textile Department, for her assistance with dating the fabrics of the eighteenth century dresses and the information from *The Gazette and New Daily Advertiser* about silk measurements in 1765.

Finally, I should like to thank Mrs Leslie Ginsburg (Miss Madeleine Blumstein), of the Victoria and Albert Museum Textile Department, for her help with dating the costumes and information about the model fashion dolls and *The Academy of Armory* by Randle Holme. Her interest, help and advice during the preparation of this book have been invaluable.

So much has already been written about costume that I feel some explanation is due for producing yet another work on the subject. There are already a few books containing some patterns of women's costumes, notably *A History of Costume* by Carl Koehler, *Dress Design* by Talbot Hughes and *Histoire de Costume* by Maurice Leloir, but there is very little information available about pattern cutting and the construction of dresses. This book deals with the period c.1660–1860 and will be followed by the publication of a volume covering the period from c.1860 into the twentieth century. It is a practical guide to cutting period costumes for use with the books listed on page 76 and is not intended to be a complete history of women's costume of the period. I hope it will prove useful for craft-work in schools and colleges, for people of any age who would find making model dolls and dressing them in period costume an enjoyable hobby, for students of dress and historic costume and those working in the amateur and professional theatre.

Unfortunately there are bound to be some gaps – due in the early years to shortage of material and in the later years to shortage of space, but the costumes I have selected give a general outline of two hundred year's fashions in dresses. In addition to the studies of dresses with details of their construction and scale patterns ($\frac{1}{8}''=1''$), I have given a brief history of pattern cutting and dressmaking, composed of extracts from contemporary letters, magazines and books, translated and edited where necessary. (I offer no apologies for using French sources of information, since French fashions and fabrics were constantly crossing the Channel. The main difference between French and English dresses, then as now, is that the English styles are not quite as exaggerated as the French and the cut may be a little less complicated). Anyone attempting to make a model or a full scale costume is advised to read this history first, where much supplementary information on construction will be found.

All the dresses have been dated from contemporary prints, portraits, fabrics, fashion-plates or photographs. The eighteenth century specimens are the most difficult to date and therefore the type of fabric used was the deciding factor in several cases. Fashions overlap each other and change gradually. For that reason I have claimed a certain amount of latitude with 'circa'. Usually a style is worn first by the young and fashionable and then adopted more widely. It finally disappears with provincial society and the older generation, who are the last to accept it.

I should like to make it clear to students that it is not necessary to unpick costumes in order to take patterns. The dresses in this book were measured carefully and the patterns are accurate to within approximately $\frac{1}{4}''$. Any inaccuracies are due to the difficulty of showing details under $\frac{1}{4}''$ when reduced on $\frac{1}{8}''$ squared paper.

DESIGNED BY ALAN MYCROFT · PRINTED IN GREAT BRITAIN BY LOWE & BRYDONE PRINTERS LTD

Pattern cutting and dressmaking c.1660-1860

A selection of extracts from contemporary sources

The purpose of this selection of extracts is to show, by means of contemporary accounts, how news of the latest fashions was exchanged and to give a general idea of early pattern construction and dressmaking methods.

News of the changing fashions was conveyed by letters, newspaper accounts and by little dolls dressed in the latest styles, supplemented from c.1770 onwards by engraved plates printed in magazines. From c.1790 these were coloured by hand. Dressmakers would have shown these fashion-plates to their customers as we use a pattern book today.

There is very little detailed information on the subject of patterns and dressmaking until the end of the eighteenth century. Prints show tailors measuring ladies for corsets and gowns, while diagrams of patterns with instructions for making up the garments are given in a few books, the earliest one I have been able to find for this period being the Lady's Riding Coat from *Le Tailleur Sincere*, a book printed in 1671. *L'Art du Tailleur* and *L'Art de la Lingere*, published in 1769 and 1771 respectively, contain interesting information on the varying measurements of cloth as well as patterns and instructions for dressmaking.

At the end of the eighteenth century there are several patterns of women's garments included in pamphlets for those desirous of doing 'good works'. The earliest advertisement I have found for paper patterns, which were sold to professional rather than home dressmakers, is in *The World of Fashion*, October 1836.

From c.1840 home dressmaking rapidly gained in popularity with the middle classes and their large families of daughters. There are books which give diagrams of patterns and information on the construction of dresses. These books were supplemented by the printed paper sheets of full-size bodice and sleeve patterns which were included in magazines. The earliest ones I have found are French and date from 1844, although there are earlier magazine patterns for embroidered cuffs and collars.

All the dresses illustrated in this book were stitched entirely by hand and some of the workmanship is exquisite. Hand sewing was not generally replaced by mechanical means until c.1860, although the first lock-stitch sewing machine, invented by Elias Howe, was patented in Washington in 1846, followed in 1851 by Isaac Singer's machine. After c.1860 it becomes increasingly rare to find a costume made entirely by hand. 1860 seems therefore to be the logical date at which to conclude this study of costume. The advent of the sewing machine enabled the dressmaker to make far more complicated dresses with quantities of trimming. The wider variety of styles and more rapid changes of fashion require a separate volume to cover them adequately.

Le Tailleur Sincere – contenant ce qu'il faut observer pour bien tracer, couper et assembler toutes les principales pièces qui se sont dans la profession de Tailleur (1671)

BENOIT BOULLAY
The Victoria & Albert Museum
A Lady's Riding Coat
(*Pour un manteau de femme à cheval*)

Take a square piece of cloth and, starting with the back, leave a quarter of the height to make the curves, allowing the same at the back as at the shoulder. These can be drawn out to form a semi-circle in the way I have shown already, for *La Robe de Prince* and *La Robe de Palais*. (From *Pour la Robe de Prince* – 'It is necessary to round off the back curve twice . . . as the robe will hang badly if only one curve is made'). When the curves have been marked, the lengths must be taken. They may be half an ell (approx. 21 French inches) and a twelfth (approx. 3½ French inches). [Author's note: 1 English ell=45 English inches: 1 French ell=approx. 43 French inches, which is equal to approx. 46½ English inches.] Place a thread on the corner of the square marked A and take it down the centre back to point F. Swing it out to the side as far as point E.

After taking the length of the front, measure the breadth of the shoulders of the person who will wear the coat. A sixth (approx. 7¼ French inches) could be allowed for this measurement, three twelfths (approx. 10¾ French inches) for the curve of the neckline and a third (approx. 14½ French inches) for the measurement from the front to the side seam at point H. However, it is always better to take the measurements on the figure, as the front is adjusted to fit the body by means of two wide ribbons, which are attached under the fronts beside the armholes. The ribbons wind round the back and come to tie again in front beneath the coat, so that the material in the back and sides is pleated and floats gracefully. When the front and back are joined together, the curve marked C is pleated in to fit the width of the shoulder yoke. The side is joined up and the curve marked D forms the armhole. The curve of the collar, which is marked L, is pleated to fit into the neckline. The sleeve is pleated where necessary to fit the armhole.

The Academy of Armory and Blazon (Book III) (1688)
RANDLE HOLME
The Victoria and Albert Museum
Terms used by Taylors

In a WOMAN'S GOWN there are these several parts, as
The STAYES, which is the body of the gown before the sleeves are put to or covered with the outward stuff: which have these peeces in it and terms used about it.

The FORE PART, or FORE-BODY, which is the breast part which has two peeces in it.

The TWO SIDE PARTS, which are peeces under both arms on the sides

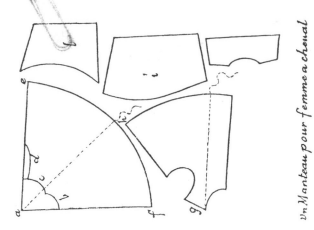

1 A pattern for a Lady's Riding Habit. From 'Le Tailleur Sincere'.

The BACK

The SHOULDER HEADS or SHOULDER STRAPS; are two peeces that come over the Shoulders and are fastened to the Fore-body: through which the Arms are put.

SCORING or STRICK LINES on the canvice to sew straight.

STITCHING is sewing all along the lines with close stitches to keep the whalebone each peece from other: cleaving the whalebone to what substance or thickness the workman pleaseth.

BONING THE STAYES, is to put the slit bone into every one of the places made for it between each stitched line which makes Stays or Bodies stiff and strong.

CORDY-ROBE SKIRTS to the Stays are such Stays as are cut into Labells at the bottom, like long slender skirts.

LINING THE BODIES or STAYS; is covering the inside of the Stayes with Fustian, Linen and such like.

BINDING THE NECK is sewing Galloon at the edge of the Neck.

EYLET HOLES or EIGLET HOLES, little round holes whipt-stitched about, through which laces are drawn to hold one side close to the other.

The STOMACHER is that peece as lieth under the lacing or binding on of the Body of the Gown, which said Body is sometimes in fashion to be.

OPEN BEFORE, that is to be laced on the Breast.

OPEN BEHIND, laced on the Back, which fashion hath always a Maid or Woman to dress the wearer.

The PEAKE is the bottom or point of the Stomacher whether before or behind.

A BUSK, it is a strong piece of Wood or Whalebone thrust down the middle of the Stomacher to keep it straight and in compass that the Breast nor Belly shall not swell too much out. These Busks are usually made in length according to the necessity of the persons wearing it: if to keep in the fullness of the Breasts then it extends to the Navel: if to keep the Belly down, then it reacheth to the Honor.

COVERING the Bodies or Stays, is the laying the outside stuff upon it.

The WINGS are WELTS or PEECES set over the place on top of the Shoulders, where the Body and Sleeves are set together: now Wings are of diverse fashions, some narrow, others broad: some cut in slits, cordyrobe like, others scalloped.

The SLEEVES are those parts of the Gown as covers the Arms: and in these there is as much variety of fashion, as days in the Year.

The SKIRT or GOWN SKIRT: is the lower part of the Gown, which extends from the body to the ground these are made several fashions, as,

OPEN SKIRTS, is open before, that thereby rich and costly Petticoat may be fully seen.

TURNED UP SKIRTS, are such as have a draught on the Ground a yard and more long; these in great Personages are called Trains, whose Honor it is to have them born up by Pages.

BEAVERS, ROWLS, FARDINGALES: are things made purposely to put under the skirts of Gowns at their setting on at the Bodies; which raise up the skirt at that place to what breadth the wearer pleaseth, and as the fashion is.

SKIRTS about the Waist, are either whole in one entire peece with Goares, or else cut into little laps or cordy-robe skirts: Gowns with these skirts are called Waistcoat Gowns.

WAISTCOAT is the outside of a Gown without either stays or bodies fastened to it; it is an Habit or Garment generally worn by the middle and lower sort of Women, having Gored skirts, and some wear them with Stomachers.

GOARE is a Cant or three cornered piece of cloth put into a skirt to make the bottom wider than the top: so are Goared Petticoats.

PETTICOAT is the skirt of a Gown without its body; but that is generally termed a Petticoat, which is worn either under a Gown, or without it: in which Garment there are,

PLEATING, that is gathering the top part in into Pleats or folding to make it of the same wideness as the Waist or middle of the wearer.

LACEING is setting a Lace of Silk, Silver or Gold about the bottom of it.

BORDERING is the lining of the Petticoat skirt or bottom in the inner side.

BINDING is the sewing of some things (as Ribbon, Galloon or such like) on both sides the Edge of the skirt to keep it from ravelling; sometimes it is done by a Hem: the top part of the Petticoat hath its Binding also sewed about the Edges of it, when pleated: which keeps the Pleats in their Pleats, the ends helping to make it fast about the wearer's Waist.

HEM, is the turning of the Edge of the cloth in; two fold or more, then sewing it up, keeps it from ravelling.

TUCKING, is to draw up the depth of a Petticoat being too long by folding a part over another.

POCKET, or Pocket holes: are little Bags set on the inside, with a hole or slit on the outside; by which any small thing may be carried about.

A MANTUA, is a kind of loose Coat without any stays in it, the Body part and Sleeves are of as many

3

fashions as I have mentioned in the Gown Body; but the skirt is sometimes no longer than the Knees, others have them down to the Heels.

THE RIDING SUITE for Women

The HOOD

The CAP

The MANTLE, it is cut round and is cast over the Shoulders to preserve from rain or cold.

The SAFEGUARD, is put about the middle, and so doth secure the Feet from cold and dirt.

The RIDING-COAT, it is a long Coat buttoned down before like a Man's Jacket with Pocket-holes: and the sleeves turned up and buttons.

A Seamster

The Seamster or Seamstry work follows next in order to that of a Taylor; this being work to adorn the Head, Hands and Feet, as the other is for the covering of the Body; nay, very often the Seamster occupieth the room and place of a Taylor in furnishing the Nobility and Gentry with such conveniences as serve the whole body, especially in the Summer season. I shall therefore give you the Terms used about their Employ and then the names of such pieces of work, as is usually done by them.

Terms Used By A Seamster

PATTERNS, Paper cut in fashions according as the Work is to be made.

CUTTING

SHAPING, the ordering the Cloth to be cut.

HEMMING, is sewing up the edges of Linen to keep it from ravelling.

SELVAGE, the outside of the Cloth.

SEAMING, is sewing two selvages together.

RAVELL, vulgarly ROVE, when threads come out of the edges of the cloth.

Names Of Things made By Seamsters

SHIRT or SHIFT for a Man.

SMOCK or WOMAN'S SHIFT

RUFFS, pleated Bands of two or three heights.

ROUND ROBINS, narrow Ruffs only about the Doublet Collar.

CRAVATS, CUFFS

RUFFLES for the hands, both Plain and Laced.

SLEEVES, BIBS, BIGGINS

HANDKERCHIEFS for Women's Necks, both round and square.

WHISKS to be worn with a Gown.

A ROMAN DRESS, the Mantua cut square behind and round before.

WOMEN'S HEAD DRESSES

WOMEN'S SLEEVES

Letters to and from Lady Suffolk from 1712–1767, with notes by J. W. Croker. (Volume I) (1824)

The Victoria and Albert Museum

Lady Lansdowne to Mrs Howard

Paris, 20th August 1727

'. . . I have sent you a little young lady* dressed in the court dress, which I desire you would show to the queen and when she has done with it, let Mrs Tempest have it†. She was dressed by the person that dresses all the princesses here'.

---

*A doll dressed as a pattern of the fashion.
†A celebrated milliner – her portrait is still to be seen on the painted staircase at Kensington Palace.

The Purefoy Letters No. 447, July 15, 1739

H.P. To Anthony Baxter, London

I desire you will send me . . . fine thick printed cotton enough to make two wrappers for my Mother, they must be of two different handsome patterns. You must also send a neat white quilted calico petticoat for my Mother which must be a yard and four inches long.

The Purefoy Letters No. 448, August 5, 1739

Henry Purefoy to Anthony Baxter

I received all the things in the box and have returned you the Marseilles Quilt petticoat by Mr Eagles, the carrier. It is so heavy my mother cannot wear it.

The Purefoy Letters No. 457, June 11, 1741

E.P. to Henry Lloyd

I desire you will send me a very good whalebone hoop petticoat of the newest fashion. It must be three yards and a quarter round the bottom and it must draw in a top for a waist half a yard and a nail round (20$\frac{1}{4}$"), and the length upon the hip to the bottom a yard and half a quarter (40$\frac{1}{2}$"). The last hoop you sent me was so big a top it would not draw in to my waist by half a quarter of a yard (4$\frac{1}{2}$").

To Henry Lloyd at Long's warehouse
the corner of Tavistock Street in
Covent Garden, London

The Purefoy Letters No. 232, February 23, 1743

E.P. To Mrs. Mary Sheppard

I received Mrs Sheppard's letter. I hope the maid will do if she can sew well, that is to work fine plain work as mobs and ruffles. If she comes she must bring a Character of her Honesty from the person she hired with last.

The Purefoy Letters No. 471, May 17, 1746

I have sent a blue Damask gown and must desire Nelly to get it cleaned or dyed of any colour it will take best. I have sent some of the same that was cleaned before to be done with this, that it may be all of a colour if it is required to be cleaned or dyed with it.

They say satins are much worn, I desire to know if they be; if they are, pray send me some patterns of a beautiful green satin and some patterns of a fine pretty deep-blue lutestring, and the prices of them.

To Thomas Robotham, London
From Elizabeth Purefoy

The Purefoy Letters No. 484, September 2, 1753

I desire you will send me three quarters of a yard of black silk for an Handkerchief for my neck, three quarters of a yard every way or wider if any – it must

2 A letter giving instructions for trimming a sack dress and petticoat, from Christine Williamson to her brother Edmund, 1764. Bedford County Archives.

be square. And send me a fine Cotton for a Gown with a Cinnamon or yellowish ground flowered very handsomely with shades of colours, and enough for another gown of fashionable cotton with a white ground flowered with colours, of a crown a yard. I have black lace to put about the Handkerchief. If I don't like the gowns I will return them you again.

For Mrs Anne Baxter
a Linen Draper in Dartmouth Street
near the Cockpit, Westminster, London
From E.P. (Elizabeth Purefoy)

The Gazeteer and New Daily Advertiser, (February 5, 1765)

The British Museum

The silk manufacturers, I find, are praying for relief and engaging public compassion in their favour. I am neither their opposer nor advocate; my observations I confine to the breadth of their goods, which in general are only nineteen and a half to twenty one inches, yet they sell them for half an ell, that is, twenty two inches and a half. The lustrings too are only from twenty three inches and an half to twenty four inches, which they call three quarters wide, that is twenty seven inches.

I pray a fixed standard for the breadths (within the selvedge) of all silk; conceiving the present practice a manifest disgrace to the British manufacture.

Mercator

Descriptions des Arts et Métiers faites ou approuvées par Messieurs de l'Académie Royale des Sciences. L'Art du Tailleur – contenant Le Tailleur d'Habits d'Hommes: Les Culottes de Peau; le Tailleur de Corps de Femmes et Enfants: L'Art de la Couturiere et la Marchande des Modes (1769)

FRANÇOIS ALEXANDRE DE GARSAULT

The British Museum and the Victoria and Albert Museum

The Tailor (Le Tailleur d'Habits d'Hommes)

Chapter III On Fabrics

There are so many fabrics of varying widths from which garments are made that I would lose sight of my objective in attempting to give a detailed account here. It is necessary to confine this study to pointing out the ones most frequently used, with their different ell measurements.

FOR THE TOP LAYER

Woollen Materials

The cloths are 1 ell (approx. 43 French inches), 5 quarters (approx. 54 French inches), or 4 thirds (approx. 58 French inches) in breadth.

Silk, Gold and Silver fabrics are about half an ell (approx. 21 French inches) in breadth.

FOR THE LININGS

Cotton cloths are about half an ell (approx. 21 French inches) in breadth. Taffetas for linings are two thirds (approx. 29 French inches) in breadth. [Author's note: 1 English ell=45 inches: 1 French ell =approx. 43 French inches, which is equal to approx. 46½ English inches].

The Corset Maker for Women and Children (*Le Tailleur de Corps de Femmes et Enfants*) No. 17   The Train of a Court Dress

It is made of narrow fabric and is very long, being two ells and a half (approx. 107 French inches) in length. There are six pieces of fabric in the width. Each of these is seven sixteenths wide (approx. 19 French inches). Begin by sewing all the widths of fabric together and then fold the whole piece in half lengthwise. Cut the curve from 1 to 3 as shown in the diagram.

The train of a dress does not need to be lined, unless it is in a brocaded fabric, when the wrong side must be concealed.

The whole of the top edge is pleated from 1 to 2. All these pleats, when brought together, form part of a circle. Four or five hooks are sewn on the edge of the pleats at intervals on either side. Altogether there are ten hooks to be attached to the loops which are sewn at the bottom of the bodice. Two buttons are placed on the second piece of fabric at each side, at the same distance from each other, with a loop behind them on the wrong side of the fabric. A tassel is sewn on the end of each loop. When the loop is caught round the button it lifts up part of the skirt. The train trails on the ground.

The Art of the Dressmaker (*L'Art de la Couturiere*)

Before the year 1675, the Tailors usually made all the clothes worn by both men and women, but in that year Louis XIV decided to give women the right to dress their own sex and since this time the Tailors have kept themselves apart. He created a Company of Dressmakers under the title 'Les Maîtresses Couturieres' and gave them statutes which allowed them to make wrapping gowns, skirts, jackets, hongrelines (which are no longer made) dressing jackets, bodices and other work for women, girls and children of either sex until the age of eight years, but nothing for men, nor the trained over-skirts for gowns, nor corsets.

N.B. The corset makers reserved the right to make corsets and the trained over-skirts for gowns. They shared with the dressmakers the right to dress children until the age of eight years.

The dressmaker has no special tools. A thimble, some needles, some thread, some silk, a pair of scissors and a flat-iron are sufficient for her work.

THE MEASUREMENTS

The measurements are taken with strips of paper following the tailor's method, marking them with

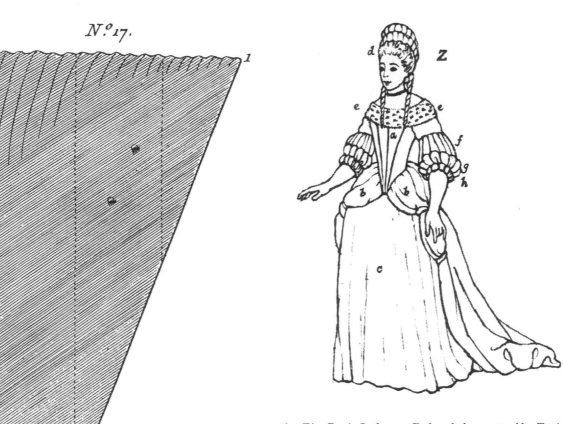

notches. The following are the ones needed for a gown and a petticoat, which are essential for the dressmaker.

(a) The width from one fastening to the other. (b) The neckline. (c) Pleat. (d) *Remonture et entournure** (e) Front. (f) Waist. (g) False front or *compere* (if desired). (h) Sleeve. (i) Back. (l) The width round the hem. (m) The front of the petticoat. (n) The back of the petticoat. (o) The side of the petticoat. (p) *Biais de la Robe*†. (q) The back without a train‡. (r) The front to the ground.

_____

*The term *remonture et entournure* means that the front needs to be several inches longer than the back, so that the *remonture* or part which tailors refer to as the shoulder piece may, after covering the shoulder, be joined to the armhole which is then called the *entournure*. This being in place, joined to the ends of the neckpiece, holds the gown in position from the arm to the nape of the neck.

† *Le Biais* is the place where the gores are attached.

‡With regard to the length of the train, it may be made longer or shorter, as desired.

4   *Fig Z. A Lady; a. Body of the gown; bb. Trained overskirt of the gown; c. Petticoat; d. Hairstyle completed with rows of ribbons; ee. Lace collar. This mode, except for the hairstyle, is still worn at Court as ceremonial dress under the name of 'Robe de Cour' or 'Grand Habit'. Plate II from 'L'Art du Tailleur'.*

3   *A pattern of a train for a court dress. Plate XIV from 'L'Art du Tailleur'.*

THE MEASUREMENTS FOR AN ORDINARY GOWN AND PETTICOAT.

The dressmaker generally uses narrow fabrics about half an ell (approx. 21 French inches) wide.

FOR THE GOWN.

Length – an ell and a third (approx. 57 French inches).

Width of the back – two ells (approx. 86 French inches), or four widths joined together.

Width of the two fronts – an ell (approx. 43 French inches), or two widths.

Width of the two gores – one quarter (approx. 11 French inches). Allow half this measurement for each one.

For each of the two sleeves – a third (approx. 14½ French inches) square.

For the two rows of flounces for each sleeve – three quarters (approx. 33 French inches) of fabric cut lengthwise.

FOR THE PETTICOAT

Length – two thirds (approx. 29 French inches).

Width – two ells and a half (approx. 107 French inches), or five widths joined together.

THE GOWN

Following your measure cut to the correct length all the pieces of fabric which are needed to make your gown – the four pieces of the back, AA, fig. 1, and the two pieces, one for each front, B, fig. 2. These should be cut a little longer by several inches to allow for the *remonture* and *entournure* explained above. Cut the sleeves, o, fig. 6, and the flounces, pp. fig. 5. Cut the same for the lining.

Assemble the pieces of fabric for the back, stitching one to the other. When all the back, AA, is assembled, pleat half across the width and immediately unpleat it. A light impression of the pleats will be left on the cloth which will show you where you should cut the gores cd, which are joined to both the end widths. These gores are cut to slope outwards, so that at point d they are a *demi-quart* (approx. 5½ French inches) wide.

Take away the gores and cut the armholes e. Cut f as far as the hips, following your measure. You leave the extra, g, in its entirety for the pleats and the distance round the gown. You cut the same for the two fronts, B.

We have just seen that the gores are only half the length of the gown. It is necessary to add that we are referring here only to a round gown to be worn without a hoop petticoat (*panier*). If it were to be placed over a hoop petticoat these gores would not be long enough to reach the hips. In this case they would have to be cut out of an extra piece of fabric.

Tack the lining on top. To tack, or to baste, is to make long stitches which may be about two inches apart, to attach the lining smoothly on top. This tacking is permanent.

Make a row of tacking stitches on the right side from top to bottom of the back of the gown to secure it. You will remove these tacks when the neckline and skirt have been finished.

Arrange the six pleats at the back as shown in fig. 3, one wide pleat in the middle of two narrow ones. The arrangement of half the back pleating is shown in h. Stitch the gores cdcd along the last of the pleats at the side as far as the hem, and then arrange three or four pleats, securing them at the hips, mm, with some herring-bone stitches.

Form the pleat on each front, qq, fig. 4, as far as the top of the *remonture* and make two or three side pleats, nn, fig. 3. These are secured like the others.

Stitch the neck piece, x, fig. 3, which should measure a finger's-breadth on the right side. It is always made of the same fabric as the gown. Fold it over and stitch it down on the inside of the front.

Make a stay on the dotted line, fig. 3, across the back pleats to hold them in position, as they are not stitched to each other. This stay is made on the wrong side in herring-bone stitch at a distance of a twelfth of an ell (approx. 3¾ French inches) below the neckline.

Stitch the *remonture* s, fig. 4, to the armhole l, fig. 3, joining the neckpiece at the back.

Attach the *quarrure*, a rectangular piece of linen or taffeta, which is stitched on the wrong side above the

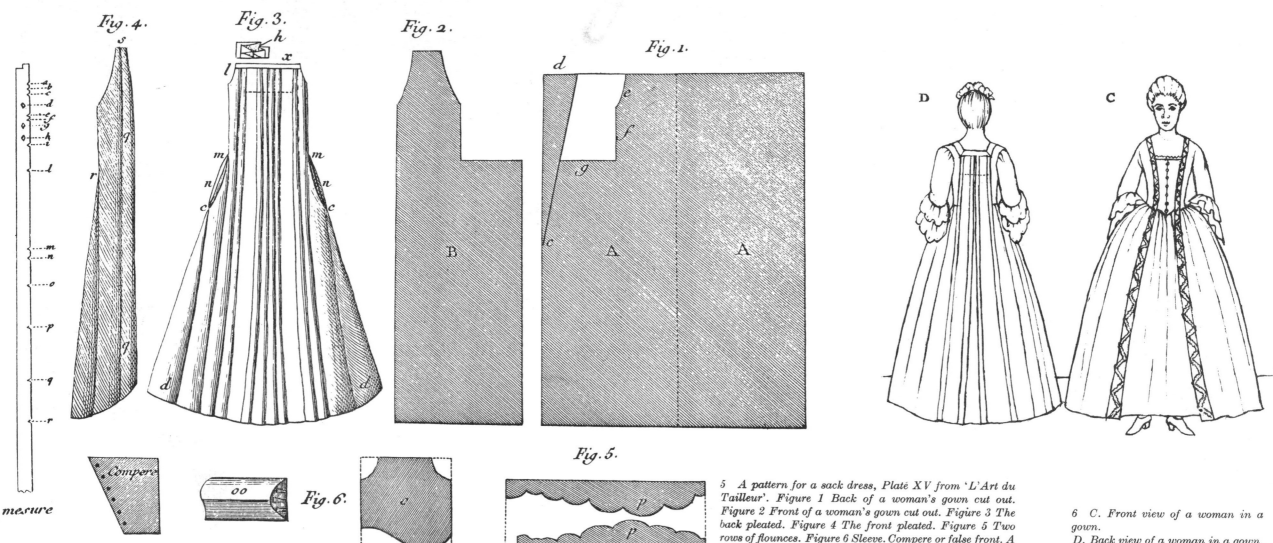

5 A pattern for a sack dress, Plate XV from 'L'Art du Tailleur'. Figure 1 Back of a woman's gown cut out. Figure 2 Front of a woman's gown cut out. Figure 3 The back pleated. Figure 4 The front pleated. Figure 5 Two rows of flounces. Figure 6 Sleeve. Compere or false front. A measure with notches.

6 C. Front view of a woman in a gown.
D. Back view of a woman in a gown. Plate III from 'L'Art du Tailleur'.

lining. This covers the width of the back pleats from the neckline to the waist. It can then be slit open if desired, from the bottom towards the top at the centre back. Tapes or cords are attached here, which are tied if the wearer wishes to be tight-laced.

Make up the gown by joining the two fronts to the back from the armhole, l, fig. 3, as far as the hips, mm, with back stitch and running stitch, the method used for sewing seams. Leave an opening eight inches deep between the side pleats, nn, for the pocket. Continue with the seam and sew the gores on the sloping side to the fronts, as far as the hem.

N.B. The side pleats of round gowns need to be joined together at the bottom of the pocket opening where the gore begins at c. However, for gowns made to be worn over a hoop petticoat the pleats are not formed at the side. The gores must be taken up as far as the hips and the pocket opening is made by the side of the gore and the front.

Line the sleeves, oo, fig. 6. Make them up and gather with running stitches in order to back stitch them to the armholes. Sew the sleeve flounces, pp,

fig. 5, with the narrowest one on top. Make a hem all round the bottom of the gown and on each side of the pocket opening. Stitch these hems. Border the hem of the gown with tape of the same colour as the fabric.

N.B. The greatest difficulty to be found when using fabrics with designs of flowers or divisions, is that of matching and arranging the material correctly while cutting as economically as possible. It is a matter for genius and talent.

At the present moment, as gowns are worn open at the front, the bosom is covered by a row of ribbon bows (an échelle de rubans) mounted on a stomacher piece, or by a false front (a compere). The false front comes within the province of the Dressmaker. The ribbon front, being regarded as a trimming and decorative feature, is within that of the Milliner (Marchande des Modes).

The false front, plate 15, is made of two pieces. These are both arranged to be cut from a square of cloth measuring about a third (approx. 14½ French inches) on all sides, so that one edge of each piece is sloping. Line both of them. A row of buttonholes is worked on

the left piece along the sloping edge and a row of little buttons is stitched on the right one. Both parts of the false front are stitched under the front of the gown so that the sloping edges can button over the bosom from the neckline to the waist.

A Pet-en-l'air is the name given to the top part of an ordinary gown when it hangs approximately a foot below the waist at front and back.

THE PETTICOAT

After cutting the five widths for the petticoat square across and the correct length, join them together, line them and tack the lining down. The top is then pleated up and the petticoat is closed from waist to hem. There are some petticoats where only the pocket openings at each side are left for plackets, but with others a third opening is made at the centre back. For the first type, cords or tapes are attached to one of the side openings to pull in the skirt; with the others, cords are sewn to the opening at the back. All these openings are hemmed. Hems are made at the top and the bottom of the petticoat with tape of the same colour as the fabric.

Descriptions des Arts et Métiers faites ou approuvées par Messieurs de l'Académie Royale des Sciences. L'Art de la Lingere (1771)

FRANÇOIS ALEXANDRE DE GARSAULT
The British Museum and the Victoria and Albert Museum

Chapter I The ell (l'aune) and its divisions reduced to feet (pieds), inches (pouces) and twelfths of an inch (lignes)

The ell measure, a pair of scissors, a needle and a thimble are the only tools the linen draper requires. The ell is the measure which she uses to determine the quantity of linen for which she is asked, or which she judges necessary for any garment within her province. Her terms of expression are the ell, or divisions of the ell [the ell used here is the Parisian ell (l'aune de Paris)], and are not understood by most people. On the other hand the King's foot (le pied de Roi), containing twelve inches, and its subdivision into twelfths of an inch (lignes) are familiar to almost everyone, and every measurement can be reduced to these terms.

The Parisian ell is fixed at 3 feet 7 inches and 8 twelfths. The ell is generally marked on a wooden ruler one inch wide and half an inch thick. It is divided on both sides of its length, on one side into four quarters, the last quarter into two eighths, the last eighth into two sixteenths. On the opposite side it is divided into thirds, the last third into two sixths and the last sixth into two twelfths. The divisions are usually marked with golden nails. Both sides are edged with iron or copper to keep it permanently true.

Instructions for Cutting out Apparel for the Poor. Principally intended for the Assistance of the Patronesses of Sunday Schools and other Charitable Institutions but useful in all Families (1789)
British Museum

AUTHOR'S NOTE

> *This book gives patterns, instructions for making up and quantities of material required for aprons, bonnets, caps, cloaks, petticoats and shifts for girls and women. There are also stay patterns for girls and a few garments for men and boys.*

GOWNS

May be made of stuff or grogram. The former is best for children. There are such a variety of widths and prices that it is not easy to ascertain the value or quantity for the different sizes of gowns; or to give any directions about the larger sizes, as they are generally made (even amongst the poor people) by some whose particular employment it is.

7 *The interior of a Lady's wardrobe showing the garments hung on pegs either by loops or the armholes. From an engraving by Chodowiecki, 1774.*

8 *The engraving shows a corset maker who is taking measurements and another who is cutting the body of a gown. A dressmaker is unfolding cloth and some girls are assembling and stitching various pieces. Plate XIII, from 'L'Art du Tailleur'. By courtesy of the Trustees of the British Museum.*

9 *The engraving shows a linen draper's shop. The proprietress carries a roll of cloth under her arm to show to a lady, in front of whom two assistants are measuring a length of cloth; several other girls are serving in the shop. Plate 1 from 'L'Art de la Lingere.' By courtesy of the Trustees of the British Museum.*

7

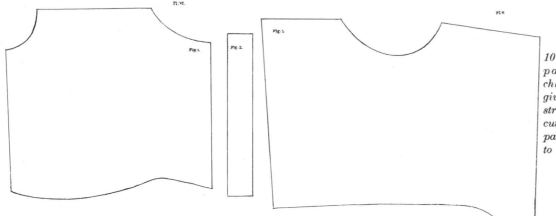

10 A full-size pattern of a child's bodice given in 'Instructions for cutting out Apparel'. Reduced to scale $\frac{1}{4}'' = 1''$.

GOWN NO. 4 (OR SMALLEST SIZE)

Three yards of stuff half a yard wide at 7d per yard make the gown. Half a yard and one nail for the body and sleeves. The breadth doubled down the middle and the half body (Pattern, Plate V, Fig. 1) placed with the selvedges at the top. The shoulder straps (Plate V, Fig. 2) out of the slope at the bottom. The rest of the piece makes the sleeves (Pattern, Plate VI, Fig. 1) the selvedge at the top. The remainder of the stuff cut in three breadths for the skirt, open before, the middle breadth cut about one nail longer than the others, for the slope. The bottom will allow of a broad hem sloping at the corners. This gown will generally require a tuck for a child six or seven years old.

The Taylor's Complete Guide, or a Comprehensive Analysis of Beauty and Elegance in Dress. Containing rules for cutting out garments of every kind and fitting any person with the greatest accuracy and precision, adapted to all sizes, pointing out in the clearest manner the former errors in the profession and the method of rectifying what may have been done amiss. Rendered plain and easy to the meanest capacity (1796)

THE WHOLE CONCERTED AND DEVISED BY A SOCIETY OF ADEPTS IN THE PROFESSION

The British Museum

Section IV   Chapter I   Of Ladies Habits

The present mode of making Riding Habits is much out of the regular method, for such short waists and broad lapels, buttons set so wide and other incongruous maxims that the maker, with all his application, is totally incapable of setting the beautiful finishing of nature in any point of view fit for public inspection.

A few years ago it was a distinguishing merit in the Habit maker to equip a Lady neatly in these habiliments of Diana even when taste was in uniform with the shape of the body. What must it be now, when the rage of extravagance has stripped us of every guide that nature pointed out as a direction for fitting the body? What will future workmen say when we declare the difference and quick transition of fashion in these particulars between 1793, when we were wont to cut waists full nine inches long from under the arm down

to the hip (which by the bye is the choice way of measuring for the length of the waist), and in the year 1796 we have been obliged to cut them but three inches in the same place for the length to figures of the same height and stature?

Habit making is a neat and delicate piece of practice and understood but by few and though by many may be thought a part of the Taylor's branch, is quite dissimilar and as different as joinery and cabinetmaking. Considering the improvement of dress and manners, the popularity, riches and industry of this country within the last thirty years it becomes not only a matter of merit but a course of necessity for every man to make himself acquainted with every part of his business for his own benefit. The luxury and profusion of the times require it. At the era we have mentioned, where there was one Habit made, there are fifty now – for you hardly see a Franklin's wife, or farmer's daughter at a market, fair, or country wake without a Riding Habit on.

With respect to the measuring for a Habit, take the following method:

First measure under the arm straight down to the hollow by the hip, there mark your measure which will be the length of your body. Next down the back seam to the hip, then across half the back. Mark the measure and then proceed to the elbow and down to the hand. Next measure round the arm at the top, and afterwards in as many places as you think proper. Be very correct in measuring round the wrist, as it must fit close and neat. Then measure round the body as for a coat. With respect to the breast be delicate and judicious and take half across with a proper consideration of ease for the rising prominency. Measure likewise from the top of the shoulder to the bottom of the stays before, or to what length the Lady may wish or as the ruling fashion may suggest. Then take the length of the petticoat from the hip to the ground and any other part you think proper.

Take your cloth and measure and cut off the petticoat first. Then lay your cloth straight and cut the edges where the seams are to be, exact by a line. Open the petticoat piece to the full width and cut your placket holes six inches from the seam in the front

11   The back and front jacket pattern of a Lady's Riding Habit with the skirt or basque attached, another jacket to be cut in one piece on the cross grain of the fabric and a sleeve. Plate C from 'The Taylor's Complete Guide'.

breadth. Mark a line from the top of the placket holes to two inches down at the centre front. Cut this off to hollow it, so that it will not be too thick and clumsy in the binding. After your seams are sewn up, you will find 12″ more in the back breadth than the front, as is required for Habit Skirts. In pleating up the petticoat to the width of the waist, mind you lay all your pleats towards the hip in front. Leave about 3″ plain at the centre front and make the rest of the front breadth pleat towards the back. Mind you lay all your pleats full at the hips. This will give a swelling appearance to the petticoat and add much to the effect. Should you want half a breadth more in, take the remaining part of the cloth and split it in two and put the pieces on each side, then the petticoat will hang properly and the seams not out of their places. After it is pleated put a band of cloth three inches wide at the top of the petticoat. In the front make fobs for the watches.

In cutting the Jacket part of the Habit pray be a little circumspect as some taste and genius is required.

First mark the back according to the plate and hollow it with discretion, for if you should do it to excess you will spoil the economy and fitting of the whole Habit and make it wrinkle both across the back and under the arm (a common error you too frequently see). Observe also you cut the top of the back wide in the shoulders, for women are in that part proportionately bigger than men, up to the back of the neck.

In order to make the back and fore part both in unity, lay the hip of the back to the hip of the forepart and stretch the back up as high as you can. Mark your fore part shoulder across and cut it to the likeness of the plate, with an agreeable pigeon breast and beautiful small waist, adequate to your measure. Be careful how you cut the shoulder of the fore part, for should you make it too short, though but one quarter of an inch, your Habit will wrinkle under the arm and across the back.

Draw the sleeve in at the bend of the arm a little, for the Ladies through custom have a manner of holding their arms more upon the bend than men.

Clear your armhole before you put in the sleeve, which bear on the back scye to the sleeve up as high as the shoulder seam; then bear on the sleeve on the shoulder to the front and make the body with large scye pieces, as the friction of the arm against the stays very soon wears them out.

Cut the collar. Make a large slit at the hand so that the sleeve may come off easy. A Denmark sleeve with four buttons is most suitable to draw off and may be made to button close and neat to the wrist. We would recommend the skirts to be rantered on, as the body will by this means look much neater in the wearing.

We have in the course of our practice met with Habits where the seam of the sleeve has turned upon the top of the arm. The defect arose from not having pitched the sleeve right. The proper way of doing this is to take the Habit body, lay it with one hand two inches from the hip and the other hand in the arm hole, and where it folds, which may be about two inches from the shoulder seam, double it under the arm. Then double it from back scye to before and where the mark falls there let the seams of your sleeves be put, as that is the right way of dividing the arm hole in four parts, which will cause the sleeves to hang true without twisting.

Before we leave the subject of Habits, we wish to impress our students with a few material hints relative to alterations of such as may fall into their hands for amendment, being injudiciously made by other people.

A thing of this kind lately came under our inspection by an insignificant person of the Trade with a woeful complaint of the great danger he stood in of losing the countenance of a lady of the first fashion, whose recommendation had brought him into repute. We commiserated his case and learnt that the great grievance was a complaint in the petticoat, which seldom happens with people of any practice. This fault was that the petticoat would not hang down straight before but rose up on the belly, which totally disfigured the lady and shewed her in front in a situation which circumstances had not in the least entitled her to. This fault was due to the petticoat being too much hollowed before, which dragged it up and made it stand out so in the middle; as the hollowings were not cut off this matter was easily remedied. We told him to let down two inches before and that would settle the business. Had the hollowing been cut off the whole dress would have been spoiled, but after this matter was adjusted he carried and fitted on both jacket and petticoat, which sat extremely neat upon the Lady and gave great satisfaction.

The Book of Trades (Part III) (1804)
Privately owned by Miss Anne Buck
The Ladies' Dress-Maker

The business of a mantua-maker, which now includes almost every article of dress made use of by ladies, except, perhaps, those which belong to the head and the feet, is too well known to stand in need of description.

The plate is a representation of a mantua-maker taking the pattern off from a lady by means of a piece of paper, or of cloth. The pattern, if taken in cloth, becomes afterwards the lining of the dress. This business requires, in those who would excel in it, a considerable share of taste but no great capital to carry it on, unless to the act of making is united the business of furnishing the materials.

12   The Mantua-maker. From 'The Book of Trades.'

The mantua-maker's customers are not always easily pleased: they frequently expect more from their dress than it is capable of giving.

The mantua-maker must be an expert anatomist; and must, if judiciously chosen, have a name of French termination: she must know how to hide all defects in the proportions of the body and must be able to mould the shape by the stays, that while she corrects the body she may not interfere with the pleasures of the palate.

It will therefore be readily admitted that the perfection of dress and the art of pleasing the fair sex in this particular cannot be obtained without a genius.

The business of a mantua-maker, when conducted upon a large scale and in a fashionable situation, is very profitable; but the mere work-women do not make gains at all adequate to their labour; they are frequently obliged to sit up to very late hours, and the recompense for extra work is in general a poor remuneration for the time spent.

The price charged for making dresses cannot be estimated: it varies with the article to be made; with the reputation of the maker; with her situation in life; and even with the season of the year.

Advertisement in 'Le Beau Monde', (October 1807)
The British Museum

To Ladies and Gentlemen,

Ladies' Riding Habits and Fashionable dress for Gentlemen. Dietrichsen, Ladies' Habit maker at his old established warehouse, No. 12 Rathbone Place, Oxford Street, London, begs leave to return his sincere acknowledgements to the Nobility and Gentry for their repeated favours during a series of years and particularly for the very numerous additional customers and increased number of orders for Ladies' Riding Dresses, with which he has been favoured, during the last season in particular, to merit a continuance of which, the utmost attention to Fashion and Fitting will always be observed.

The Lady's Economical Assistant or The Art of cutting out and Making Wearing Apparel   (1808)
by A LADY
The British Museum

The great waste occasioned by the usual mode of cutting out linen etc. for all articles of clothing has induced me to take some pains in calculating the different widths and lengths of various materials, so as to cut out wearing apparel to the greatest advantage.

I have given directions for making all sorts of baby linen and complete dresses for children from one to two years of age, and from four to five, which, with very little alteration, will suit all the intermediate years. Also several articles of wearing apparel for women that are not likely to be much affected by fashion [Author's note – night jackets, night shifts, shifts, skirts for poor women]: and directions for making men's shirts and night caps.

To avoid damaging the patterns in the plates, the best way is to trace them on thin paper, then to cut out the pattern thus traced, accurately. By marking each paper with the number of the plate, there cannot be any mistake.

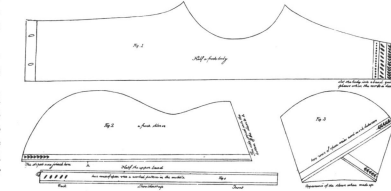

La Belle Assemblée   (October 1808)
The British Museum

An extract from a letter on dress

'. . . I am sure you will give me credit for not running into debt with my milliner . . . That malicious little S – sent to borrow my new polonese robe, or if I would have the goodness to send her the name of my dressmaker. I dislike the insidious little puss and am determined to punish her when it is in my power. So I sent my compliments and that my robe was in the hands of my maid who was making some alterations on it; that I was my own dressmaker, or at least designer, and that my name was at her service!'

14   Two ladies examining a fashion doll. From a watercolour of an Academy for Young Ladies by Edward Burney, c.1813. The Victoria & Albert Museum.

Royal Ladies' Magazine and Archives of the Court of St. James's.   (January 1832)
The Gallery of English Costume
To Correspondents

In answer to Mrs. L. we inform her that the drawings of the fashions are made from beautifully formed paper models, which may be seen and purchased – as, for the purposes of the Magazine, they are useless after the copies are published.

13   A full size pattern of a child's bodice and sleeve. From 'The Lady's Economical Assistant'. Reduced to scale ¼" = 1".

15 *Ladies looking at a fashion doll with three dresses. The flat box on the table in which the doll and dresses appear to have been packed indicates that they may be 'the beautifully formed paper models' referred to in the 'Royal Ladies' Magazine', January, 1832. From a French woodcut, c.1830.*

Advertisement in 'The World of Fashion' (October 1836)

The Gallery of English Costume

WHO SETS THE FASHIONS?

MADAME AND MRS. FOLLET

The Principal Fashions of the day emanate in no small degree from Madame F.'s inventions at Paris and supersede the borrowed Fashions of some of the English periodicals, embracing every new style of dress, exquisitely formed in the exact models and colours in which they are worn, consisting of full length and small size French paper. Millinery and dresses of every description, sleeves, trimmings, etc., etc., – sold at 10s per set (comprising four articles) packed for any part of the Kingdom, at 3s extra.

To Ladies in Business requiring their own materials made up during their stay in London, Madame and Mrs. F.'s establishment offers a combination of first rate ability, with most moderate charges.

IMPROVED ART OF FRENCH AND ENGLISH PATTERN TAKING, CUTTING AND FITTING.

Madame and Mrs. F. give finishing instructions to Ladies commencing Business and to young persons who have been neglected in the same and render them perfectly competent to take patterns, cut out and fit the most difficult figures with a facility scarcely to be credited and certainly not excelled. Lessons also in Millinery. The Improved French measurement for corsets in one lesson. Terms from 2 guineas to 5 guineas. Private rooms are appropriated. N.B. All letters, remittances and Post Office orders must be Post paid. Madame and Mrs. Follet, Milliners and Court Dressmakers, 53 New Bond Street and Rue Richlieu à Paris.

***A Young Lady can be admitted as Junior Partner.

Advertisement in 'The World of Fashion' (April 1837)

The Gallery of English Costume

Paris, March 25, 1837

A letter just received from Mr. Smith of St. Paul's Churchyard, London and Boulevard des Italiens, Paris; who is now in Paris,

'Madame – on arriving at Calais on Sunday evening, Madame and myself made the best of our way to Paris and have since visited more than forty of the principal Marchandes des Modes. All of them were preparing for Longchamps and certainly some splendid articles were ready. Thursday and Friday we went to the Boulevards and Champs Elysèes and of course saw everything that was to be seen. The weather being very cold, it was not so grand and imposing as it has been on former occasions. We are now much occupied in selecting and have procured some of the most beautiful Dresses, Pelisses, Mantles, Pelerines, Capes, Tippets, Sleeves etc.; you ever saw. The Bonnets, Caps, Hats, Turbans and Head-dresses are splendid, the materials rich almost beyond description – you will be delighted with them. We have this day forwarded by the Diligence sixteen of the newest and most beautiful Bonnets and Hats. They are very different in shape and style to what has been worn and are exact copies of those made for Madame Adelaide, the Princess, the Ladies of the Different Ambassadors and leading Fashionables in Paris. There are four Head-dresses, six Turbans and twenty six Caps all very elegant. Some of them cost from two to three hundred francs. Neither trouble nor expense has been spared to procure every novelty in Paris. There are four Dresses, two Pelisses and five Mantles, elegantly embroidered, and quite new. Today we are having packed twenty-three large boxes of Flowers and Feathers. The Flowers are so fine and so de-

liciously perfumed, you will think them growing and so blended as to produce the most beautiful colouring in the world. We are also packing about eighty dozen of the finest white chips, which we will be able to sell at from 12s to 18s each; and fifty dozen imitation Cotton Paille de Riz, almost equal and about half the price. The Agent will clear them at the Custom House, and you will receive them on Tuesday or Wednesday at the latest. Get them all copied and made up in parcels as usual. We set out on our return on Thursday and shall bring all our goods home with us, so that all may be ready on Monday, the 3rd of April.

We shall see seven dresses on Wednesday evening, now making for the Ladies Patronesses of the English Charitable Subscription Ball to be held in Paris on Monday, the 3rd of April; and by great interest have been promised models made up in materials of each, with the names of the ladies for whom they are made, and the couturiers who are making them attached'.

SMITH AND LAPOULLI

Beg to announce the arrival of the above elegant and fashionable articles, and recommend to their friends an early order. They have made them all up in paper as usual, price 20s the complete set, and all purchasers will be allowed to inspect the originals; and Ladies not visiting London shall be furnished with every information, and patterns of the materials, without any extra charge. They have also received several cases of very fine Leghorns from Italy and three cases of beautiful Rice Straw, Tissues and novelties from Switzerland, all of which will be ready on Monday next.

26, St. Paul's Churchyard and 4, Aldersgate Street, London.   March 29, 1837.

Advertisement in 'The World of Fashion' (April 1837)

The Gallery of English Costume

Fashion Unrivalled. Town and Country Milliners and Dressmakers are respectfully invited to inspect the new Fashions just imported by Madame and Mrs. Follet, from their house at Paris, replete with every novelty and design and formed with exquisite taste, in coloured French paper, consisting of Morning, Evening and Dinner Dresses, Headdresses, Dress Hats, Caps etc.

Sold in sets comprising four articles at 10s, packed for any part of the Kingdom at 3s extra.

All Letters and Remittances must be Post Paid.

Assistants in Millinery and Dressmaking according to the required qualifications promptly supplied (Prospectuses gratis). Finishing instructions given in Millinery or Dressmaking to those who are not quite proficient in the business. Private rooms are appropriated and terms moderate.

Madame and Mrs. Follet, Milliners, Court Dressmakers, and Original Importers of French Paper Fashions.

53, New Bond Street, London and Rue Richlieu, Paris.

The Workwoman's Guide   (1838)

by A LADY

The British Museum

The Author of the following pages has been encouraged to hope that in placing them, after much deliberation, in the hands of a printer, she is tendering an important and acceptable, however humble, service to persons of her own sex, who, in any condition of life, are engaged by duty or inclination in cutting out wearing apparel in a family or for their poorer neighbours. She trusts in particular that Clergymen's Wives, Young Married Women, School-mistresses, and Ladies' Maids may find a fast and serviceable friend in the 'Workwoman's Guide'.

To assist the unpractised in understanding the written descriptions, almost every pattern is likewise drawn twice, so as not only to represent its appearance when cut out, but also when made up. The difficulty of describing irregular and complicated shapes has been obviated by enclosing each in a square, marked with a scale of nails. In a charity school in which the Author was much interested, and for the use of which her collection of patterns was originally begun and her drawings made, girls from ten to sixteen years of age were in the constant habit of cutting out correctly and easily with no other guidance than the drawings.

Dress, it seems, has of late been admitted by philosophical critics to the dignity of a fine art: it both requires and cultivates taste, and the consideration of a pleasing effect and air in dress is first applied in the cutting out.

No one who has not been a frequent visitor in the homes of the poor, is aware of the extravagance and waste usual among women of a humble class, arising from their total ignorance in matters of cutting out and needle-work, nor how much instruction they want on those points even to the making of a petti-coat and a pinafore. The same ignorance and unskil-fulness, and the same consequent waste of laborious and scanty earnings is common among our female household servants; who, by putting out their clothes to dressmakers, pay nearly half as much for the making up as for the materials. The direct saving of expense upon articles of dress, were they qualified to work for themselves, would, with all persons in these conditions of life, be an important annual item; and the thrifty disposition, the regularity and neatness, the ideas of order and management inspired by the conscious ability and successful exertion in one leading branch of good housewifery, cannot be too highly prized or diligently cultivated; for the result is moral.

Extracts from some of the chapters

Chapter III

Articles of clothing are measured by cloth measure:
2¼ inches make 1 nail   4 quarters make 1 yard
4 nails make 1 quarter   5 quarters make 1 English ell

Chapter IV

A workbox should contain six or eight of the useful sized white reel sewing cottons, black cotton and

10

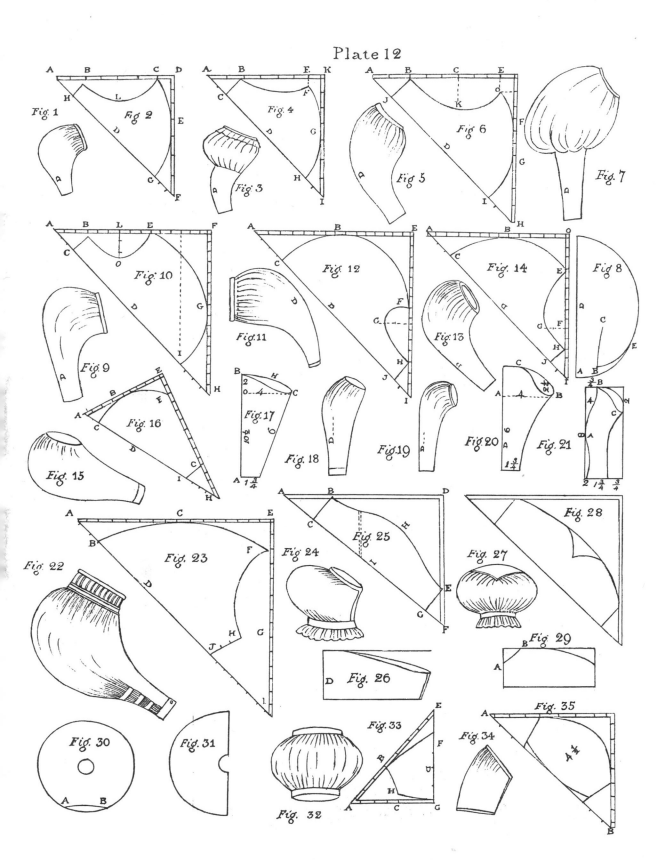

Plate 12

silks, white, black and coloured; a few useful tapes, bobbins, galloon, buttons of all kinds; hooks and eyes. An ample needlebook containing a page of kerseymere for each sized needle, not omitting the darning, glove, stay and worsted or carpet needles.

There are various kinds of scissors; the most useful are,

> A large pair for cutting out linen: A medium size, for common use: A small pair, with rounded points: A smaller pair, with sharper points, for cutting out muslin work, etc.: Lace scissors with a flat knob at one of the points: Buttonhole scissors.

Chapter VI

It would be useless to form scales for the different kinds of dresses, as shapes vary so much, therefore none will be introduced excepting for children and young persons; as, however, the dress forms one of the most important parts of a person's wardrobe, all general observations for cutting out that can be reduced to rule will be given. At the same time it is strongly recommended to all those who can afford it, to have their dresses made by a mantua maker, as those which are cut at home seldom fit so comfortably or look so well as when made by persons in constant practice. It would be very advisable, as a practice, for persons little acquainted with cutting out, to purchase cheap print for poor children's dresses and by fitting them on much experience and nicety might be acquired at little waste or expense.

The Tailor's Masterpiece (1838)

GEORGE WALKER

The Gallery of English Costume

[There are different editions of this book in the Victoria and Albert Museum and the British Museum]

The Art of Cutting Ladies' Riding Habits, Pelisses, Gowns, Frocks, etc.

> *Directions to take the measure for a Habit or Pelisse, etc.*

It is necessary in the first place to observe that the Lady should be suitably dressed for the purpose of taking the dimensions correctly. She ought to have on the same corsets as she intends to wear with the garments you are taking measure for. As a Habit is worn only over a thin underdress such as a plain silk or cotton body lining, as it is termed, or a Habit Shirt, therefore the plainer or thinner the dress measured over, the more preferable.

All measures given in the examples of this work are given in inches and parts of inches unless otherwise particularly specified.

Copy of the measure for a Habit for a medium sized person, say 5 feet 4 inches high.

Breast	Waist	Lapell	Front
33	23	17	57

Make four marks on the centre of the back as at A, B, I and D (see figure 1) from whence the principal dimensions are taken. Make the first mark at the bottom of the neck as at A, taking as a guide the prominent bone. In all cases this is the proper height to measure from, whether the garment is required low or high to the neck. Next mark the centre between the shoulders, which is done by placing an inch measure across the back from the centre of the two back scyes and where it crosses the back seam make a mark as at B. The third point marked I, by which the bottom of the armhole is correctly ascertained, is merely to carry the tape round the body close under the arms. The fourth point is made at the most hollow part, as at D, from which the balance or length of shoulder strap is taken. Take the length of the back from A to B, to the mark opposite the bottom of the armhole, to the waist as at D, and to the bottom of the skirt.

Directions to form the back according to Plate 18

First suppose the line with letter A at either end to be the edge of a piece of paper from which to cut the shape of the back. Make a mark at B for the top of the back seam. Mark D (centre point between the shoulders) and C (waist). Draw DE at right angles and make a mark for the width of the back according to the fashion of the day, for whether the back is required wide or narrow it is entirely immaterial, as it will not have the least effect on the fit, for whatever variation of fashion may take place with regard to the width of the backs, corresponding effect will be produced upon the fore part and sleeve.

Directions to form the fore part according to Plate 18

In the first place draw a line to proceed as from A to H, upon paper, for it is advisable to cut the fore part out from a sheet of paper before the cloth is cut, which gives the advantage of placing it on the cross or bias and also to make the most of the cloth.

For the bust dart it is necessary to be cautious not to run too suddenly a point at Z. The person who can use an iron well will press the shape on all sides so as to form a round receptacle as required. Occasionally in the case of extreme large breasts it is difficult to make them answer by taking out only one dart and in such case the effect may be accomplished by shaping two pieces out, as represented by the dotted lines on each side of Z.

In case the Habit is required very tight in the waist, as they generally are, run a seam from Q under the arm to the bottom as represented by the dots.

Directions to form the Habit sleeve

As Habit sleeves are subject to so much change in style, it is necessary to treat upon them in such manner as to meet all vicissitudes of fashion. The close-fitting sleeve is the groundwork for all kinds of sleeves. It is produced in the same way as the Gentleman's Dress Coat sleeve and was fashionable to Ladies' Riding Habits about the commencement of the nineteenth century as well as in the year 1838. See Fig. 1, the firm outline. It is necessary to allow for the sleeve head about an inch for fullness as per dotted line from C to B. This fullness may be carried to any extent that fashion demands, for instance, in

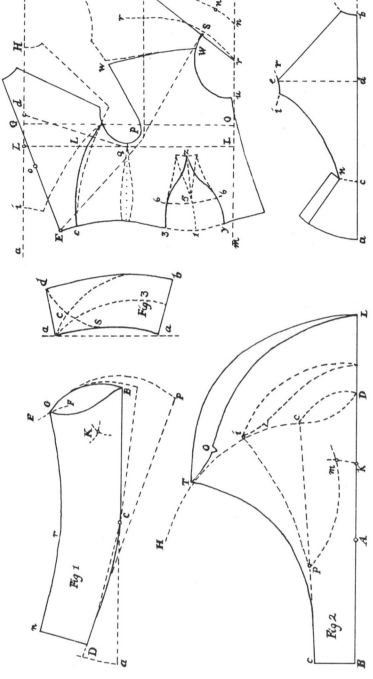

17 *Front and back views of a Lady wearing a Riding Habit. Plates 16 and 17 from 'The Tailor's Masterpiece'.*

18 *Skirt patterns with construction lines. Plate 19 from 'The Tailor's Masterpiece'.*

19 *Bodice and sleeve patterns with construction lines. Plate 18 from 'The Tailor's Masterpiece'.*

1838 many sleeves were carried out to P. In putting in the sleeve part, place the top of the hind seam to the middle of the back scye.

The sleeve, commonly called the Pelisse sleeve, with only one seam, and that to be underneath the arm, is represented by Fig. 2. The firm outline was fashionable in 1834. The sleeve may be formed larger or less at pleasure, for instance the full width of the sleeve might be made either at H or T and the head, to correspond with any width of sleeve, might be made higher or lower than the point at L – for instance, see the dotted sleeve head formed from i.

Directions to form the skirt, commonly called the Petticoat of a Habit

Suppose the cloth to be 28″ wide on the double and KA and 4Q to be the edges of it. Form the hind part of the skirt first. Measure 54″ at the double edge of the cloth as at A. The shape KVTZZ is the back skirt. AT is the ordinary skirt length. ZZ is the length for a Riding Habit (½ or ¾ yard, to fancy, longer than AT). The front breadth is cut exactly the same but check the front length to see if it corresponds with the measure of A to 2. This completes the sloped Habit skirt, from which, as a principle, any other skirt can be formed to accord with the fashion of the day.

The back and front breadths of the Habit skirt being both of the same width, will require pleating or puckering in to the size so that the seams will fall at the sides, in order to have the pocket holes, or apron of the skirt, at the usual place; it will, however, also be observed in the treatise upon the Habit skirt with plain front, that the side seams of the above skirt need not be cut from V to T, but the whole width of the skirt may be left on the back skirt and the front breadth cut so much the less, as represented from E to U.

Suppose the skirt of a Habit to be required wider than what has previously been described, say to put the whole width of the cloth in the back breadth, it is merely to cut the said back breadth square across top and bottom and to the length required, and join it to the side seam of VTZ and EWU. If the full breadth of cloth is required in both back and front breadth this would become a straight or parallel skirt, whereas that previously described is commonly called the sloped skirt. The straight skirt only requires cutting square across the top and bottom for the back breadth, and also for the front breadth if the measure falls the same before as behind. If not, simply lower or raise it.

Having defined a method whereby Habit skirts may at all times be correctly formed according to the variations of figure, fashion or fancy, I shall proceed to describe those calculated for walking dresses, such as Pelisses, etc:

A Pelisse skirt is formed on the same principle as the Habit skirt, although generally made open up the front, the lengths and widths according to fashion. The method laid down for the Habit skirt first treated on produces a medium size but the fashions of Pelisses are liable to greater extremes. It may be necessary to treat them more explicitly, for instance in 1817, when cloth Pelisses were almost universally worn, the style adopted was very short waisted, so that the skirt was sewed on nearly close under the arm. At this time the skirts were cut very narrow towards the top and the fullness put into the space of about four inches behind so that the front and sides were quite plain. The fullness being put so close together behind did not give the room required for the hips, to allow the sides to set free. Consequently for a Pelisse with an extreme narrow skirt it is necessary to shape on at the side seams, to give room for the hips, about a couple of inches upon both front and back

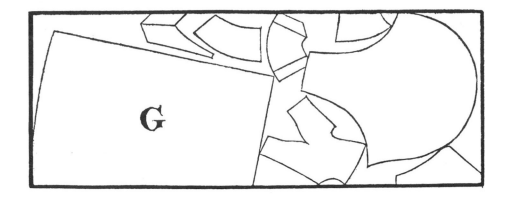

G

G HABIT or PELISSE is represented in the plate, and the quantity of cloth required for the same would be as follows, viz. for the Jacket or body part, nearly a yard of cloth, and suppose the skirt a yard long, would take 2 lengths, making 3 yards for a Pelisse, and for a Habit would require as much more cloth as the extra length of skirt, say $\frac{3}{4}$ of a yard longer than the walking length, would be $4\frac{1}{2}$ yards for the Habit; this allows the two full breadths of the cloth in skirt except taking the collars, &c. off the front breadth, as marked; but in case the two full breadths are put in the petticoat, it will require a $\frac{1}{4}$ of a yard more, and contrariwise in case of the narrow skirt and sleeves as worn in 1817, the sleeves then cut off the front breadth, which takes half a yard less cloth. This calculation of length is for a person, in height, about $5\frac{1}{2}$ feet, therefore according to any extra length of skirt required the calculation would be easily made. It may be observed that in 1817, the whole width across the top of the sleeve was about 18 inches, whereas the sleeve in the plate is calculated at 23 inches, as they were worn in 1827. In 1837 they were worn 28 inches wide across, and at the same time also the petticoat or skirt had the two full breadths of cloth in, and made in length for a person of medium height $1\frac{3}{4}$ yd. long, which took $3\frac{1}{2}$ yds. cloth and $1\frac{1}{2}$ yrd. for the body and sleeves, made 5 yrds for the Habit. In 1838 the sleeves were made nearly as close as men's sleeves, so that $4\frac{3}{4}$ yrds. made the Habit.

20 A Pattern layout for a Riding Habit or Pelisse. Plate G from 'The Tailor's Masterpiece'.

breadths as at P, running it out at the bottom to the original line as at W. Also run it out at the top as to E with a shape as per model, which forms a hollow a portion of the way below the top. Without this precaution the skirt would not set hollow to the sides and if tight at the hip would gape and set, or hang rather ill down the front.

In case it should be fashionable to have a Pelisse skirt as wide at the top as at the bottom, the back breadth is formed on the square both at top and bottom, and the front also. In this as in other cases the top of the front breadth must be attended to in order to ascertain how much it will require to be sloped across the front, or whether a slope be required or not, for it depends upon the form of the body part at the bottom of the waist in front.

Be very careful to take the length from both centre front neck and centre back neck to the ground, as that distance is fixed. If this is not done the set of the skirt may not be correct at the front, particularly as a Pelisse is generally cut to open all the way down in front and if the waist is not properly measured at front and back, the skirt will not set properly, unless what is deficient in one is added to the other.

Habit or Pelisse collars are cut various ways to fancy, but generally upon the following principle viz: the sewing on edge is cut about an inch hollow from a straight line as represented from *a* to *a*, Fig.3, Plate 18, and the seam behind on the square of the sewing on edge. First suppose a collar required for a Habit or Pelisse which will be closed to the top. The length of the sewing edge should be about $\frac{1}{2}''$ bigger than the gorge is, as from *a* to *a*. Then, according to fancy, the fall down may be shaped square as *adb*, or round as *acb*. If a lapel and collar are required it is necessary to run from about 4" off the front as represented from *s* to *c*. For a plain roll front, shape the collar as from *sc* to *b*, for the frock style of collar *scdb*. In case of a Pelisse collar being required more circular, it is only to commence with a larger hollow from the straight line, and then proceed as before.

The Ladies' Hand-book of Plain Needlework (1842)
The British Museum

Introduction

To become an expert needle woman should be an object of ambition to every British fair. Never is beauty and feminine grace so attractive as when engaged in the honorable discharge of household duties and domestic cares. To learn how to fabricate articles of dress and utility for family use, or, in the case of ladies blessed with the means of affluence, for the aid and comfort of the deserving poor, should form one of the most prominent branches of female education. And yet experience must have convinced those who are at all conversant with the general state of society, that it is a branch of study to which nothing like due attention is paid in the usual routine of school instruction.

No one can look upon the Needle without emotion; it is a constant companion throughout the pilgrimage of life. We find it the first instrument of use placed in the hand of budding childhood, and it is found to retain its usefulness and charm even when trembling in the grasp of fast declining age. The little girl first employs it in the dressing of her doll, then she is taught its still higher use, in making up some necessary articles for a beloved brother or a revered parent. Approaching to womanhood, additional preparation of articles of use, as ornaments for herself and others, call for its daily employment; and with what tender emotions does the glittering steel inspire the bosom, as beneath its magic touch, that which is to deck a lover, or adorn a bride, becomes visible in the charming productions of female skill and fond regard. To the adornments of the bridal bed: the numerous preparations for an anxiously-expected little stranger, and the various comforts and conveniences of life, the service of this little instrument is indispensable. Its friendly aid does not desert us even in the dark hour of sorrow and affliction. By its aid we form the last covering which is to enwrap the body of a departed loved one, and prepare those sable habiliments, which custom has adopted as the external sign of mourning.

Chapter I Instruction in the preparation of body linen
The lady who is intending to engage in the domestic employment of preparing the linen necessary for personal and family use, should be careful to have all her materials ready and disposed in the most systematic manner possible, before commencing work. We shall proceed to give plain directions by which any lady may soon become expert in this necessary department of household uses, merely observing that a neat work box well supplied with all the implements required, including knife, scissors (of at least three sizes), needles and pins in sufficient variety, bodkins, thimbles, thread and cotton, bobbins, marking silks, black lead pencils, etc., should be provided and be furnished with a lock and key, to prevent the contents being thrown into confusion by children or unauthorised intruders.

The lady being thus provided and having her materials, implements, etc., placed in order upon her work table, to the edge of which it is an advantage to have a pincushion affixed by means of a screw, may commence her work, and proceed with it with pleasure to herself and without annoyance to any visitor who may favour her with a call. We would recommend, wherever practicable, that the work table should be made of cedar and that the windows of the working parlour should open into a garden, well supplied with odiferous flowers and plants, the perfume of which will materially cheer the spirits.

Chapter IV Explanation of Stitches
Running
Take three threads, leave three and in order that the work may be kept as firm as possible, back-stitch

21 A detail showing bodice drapery on a stand. From a fashion-plate in 'Petit Courrier de Dames', November 1839. The Victoria & Albert Museum.

occasionally. If you sew selvedges they must be joined evenly together.

Gathering
You begin by taking the article to be gathered and dividing it into halves and then into quarters, putting on pins to make the divisions. It must be gathered about twelve threads from the top, taking three threads on the needle and leaving four, and so proceeding alternately until one quarter is gathered. Fasten the thread by twisting it round a pin; stroke the gathers, so that they lie evenly and neatly, with a strong needle or pin. You then proceed as before, until all the gathers are gathered. Then take out the pins and regulate the gathers of each quarter, so as to correspond with those of the piece to which it is to be sewed. The gathers are then to be fastened on, one at a time, and the stitches must be in a slanting direction. The part to be gathered must be cut quite even before commencing, or else it will be impossible to make the gathering look well.

AUTHOR'S NOTE
The word PLAIT, *as used in the next two extracts, has two meanings. The word following in brackets gives the present day term.*

The Ladies Handbook of Millinery, Dressmaking and Tatting (1843)
The British Museum

First, the materials for the intended dress must be procured, and it is advisable, whenever practicable, to get them all at the same time. The necessary requisites are the material, the lining for the body and skirt, wadding, covering, hooks and eyes, silk thread and what is called stiffening muslin. You will require all these for a silk dress and most of them for those of other fabrics.

Proceed to cut out the dress, first measuring off the number of breadths of the proper length for the skirt (which is, of course, to be regulated by the height of the wearer). If tucks are to be introduced into the skirt a proper allowance must be made for these, as also for the turnings both at top and bottom. You next cut out the sleeves, as being the largest parts of the garment except the skirt. In cutting out the sleeves you must first prepare a paper pattern of the required shape; then double the lining, and cut it exactly the shape of the paper, leaving about an inch all round for the turnings in. You will thus cut the sleeve linings both together and will avoid some labour and all danger of making one larger than the other. Double the silk, or other material, so that both the wrong sides may face each other and cut the sleeves by the linings just prepared. To secure exactness it is best to tack it to the material. Be careful to lay the straight side of the pattern to the selvedge of the silk.

Take the proper measures for the front and back of the body by fitting a paper pattern to the shape of the person for whom the dress is intended. The paper should be thin and you commence by folding down the corner the length of the front, and pinning it to the middle of the stay bone. Then let the paper be spread as smoothly as possible along the bosom to the shoulder, and fold it in a plait (dart) so as to fit the shape exactly, and bring the paper under the arm, making it retain its position by a pin. From this point you cut it off downward under the arm, and along the waist; the paper is then to be rounded for the armhole and the shoulder, and you must recollect to leave it large enough to admit of the turnings. In the same manner you proceed to form the back, pinning the paper straight down, and leaving sufficient for the hem, you fit it to the shoulder and under the arm, so as to meet the front.

You will thus have an exact pattern of half the body. The linings are to be cut by the pattern and the silk by the linings. You must take care to cut the silk on the cross way of the silk and in two separate pieces, which are afterwards joined in the middle. If the plait (dart) made in the pattern be very large, it must be cut out on the silk, or the body will not fit well to the shape; if small, it may be left, but we think that in all cases to cut it out is the preferable method.

It is not generally advisable to cut out the half of the back all in one piece, as it fits better with pieces joined at the sides; these are called side bodies; and this method should always be adopted, unless the lady has a very flat back: in that case it is best to cut the half all in one piece. The backs must be cut straight and it is best to tack the material to the lining before cutting it.

Begin to make the garment by running or seaming the breadths of the skirt together. Be sure that it is

made full; a narrow or straight skirt is now completely and very properly exploded. Run the seams as evenly as possible, fastening the ends to your knee or to a pincushion screwed to the worktable to hold them firmly. Run the lining together in a similar manner and fasten each of the outside seams to a corresponding one in it; after which turn the edges at the top down on the inside, and sew them firmly together. Between the lining and the silk it is usual to introduce some kind of material, as stiffened muslin or wadding, to hold the bottom of the dress in its proper place. This is fastened to the lining and the silk is hemmed down upon it.

Care must be taken that no stitches appear on the right side. An opening in one of the seams must be left for the pocket hole, which must not exceed one quarter of a yard in length. You run the silk and the lining together as at the top, and make a plait (pleat) which is to be folded over on the right side. This is secured at the bottom, and conceals the opening. Having thus completed the skirt, to which flounces may be added, or into which tucks may be introduced, if deemed advisable (they seldom are in silk dresses), you proceed to make the sleeves, running up a cord on one side of the silk, or other material. Fold both the silk and the lining the same way, stitch them together and leave an opening at the wrist. You then turn the sleeve and the edges, being on the inside, are not seen. The sleeve being thus seamed up, it is, if full, to be gathered, or done in small plaits (pleats) at the bottom, to the size of the wrist. The gathers, or plaits, are set into a narrow band, lined, and you cord as you please, or as is most in accordance with prevailing fashion. You next put on the trimmings at the top of the sleeve, and then set it into the arm-hole with small plaits (pleats). Some put on the trimmings after the sleeve has been set onto the body, but it is a most incorrect and inconvenient practice.

The next thing to be done is to put the several parts of the body, or waist, together. This should be done slightly and the body tried on, in order that the fit may be made as perfect as possible. When this is done, sew the parts firmly together and put a cord over all the joinings, except those under the arms. Fasten the plaits (darts) down on the fronts, hem the parts which require it, cut the proper shape round the neck and see that the armholes are so made as to be easy and agreeable. Then hem the back, stitch the dress up the front as firm as you can, and do the same at the shoulders, the side bodies and under the arms; after which, you must put a cord or a band at the waist and must also insert a cord round the neck. This cording of the neck and waist require much care and attention, as, if not done properly, the appearance of the dress will be spoiled. In case you prefer a band to a cord at the waist, it must be lined and the lining must be put on first and afterwards covered with the material of which the dress is composed. If there be any trimmings on the body, they must be put on before the sleeves are set in. A cord must be set round the armholes, as neat as possible.

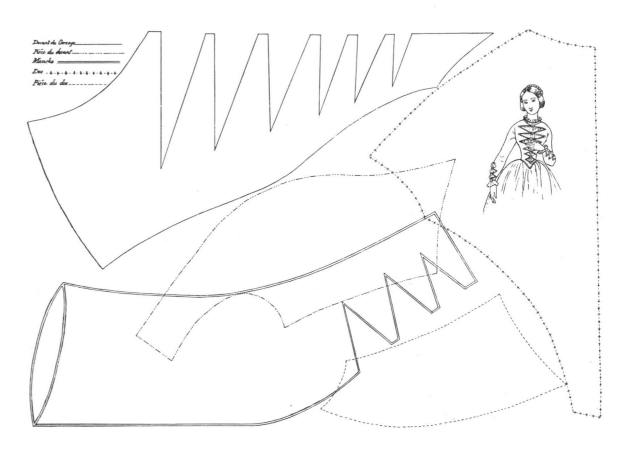

22 *A full-size printed paper pattern of front and back bodice and sleeve. From 'Petit Courrier de Dames', September 1844. Reduced to scale $\frac{1}{4}'' = 1''$. The Victoria & Albert Museum.*

The body being now finished, you have only to set it onto the skirt, which is to be doubled more at the front than at the back, in order to form the slope. You gather the part not plaited (pleated) and join it to the body. In setting on the back, it is best not to gather it, but to fold each gather as you proceed. This secures an evenness not otherwise easily to be obtained. The depth of the slope varies, and no certain rule can be given, except that in all cases the skirt must be a little shorter before than behind, otherwise much inconvenience will be found in walking, especially where it is the fashion to wear the dress of a considerable length.

Tucks, with or without open work between them, have an exceedingly neat appearance and never look out of fashion. They are especially proper in black and white dresses and if tucks are put on, it is essential that they should be cut the straight way of the material. To cut them on the cross is decidedly improper. It is sometimes good economy to make the sleeves of a dress in two separate parts, so that the lower portion can be taken off at pleasure. For an evening dress this is found very convenient, as the under part will come off at the elbow, and a ruffle of lace can be substituted in its place, which gives a short sleeve a neat and finished appearance.

The directions here given apply principally to dresses made of stuff or silk. In those made of muslin or cotton, some slight variations occur. These latter are not always lined; indeed cotton prints for summer

wear are seldom done so; but the lining of muslin dresses is becoming much more common than it was some years since, experience having shewn that the dress, when lined through, sits so much neater upon the person than it does without. In cases where linings are omitted, a piece of some strong material must be run in at the bottom of the skirt, and firmly held down with the hem. But we think a thin lining, even for the light dresses worn in summer, is to be preferred. It is a good plan to set a cord round the bottoms of dresses; they soon wear, but the cord is a great advantage, as, when it gets unsightly, a new one can with little trouble be put in its place and the dress remains the same length as before.

The Handbook of Dressmaking (1845)
MRS. M. J. HOWELL
The British Museum

Mrs. Howell has much pleasure in introducing to the notice of her friends, the Portfolio of Monthly Fashions, supplied to her direct from Paris, consisting of full size Morning and Evening sleeves, Bodies and Trimmings; likewise such as are desirable for Promenade Costume. Terms for the set of Twelve Articles, £1.1.0, accompanied by proper directions for making up; the half set charged 11s 6d., or three articles for 5s. 6d. Sent free to any part on receipt of a Post Office Order.

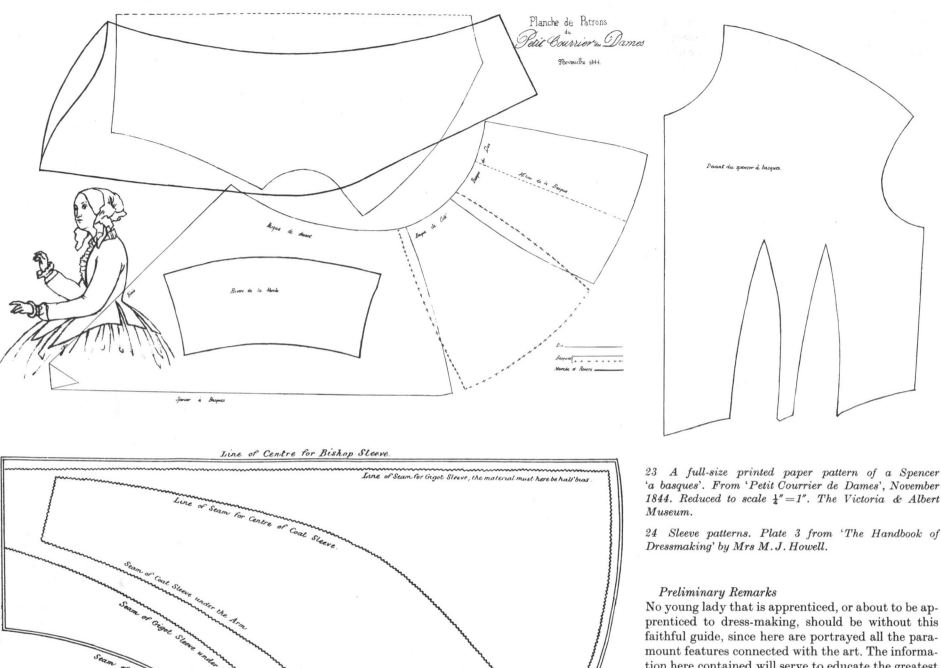

Planche de Patrons
du
Petit Courrier des Dames

Spencer à Basques.

Line of Centre for Bishop Sleeve.

Line of Seam for Gigot Sleeve, the material must here be half bias.

Line of Seam for Centre of Coat Sleeve.

Seam of Coat Sleeve under the Arm

Seam of Gigot Sleeve under the Arm

Seam of Bishop Sleeve under the Arm

Plate 3.
Key for Cutting Sleeves.

Devant du spencer à basques.

23 *A full-size printed paper pattern of a Spencer 'a basques'. From 'Petit Courrier de Dames', November 1844. Reduced to scale ¼″ = 1″. The Victoria & Albert Museum.*

24 *Sleeve patterns. Plate 3 from 'The Handbook of Dressmaking' by Mrs M. J. Howell.*

Preliminary Remarks

No young lady that is apprenticed, or about to be apprenticed to dress-making, should be without this faithful guide, since here are portrayed all the paramount features connected with the art. The information here contained will serve to educate the greatest novice in the theory of the business, allowing the practice to follow. Again no work-room should be without a copy, since it will save the principal much time and fatigue in giving various directions. Should a young lady be admitted as an apprentice, let her learn the remarks here offered. No doubt can exist as to their utility, since it often occurs, in the absence of the principal, that the apprentices are left to manage their own work.

It will be necessary for me to commence an explanation of my new system of measurement which in some degree I owe to the French, who have always taken their measures by proportions. In offering to the public my entirely novel method, I trust it will be acknowledged that I have improved even on the Continental plans.

Explanation of plates
Plate No. 1 is a high body, the bust formed by one plait (dart); from this simple pattern every description of body, cape, collar, chemisette or pelerine might be cut. This pattern admits of various changes – see Plate No. 2. It is there composed of dissected pieces intended to show the form of a stomacher, or point body, which fashion ordains at present as dinner dress. The symmetrical designs are divided into classes for the more ready explanation to the uninitiated; each class contains six numbers; the price varies from 4s. 6d. to 5s. 6d. according to the quality of the envelope. Orders, accompanied by a post office remittance, will meet with immediate attention.

On Measure Taking
The symmetrical designs afford the key to fitting at sight. They have been formed on models moulded in the highest perfection of the human form, and will enable the pupil, with the aid of the explanations here contained, to correct in the figure she requires to fit, any inaccuracy. Each envelope contains a design, complete for trying on. The pupil has only to act from every unprepared design after the same method. They will then be able to take any figure, however difficult. I proceed to lay down rules for the use of unprepared designs.

First take some soft Irish lawn or linen. Observe the yellow mark across the designed paper pattern. Be sure to place the selvedge in the same direction, which will bring the material on the direct bias in the centre. Pin the pattern very neatly on the Irish linen. Be careful to have no crease in whatever you are cutting out, or this will interfere materially with the fit. Mark round the pattern with a blue pencil. Commence cutting 1½″ from your paper pattern. It will be necessary to leave this turning at all parts, the armhole excepted. Do not cut out the plaits (darts) which form the bust. Refer as before to the yellow mark on the paper pattern of the back and side pieces as to where the selvedge must be placed. Tack your lining with coarse thread. You will leave it pinned up the front and under the arm, these being the parts most likely to need alteration, either to be taken in or to be let out, if the proportions of the figure are not entirely perfect.

To those in business, the writer would recommend a set of soft Irish linings to be kept at all times made up from the designed patterns; so that should a gentlewoman call to give an order, the measure for her dress could be accurately taken in a few seconds.

A tight sleeve pattern will be found with the case of designs which, like the body patterns, have been formed on a modelled arm. Here again it will be found necessary to make trifling alterations, according to the length or shortness of arm it may be intended for.

When you have tried on your lining body you may cut away all the superfluous turnings which are allowed at the waist, front and seams, leaving only the same width as at the armhole. By this mode you may save half a yard of silk in cutting out your body and sleeves.

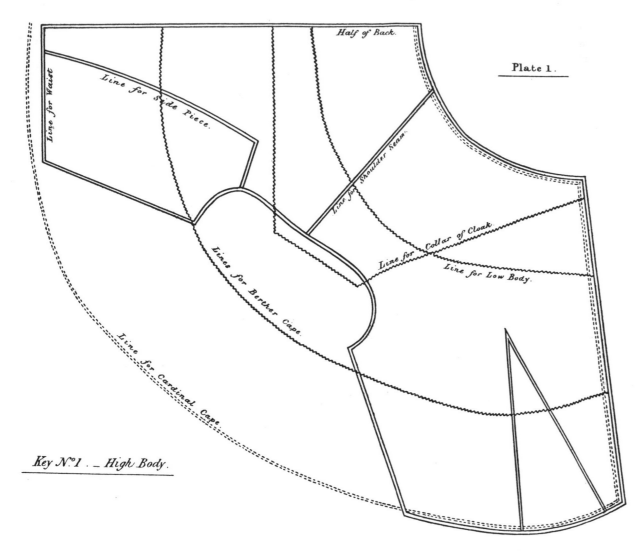

Plate 1.

Half of Back.

Line for Waist
Line for Side Piece.
Line for Shoulder Seam.
Line for Collar of Cloak
Line for Low Body.
Lines for Berthe Cape.
Line for Cardinal Cape.

Key Nº 1 . — High Body.

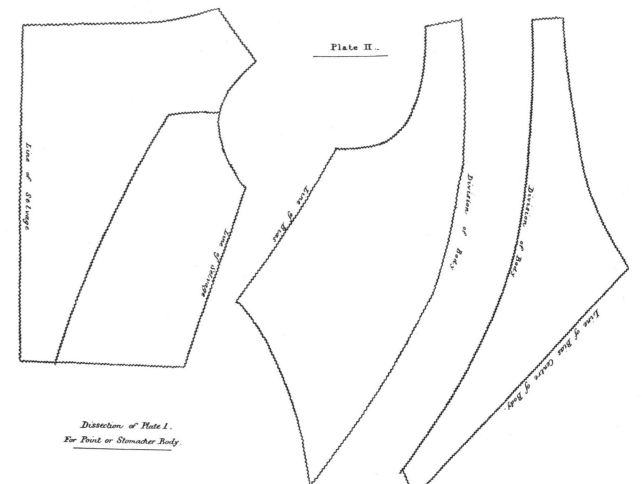

Plate II.

Line of Selvage
Division of Body
Division of Body
Line of Bias Centre of Body

Dissection of Plate 1.
For Point or Stomacher Body.

25 A high body pattern with variations. Plate 1 from *'The Handbook of Dressmaking' by Mrs M. J. Howell.*

26 A pattern of a point or stomacher body. Plate 2 from *'The Handbook of Dressmaking' by Mrs M. J. Howell.*

On Cutting out with Economy and Making up the Dress

Having tried on the lining body and finding that it fits, open the various seams. Place each piece on the silk or whatever material you have selected for the dress. Regard the way in which the threads run; your lining will prove a sure guide. Tack the body and sleeves through to the outside precisely on the blue mark, or through the line of pinholes if an alteration was made. The tacking thread will not only serve to keep the one secure on the other but will act as a guide for the inside as well as the out. In stitching the different seams of the body pay great attention in seeing that they are taken exactly to the guide line. I recommend that the felling on the tapes or ribband at the back of the seams, to admit of the steel or whalebone, be put on loosely, as in the event of these being tightened the nice appearance of the body will be destroyed. In using the whalebone observe it be perfectly straight before you put it into the casings. As the best kind of whalebone is sold in rolled lengths it is desirable that you place it in hot water or in front of the fire to bring it straight, previous to cutting it in

pieces. Whether you stitch in your sleeve with or without a cord, be most particular in seeing it is not tightened. Let your sleeve at all times be rather larger than the armhole it is intended to fit.

Novices should pay great attention in the cutting out of stripes and plaids, since checks or stripes invariably require to be faced in the cutting out. In trimming your bodies, if the figure be inclined to embonpoint, be most careful in endeavouring to give as little size as possible: for this purpose introduce few or no trimmings on either the body or sleeves. If trimmings are required, make them of as neat and close an order as possible. Slight figures frequently require a little pad under the front of the armhole and under the shoulder bones. Here you may introduce a little fine horsehair – that used for stringing pearls is the most desirable. Horsehair now takes the place of the wadding formerly used; it is far superior in consequence of its elasticity. The French never use any other kind of material for pads. Slight figures look far better in bodies that are trimmed. Either capes or folds are extremely becoming.

Observe in silks and satins that are shaded, there is

an up and a down. The same remark applies to velvets and woollen cloths.

On Piping or Braiding

Silk and other orders of pipings, as well as braid, produce a pleasing, easy and agreeable description of embroidery. Pipings for working embroidery may be prepared after the following method whether in crape, gros de Naples or satin. Cut narrow strips, immediately on the bias, 2″ wide. The slightest deviation from the bias will cause the pipings to twist and spoil the effect. Join the strips together on the straight grain, fold in half and run it on the wrong side, leaving it to form a groove so that a bodkin may be pulled through it to turn it inside out. Stretch the silk where the running has taken place to its fullest extent, by holding the thumbnail firmly on the work and drawing it along. Take a rather wide turning in as this serves to give support and to fill out the pipe when turned.

This kind of trimming is worn worked in patterns round capes, for trimming on bodies and frequently as a skirt trimming. When it is worked in any kind of

pattern it will be necessary to have a guide, which is arranged after the following plan.

Select some simple embroidery pattern for the purpose. It must be pricked into holes by a small stiletto. Arrange the pattern on the material and weight the corners. A small muslin bag containing pounce (a fine powder) must be rubbed over it, so as to penetrate through each pierced hole. The design thus produced must be traced over with a drawing pencil, the pounce not being sufficiently durable.

Rouleaux are made after the same mode as the piping, with the difference that the silk is cut double or triple the width of the one described according to the size of rouleau required. Equal attention must be paid to the cutting of the material on the direct bias. A certain thickness of lamb's-wool is passed through the groove on the end of the bodkin and left in the rouleau when it is turned.

The Principals in some houses of business object to the turning of both pipes and rouleau; in such cases the silk is still cut the same width, the method in the work alone differing. The breadths must be joined in one long length, doubled and pinned through the middle. The doubling will reduce the width to 1″, and it must be doubled again, first at one edge and then the other. The lamb's-wool may be laid in the rouleau and the material felled over, where the running and the turning is objected to.

The method of tracing through the pierced embroidery pattern is equally desirable for braiding. The great beauty in braiding consists in making the different turnings perfectly pointed. When braid embroidery is finished it should be passed under a warm, but not hot, iron, the work being covered with tissue paper. This flattens the braid and adds much to the beauty of its appearance.

On Cutting out Skirts with Economy

After taking the length of the back and allowing for the hem at the bottom and a turning in at the top, you cut off from the lining muslin as many breadths as will make four yards in width when joined together. Tack all the seams together; gather up the top without any slope and slip it over the head. Tighten the gathering thread to the waist when the lining body is found to be correct. You will then have the opportunity of noticing where the pins for the top of the skirt may be placed. This of course must be regulated by the shape of the bottom of the bodice. Be careful to place your row of pins close together, as when the gathering thread is unfastened the pins will otherwise be at too great a distance.

The front breadth, by bringing it to the slope of the pins, will be found to be much shorter than the back. There are four straight breadths and four sloping: the three long ones are for the back and the shortest for the front. The sloping ones are for the side. Cut out the silk by the lining pieces. Be sure as you proceed with the breadths to tack each firmly.

In order to give the skirt a pretty "set" you must be careful to place a greater quantity of fullness on the hips than in the front, whether you gage or plait (pleat) it. I recommend that the most minute attention be paid to the arranging of the plaits (pleats) or gathers. The seam under the arm of the body will serve as a safe criterion, for where the rise of the hip takes place, there the plaits (pleats) or gathers should thicken. Be particularly careful that your skirt droops rather than catches up at the back; the latter is extremely vulgar in its appearance.

Plain skirts are much admired by the Parisians, and their method of supporting them from the figure is far more *distingué* than the plan adopted by our English ladies. With the former the crinoline or wove horsehair is introduced in wide strips into the hem of the skirt and is arranged after the following method. When the skirt lining is run together, a strip of crinoline or horsehair is cut about a quarter and a half (13½″) wide, doubled to half the width and placed inside the hem. Should it be wished to make the skirt appear very full, two straight pieces of the crinoline, of the width and thickness of that in the hem, may be laid on in bands about a quarter of a yard distant

up the skirt. These are enclosed by a piece of lining muslin. This quite supersedes the necessity of the stiff petticoat.

On Goffering

Goffering in England is done by a machine, the effect of which is stiff and ungraceful, whereas the French mode, with straws, is simple, elegant and speedily accomplished. It is necessary in the first place to take a slip of wood – (the flat boards used by silk mercers for folding their satins are desirable for the purpose). This board must be covered very smoothly with a piece of flannel, which is sewn together at the back. Over this place middle-width tapes which must be well secured at each end. The tapes should be placed at about 1½″ from the edge of the board, on either side. Proceed by folding the border or whatever trimming you may be about to goffer into three or four thicknesses, placing it immediately between the tapes. Pin the end you begin from firmly to the flannel; after which place first one straw over and another straw under, until you reach the extremity of the border. Be sure to keep the straws as closely knit together as possible. Should they be disposed to slip apart, fasten them with a pin. When the straws have been carried as far as may be desired, turn back a small piece of the fabric and fasten it with pins on either side. By these means the straws will arrange themselves closely together. Place a rather damp muslin over the straws and pass a warm iron lightly over the whole.

Next place the board at a short distance from the fire and allow the work to dry gradually. Withdraw the straws and the goffer is shewn perfect. The size, of course, depends on the straws selected. Another advantage to be derived from this mode of procedure is that should the border be of a costly nature, such as Valenciennes lace, there is no danger to be apprehended, which there might be from the destructive character of the machine.

On Pinking and Trimmings in Velvet

Pinking is an elegant style of trimming in gros de Naples: it is done by means of a punch and a block of lead. Both are very inexpensive articles. The punches are of various shapes and sizes. The gros de Naples is cut out in bias widths according to the depth of trimming chosen. The strips are then tacked one on the other, keeping the edges perfectly even. The substance should amount to about six thicknesses. They are placed on the block of lead with some paper between and struck sharply with a hammer. On its removal the pattern will be found to be perfect and well finished. Prior to the untacking of the breadths the edges of the pinking should be touched with a camel's hair brush, steeped in a weak solution of gum. This will prevent ravelling.

Velvet leaves, arranged either as flowers or in the form of a wreath, have a pretty and simple effect when placed above the flounces so as to form a heading.

The effect is extremely good for slight mourning where the trimming is of black velvet and the robe of white watered gros de Naples. The designs are cut either by punch or with sharp scissors. Before the velvet is cut out in shapes a thin paper should be gummed at the back. If the velvet be black choose the tissue paper of the darkest tint you can find. This will allow your trimmings to wear as long as your dress, otherwise the edges will become rough by unravelling.

General Observations and Rules on Padding

No definite length of material can be given for the making of a dress, since the number of yards depends on the various draperies selected.

In fixing in sleeves, be careful that the seams are arranged in their proper places, which must depend entirely on the sleeve selected.

Paddings of horsehair, as before observed, will be found indispensable. If the figure be larger on one side than the other, reduce the front and side piece a little under the arm. Should this prove insufficient, add small pads of the finest horsehair to the inner part of the body of the dress. Tight sleeves look much better if wadded if the arm be thin: this must be done with the greatest care.

I recommend amateurs to be most particular in cutting out material, such as stripes and plaids. Begin by cutting off the skirt of your dress. Then cut out the right sleeve and half the body, and for the left and opposite side of the body arrange the stripes or plaids immediately on each other so that they may face. The plaids and stripes should likewise be made to match for the skirt.

Advertisement in 'The World of Fashion' (November 1849)
The Gallery of English Costume

IMPORTANT TO COUNTRY MILLINERS.

Mrs Dewsbury, Paper Pattern and Bonnet Shape Establishment, 3 Rathbone Place, Oxford Street. Established 1834.

Mrs Dewsbury respectfully announces to her numerous customers that her show rooms are now open with a large selection of the Newest Designs in full sized Paper Patterns consisting of Dresses, Cloaks, Mantlelets, Spencers, Bodices, Sleeves etc. Also, in addition to the above, Mrs D. begs the attention of ladies in general to inspect her large and well selected stock of Bonnet Shapes, they being of the most superior style and quality. They have never failed to give satisfaction to the wearer.

Patterns forwarded to all parts of the Kingdom at the undermentioned prices: A set of twelve Articles, with Box, £1.2.0; a set of six ditto with Box, 11s. 6d. A parcel containing six Articles postage paid, 11s. 0d.; A large Article, postage paid, 3s. 6d. All remittances, per Post-office order, payable in Oxford Street, to Mary Dewsbury.

The Art of Dressmaking, containing Plain Directions in Simple Language from the Fitting of the Pattern to the Finish of the Dress (1849)
MRS CORY
The British Museum

To the Industrious Daughters of Tradesmen, and to Persons of Limited Means, this Useful Little Manual is Chiefly Addressed.

The Author has endeavoured, in as simple language as possible, to convey thoroughly her meaning in the Art of Dressmaking, and is led to believe that she has so far succeeded, that any person, with but a moderate capacity, can take a pattern by her directions and work from it better than many who have served an apprenticeship, as it is well known that apprentices are seldom taught how to take a pattern from the figure: the only way in which they acquire the knowledge is by being allowed to hand the pins to the Operator, who is always the Mistress, or First-hand.

THE ART OF DRESSMAKING

Supposing the reader to have no idea of cutting the first pattern, she is requested to take the body of an old dress and pick it to pieces, when, if made with a single plait (dart), the half-front will be something in the form shown in the Frontispiece of this little manual. The half-front is then to be laid upon a piece of undressed Holland, and a pattern cut from it, allowing the Holland to remain a couple of inches larger than the body where the dotted line is pointed out in

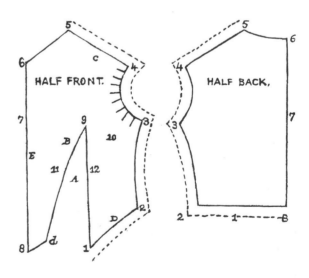

27 *A bodice pattern. From 'The Art of Dressmaking' by Mrs Cory.*

the wood-cut, and NOT cutting out the space at letter A. The half back is next taken and a pattern cut from that in a similar manner.

It must be remembered that this is not the pattern to work from, but only a necessary groundwork on which to take the paper, or working pattern.

INSTRUCTIONS FOR TAKING A PATTERN FROM THE FIGURE

First tie a piece of ribbon round the neck of the person whose pattern is to be taken, and place the Holland pattern of the half-back on the left side of her back, pinning it to the ribbon at the nape of the neck, and placing two or three pins to keep it firmly and exactly down the centre of the person's back. Then proceed to fit the left side of the front, pinning the pattern at Fig. 6 to the ribbon between the two little prominent bones of the neck. Carry it down smoothingly with the hand, placing pins rather closely to keep it firmly in its position, as low as the point Fig. 8 is required to be, then with the hand smooth tightly along, from Fig. 7 to Fig. 5, and pin Fig. 5 of the front and Fig. 5 of the back together. Next, pin tightly and carefully all along the shoulder to Fig. 4 of the front and back, being particular that the pins are kept in a direct line; that accomplished, smooth the hand tightly over from Fig. 9 to Fig. 10 and pin the pattern to the person's underdress. The next thing is to form the plait (dart), which is done by taking up the smallest perceptible piece at Fig. 9 and gradually increasing the size to be removed between the lines 11 and 12, according to the figure of the person, taking care to place each pin closely following the last in a direct line, until the length of waist required by fashion is arrived at. After this pin the front and back together at Fig. 3, as close under the arm as possible. Should the armhole be too tight, cut in the direction of the small lines as figured in the Frontispiece.

Proceed pinning the back and front together from Figs. 3 to 2, down to the waist, then take the pin out at Fig. 10 and tighten the pattern wherever it may be required by placing the pins farther in. Then trace with pins a line, whether for a high or low dress, round the armhole and round the waist.

The pattern is then to be removed, and with a needle and thread a line is to be traced where every pin is, before taking it out, being very careful in keeping a direct line, particularly in the front plait (dart) or plaits (for more may be made in the same manner), forming them with taste a little apart at the top, and gradually nearing each other towards the waist. Particular attention must also be directed in keeping the line straight round the waist, the neck at the shoulder seam and under the arm, otherwise, when the pattern is taken off on paper, the front shoulder seam will be longer than the back, or the reverse.

When the pattern has been traced out with thread, the pins are to be removed and the pattern then placed upon some stiff brown paper, to which it is to be pinned as firmly as possible, the way of the threads. Some dressmakers cut their Holland patterns the crossway of the stuff, but the straight way is to be preferred as it is less liable to give, consequently a more perfect pattern of the figure is obtained. In pinning the Holland pattern to the paper it is necessary to smooth it down and across, so that it may lie perfectly even, the pins being placed rather closely together on the outside of the tracing threads. When

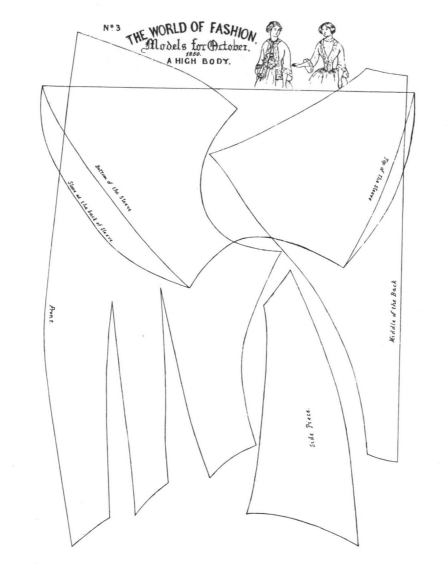

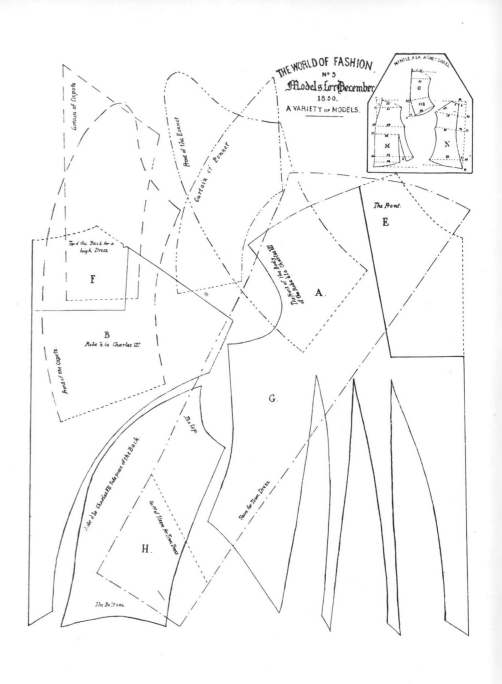

28 A full-size printed paper pattern of a bodice from 'The World of Fashion', October 1850. Reduced to scale $\frac{1}{4}''=1''$. The Gallery of English Costume.

29 A full-size printed paper pattern of various garments. From 'The World of Fashion', December 1850. Reduced to scale $\frac{1}{4}''=1''$. The Gallery of English Costume.

these directions have been attended to, pierce holes through the Holland and paper to mark out the pattern in the latter, then unpin it from the Holland and cut out through the holes. A correct pattern will then be obtained, from which a drawn, plaited (pleated) or plain body can be made.

A PLAIN BODY

Is made in the following manner: fasten the paper pattern down firmly on the stuff the dress is to be lined with, and trace the pattern correctly all round the edge with a piercer. Remove the paper, and cut out the distance from the holes you desire the turnings in to be, then lay the lining on the dress-material, exactly the same way of the threads (always). Cut out and trace the lining marks (the holes) to the outside.

In cutting the back it must be allowed to be half the width of the hem larger, in order that it may wrap, or on the front, if to be fastened before. Tack it together and try on. If the foregoing directions have been adhered to, it will fit; but should it be too loose, take it in at the seams, under the arm and at the shoulder. Having made the body fit, stitch it neatly together, just within all the tracing threads. Finish by cording top and bottom according to taste. A body lining cut in the same manner is required for a plaited (pleated) or gauged body.

TO MAKE A PLAITED (PLEATED) BODY

When the lining is cut, close the front plait (dart) from 9 to 1: then allow, if for a slight person, two breadths of silk for a front, or more if in thin material. Pin the silk at point 8 and up to 7, leaving the length of the silk hanging at the throat, then divide the breadth into about five plaits (pleats). Place the first one close to 8 and up to E, about $\frac{3}{4}''$ distance from the centre. The other four are in like manner placed near each other at the waist, and widen to nearly an inch towards the top. Place the body on your lap, so that the knee will support it as near 9 as convenient, and having the throat next you, carry the first plait (pleat) up close to 5. If a striped dress, keep the stripes at the edge of each plait (pleat). Smooth your hand to keep them tight and close to the lining, and spread them to within $1\frac{1}{2}''$ or $2''$ of 4; then tack along on to the lining where it has been pierced from the pattern and cut off. You will then find the slope from one side will work into the other, which do exactly like the last; tack the half-fronts together at the tracing thread, and then to the backs, as in the last pattern, and try on. Take in as in last pattern if required.

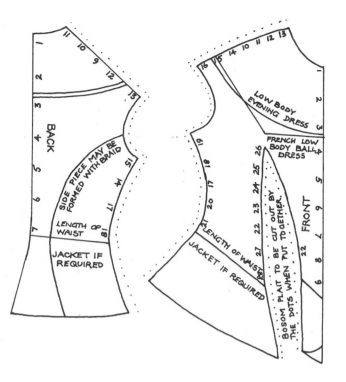

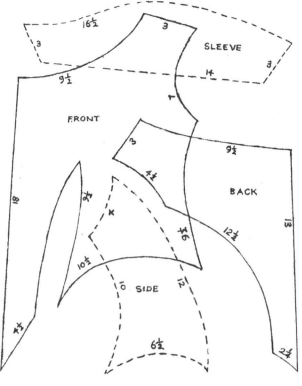

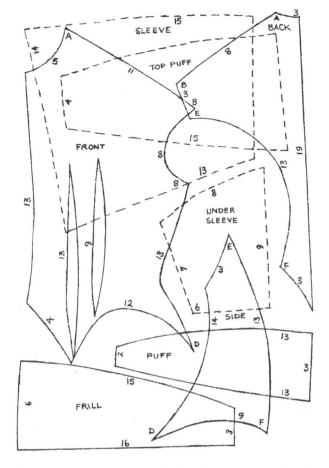

30 A full-size printed paper pattern of a bodice redrawn and reduced to scale ⅛″=1″. From 'A New, Simple and Complete Method of Dressmaking' by Mrs T. Whiteley, 1855. The British Museum.

31 The Drapery Body. It is peculiarly becoming to the figure, whether slender or stout. For a ball, white tarlatan possesses a simple elegance, as also pink, blue, black or

white net. If a more durable article be required, a black Brussels taffeta or any of the soft summer silks are as eligible. The drapery trimming of the body is of the same material as the dress. It is not given in the working pattern, being only a piece of material nine inches wide and a couple of yards long. From 'The Englishwoman's Domestic Magazine', August 1858. The British Museum.

32 A Promenade Dress. Plain silks are now preferred for this purpose in the French capital. These are made with two skirts trimmed with a vandyke of quilled ribbon, the turning of each point being finished with a small tassel. The sleeve is full and closed at the cuff. From 'The Englishwoman's Domestic Magazine', January 1859. The British Museum.

A GAGED OR DRAWN FRONT IS THUS MADE

Measure the length of the body from 5 to 8, and allow the material 1″ longer at each end. Cut it and allow for fullness as in the last pattern; trace a line to mark the middle, and proceed to run the body, leaving a plain piece at each end the length from 3 to 9. Leave the thread long enough to remain without drawing, until sufficient runnings have been made to reach to B. They may be placed, according to taste, from ¼″ to ½″ apart. Have ready a stiff brown paper pattern of the front, with the plait (dart) firmly sewn, and tack the middle of the body to the middle of the paper, up from 8 to 6, drawing it up gradually till it fits from line 12 on one side to line 12 on the other. Carry the fullness regularly up to the shoulder from 5 along to 4; tack everywhere round the outside of the pattern. Have ready the lining, and remove it on to that, tacking the two tracing lines together to make it fit. Should it not be wished to be lined to the throat, cut away to the height of a low body, when tack to the backs and try on.

Skirts are so simple, that I conclude anyone who would attempt a body would know how to make them, but I will give them a hint as to one of the best ways.

Measure the length required from the waist to the ground at the back and allow for hem and turning. Cut it and as many breadths as you intend putting into the skirt. Run all these together, after clipping

the selvedge. Cut the lining to match and tack the selvedge at every seam to it, leaving the turnings between lining and silk until you come to the last, which close up inside. Measure the length in front from point 8 to the feet, just letting it clear the ground, turn in, in a sloping direction, the front quarter of the skirt regularly along till you arrive at the back quarter, which will not require any slope. Gather it and sew the front quarter on just under the waist cording from 8 to 2, the back quarter from 2 to 8, the other half in like manner.

No directions can be given for sleeves as fashion alone guides the shape of them.

In conclusion the Authoress will be happy to impart further instruction to those who may wish to be perfected in the Art of Dressmaking.

Her terms are seven shillings and sixpence for the course of six lessons, including patterns of Mantle, Sleeves etc. On Mondays, Wednesdays and Fridays, she receives pupils at her own residence, No. 8, Constitution Row, Gray's Inn Road (opposite Cromer Street); and on the alternate days she gives lessons at the residences of pupils, if in parties of four, at One Guinea the course.

The World of Fashion (August 1850)
The Gallery of English Costume

We this month present to Our Subscribers and the

Public, in addition to the customary Attractions of this favoured Magazine, the

FIRST COLLECTION OF PATTERNS

for fashionable Dresses and Millinery which we propose continuing every month in order that Ladies of Distinction and their Milliners and Dressmakers may possess the utmost facilities for constructing their costumes with the Most Approved Taste and in the Highest and Most Perfect Style of Fashion. These IMPORTANT NOVELTIES will be Supplementary and in addition to the present Attractive features of *The World of Fashion* and WITHOUT ANY ADDITIONAL CHARGE, the price of this Magazine the Only Authority for Ladies' Fashions, being still ONE SHILLING ONLY. It will, therefore, always be the Cheapest, as well as the Most Elegant and Authentic publication of the kind.

The Models for August 1850, which are given in the present number of *The World of Fashion*, consist of the following Elegant Novelties adopted by the Ladies of the British Aristocracy

   I Model of a Full Dress
  II Model of a Bonnet
 III Model of a Capote

(These Models may be traced with ease by the peculiar style of line devoted to each as explained at the top of the large sheet upon which they are engraved).

A Pictorial Outline of Englishwomen's Costume c.1660-1860
These drawings were made from contemporary engravings, fashion-plates, costumes and photographs to illustrate the gradual change of shape and evolution of new styles. The dates given are those of the original sources but are not necessarily of the introduction of the particular fashion.

1660 1670 1680 1690 1705-10 1720-30 1740-50

1760 1780 1790 1795 1800 1805 1810 1815 1820

1825 1830 1835 1840 1845 1850 1855 1860

*c.*1660-5   Claydon House

A bodice in ivory silk, trimmed with crossway strips of ivory satin, ¾″ wide. These strips are pinked in rounded shapes and a length of ivory braid ⅛″ wide is stitched down the centre of each one. The whole bodice is mounted on top of a stiff, boned corset made of two layers of linen with ¼″ wide whalebones stitched between them. Two long bones encased in linen form the base of the narrow shoulder-piece under which the sleeve is fitted. The bodice is lined with fine white silk which has perished in places, thus revealing the boned linen foundation and the coarse linen strip stitched to the centre front to hold a wooden busk. The worked bars on the tabs were probably used to secure the petticoat or the hip pads which were worn underneath it. Unfortunately the petticoat and overskirt have not been preserved. Both garments would have been cut on the straight grain of the material and closely gathered into small pleats at the waist. The ones shown are taken from portraits of this period, as are the chemise sleeves shown with the bodice. The neckline would have been edged above by the frill or lace of the chemise.

c.1720-50   The Laing Art Gallery and Museum

A wrapping gown in bright cherry pink satin with a large brocaded design in a paler shade of pink and golden yellow, worn over a dome-shaped hoop-petticoat. As the wrap-over is not very wide, the dress might have been fastened at the waist with a brooch or ribbon tie. The bodice is close-fitting the back being cut in one piece or 'en fourreau' with the skirt. Inside the front of the bodice are two strips of linen doubled over with eyelet holes worked in them. The gown fastens by lacing through these holes over the corset or stomacher. A modesty piece, which was a gathered strip of fine linen or lace, would be pinned or stitched to the top of the corset and a tucker. which was a frilled lace edging, could border the rest of the neckline. The latter was either tacked onto the dress or was part of the day shift pulled out to show. The end of the chemise sleeve and its ruffle would have shown below the cuff of the wrapping gown. This style of dress was worn throughout the first half of the eighteenth century, being at the height of its popularity between c.1735-50. This particular gown was dated by the fabric. The detail of the bodice shows the worked eyelet holes in the linen strip for the lacing. The design of the silk was dated to c. 1707-14 . (See pages 70 and 71 for further information).

22

A BODICE C1660-65

A WRAPPING GOWN C1720-50

SHOULDER PIECE CUT IN SILK, LINED WITH LINEN AND LEFT UNBONED.

FIRST AND LAST DECORATIVE SLEEVE BANDS MEET THESE POINTS ON THE BODICE.

SIDE PANEL TO HERE.

SLASH UP THE TABS AND FOLD A SELF COLOURED SILK BRAID OVER THE RAW EDGES STITCH DOWN. THE EFFECT IS OF A CLOSE BUTTONHOLE STITCH. SMALL WORKED BARS ARE MADE IN MATCHING SILK IN THE CENTRE OF EACH TAB.

THE UNDERARM SLEEVE PANEL IS GATHERED UP WITH THE SLEEVE AT THE TOP THE BOTTOM IS LEFT SMOOTH ALTHOUGH THERE ARE SOME GATHERS IN THE SLEEVE THE TWO END DECORATIVE BANDS ARE MOUNTED ON THE EDGES OF THIS PANEL.

SHOULDER PIECE UNDER WHICH THE SLEEVE IS SEWN

CENTRE FRONT

STITCH INSIDE BODICE AT FRONT

LINEN BUSK HOLDER

UNDERARM SLEEVE PANEL

CENTRE BACK

ALL THE DECORATIVE STRIPS OF PINKED SATIN ARE CUT ON THE CROSS.

FRONT SLEEVE

GATHER AT TOP AND BOTTOM ON THE DOTTED LINES.

BAND FOR BOTTOM OF SLEEVE.

LENGTHS OF STRIPS FOR THE SLEEVE.

FRONT

BACK

THE SLEEVE IS CUT FIRST IN SILK AND THEN IN LINEN. THE PIECES ARE MADE UP SEPARATELY AND THEN PUT TOGETHER AND TREATED AS ONE PIECE OF FABRIC FOR GATHERING. THE PINKED STRIPS ARE MOUNTED ON STRAIGHT SILK STRIPS 3" WIDE THESE ARE MADE FROM 1½" WIDE PIECES FOLDED IN HALF, WITH THE RAW EDGES TUCKED IN. A STRAIGHT BAND IS STITCHED ROUND THE BOTTOM OF THE SLEEVE BEFORE MOUNTING THE 1" DEEP PLEATED SATIN.

IN BRIGHT CHERRY PINK SATIN WITH A BROCADED DESIGN IN A PALER SHADE OF PINK AND GOLDEN YELLOW. THE WHITE LINEN UNDER BODICE IS MADE UP FIRST AND THE BROCADE IS MOUNTED ON TOP. THE STITCHING GOES THROUGH TO THE LINEN. THE DART IS MADE ON THE FRONT BODICE BEFORE PLEATING THE FABRIC. THE CUFF IS JOINED TO THE SLEEVE AND THE WHOLE SLEEVE IS THEN MOUNTED ON WHITE LINEN FOR THE LINING. THE LINEN IS CUT ON THE SAME GRAIN AS THE BROCADE. THE LINEN AND THE BROCADE ARE WORKED AS ONE PIECE OF MATERIAL.

DART

FRONT LINEN UNDER BODICE

FACING STITCHED ON HERE

THE FRONT IS LEFT OPEN TO THIS POINT

THE FRONT LINEN UNDER BODICE AND EYELET HOLE STRIPS ARE CAUGHT INTO THIS TUCK WITH ONE ROW OF STITCHING.

LEAVE THE SEAM OPEN BETWEEN THESE MARKS FOR HANGING POCKETS

JOIN IN FABRIC

JOIN IN FABRIC

JOIN IN FABRIC

JOIN IN FABRIC

JOIN IN FABRIC

JOIN IN FABRIC

JOIN IN FABRIC

CENTRE FRONT

THE CENTRE FRONT WAS ORIGINALLY OPEN TO THIS MARK WHEN THE SILK WAS MADE UP AS A MANTUA

JOIN IN FABRIC THIS WAS THE HEM OF THE GOWN IN ITS ORIGINAL FORM

THE SKIRT IS LINED FROM THE HEM TO THE DOTTED LINE WITH RED GLAZED WOOLLEN FABRIC. THIS LINE IS APPROXIMATE AS THE LINING VARIES IN DEPTH FROM 28" AT THE CENTRE BACK TO 26" AT THE SIDES AND 16" OR 17" AT THE FRONT. THE WOOL IS PIECED TOGETHER VERY ROUGHLY.

FRONT

BACK

SLEEVE

MAKE A TUCK HERE

CUFF

THIS PART OF THE CUFF IS TURNED UNDER, CUT AND PLEATED TO FORM A FACING.

BODICE SIDE SEAM TO HERE.

BACK LINEN UNDER BODICE

PANEL TO COVER THE PLEATS AT THE BACK NECK. THE CENTRE BACK IS INDICATED BY THE MARK.

CENTRE BACK TO FOLD

SEW THE PLEATS DOWN TO THIS POINT.

CENTRE BACK

THE SILK WAS ORIGINALLY MADE UP AS A MANTUA (SEE PAGE 70) FROM TWO LENGTHS RUNNING STRAIGHT OVER THE SHOULDERS FROM GROUND LEVEL AT THE FRONT, TO THE HEM OF A SLIGHTLY TRAINED SKIRT AT THE BACK. THE FRONT WAS ORIGINALLY ALMOST THE SAME LENGTH AS THE MANTUA ON PAGE 70. A PIECE WAS JOINED ONTO THE FRONT SKIRT TO MAKE IT LONG ENOUGH FOR THE PRESENT STYLE, PROBABLY FROM THE SHORT TRAIN WHICH HAS BEEN CUT OFF. THE DESIGN OF THE FABRIC RUNS UP AT THE BACK AND SIDES OF THE SKIRT AND DOWN AT THE FRONT.

THE DESIGN OF THE SILK IS SO FLAMBOYANT THAT THE JOINS DO NOT SHOW, NOR THE FACT THAT THE DESIGN RUNS UP AT THE BACK AND DOWN AT THE FRONT OF THE GOWN.

c.1730-50   Snowshill Manor

The jacket of a riding habit in deep drab-coloured, worsted woollen cloth. The cuffs and collar are faced with velvet to match the colour of the coat. The skirts of the habit and inside the front of the bodice, behind the buttons and buttonholes, are lined with rose pink silk taffeta. The front and back bodice and sleeves are all lined with heavy white linen. The jacket could have been worn open over a waistcoat. The petticoat of the riding habit is missing but it would probably have been made of the same material as the jacket and worn over a hoop-petticoat. The one shown in the drawing is taken from a contemporary portrait.

c.1775-85   Snowshill Manor

A caraco jacket in slate blue and silver grey brocaded silk lined with glazed saffron yellow wool. It is trimmed round the neck and sleeves with $\frac{3}{4}''$ wide silver grey ribbon, ruched into $\frac{1}{8}''$ box pleats $\frac{1}{4}''$ apart. Detachable white lawn ruffles or round cuffs would have been tacked to the ends of the sleeves. This jacket was worn over a petticoat which could have been decorated with a flounce or made entirely of the same material as the caraco. The front is fastened edge to edge with concealed hooks and eyes. A gauze handkerchief could have been draped round the neck and tucked into the corsage in front. Inside the caraco are two loops which were probably used to hang it up on pegs.

THE JACKET OF A RIDING HABIT C1730-50

IN DEEP DRAB COLOURED WORSTED WOOLLEN CLOTH WHICH IS VERY FIRM AND STIFF TO HANDLE. THE COLLAR AND CUFFS ARE FACED WITH VELVET TO MATCH THE CLOTH. THE COLLAR IS CUT ON THE SAME GRAIN AS THE WOOL BUT THE CUFFS ARE CUT ON THE STRAIGHT. THE BALANCE MARK ON THE COLLAR MEETS THE SHOULDER SEAM OF THE JACKET

CENTRE BACK

COLLAR

A CANVAS INTERFACING IS USED TO STIFFEN THE JACKET FROM THE CENTRE FRONT TO THE DOTTED LINE
THE SKIRTS ARE NOT STIFFENED. THEY ARE LINED WITH ROSE PINK FINE SILK TAFFETA. A PANEL OF TAFFETA IS ALSO STITCHED OVER THE CANVAS INTERFACING INSIDE THE FRONT.

FRONT FACING IN PINK TAFFETA

CENTRE BACK

CENTRE FRONT

X = STAB STITCH TO HOLD PLEATS TOGETHER
----- = UNDER FOLD LINE OF PLEAT.
—·— = MEETING LINE OF PLEAT EDGE.

BACK SKIRT

FRONT FLAP TO DOTTED LINE

CUT SLIT FOR POCKET HERE. MOUNT POCKET AS SHOWN.

FRONT SKIRT

POCKET BAG IN PINK TAFFETA.

THE FRONT AND BACK BODICE AND THE SLEEVES ARE ALL LINED WITH HEAVY WHITE LINEN. "MISS BETTY" IS WRITTEN IN BLACK INK ON THE LINEN NEAR THE BOTTOM OF THE JACKET ON THE LEFT SIDE.

METHOD USED IN ASSEMBLING JACKET
1. JACKET STITCHED TOGETHER AND INTER-FACING MOUNTED AT THE FRONT.
2. COLLAR FACED WITH VELVET AND STITCHED TO JACKET.
3. PINK TAFFETA SKIRT LINING MADE UP AND EDGE STITCHED TO JACKET.
4. WHITE LINEN BODICE LINING MADE UP AND PINK TAFFETA PIECES JOINED ON AT THE CENTRE FRONT.
5. THE LINING EDGE-STITCHED TO THE JACKET.
6. LINEN AND TAFFETA CAUGHT TOGETHER AT THE WAIST.
7. CUFFS FOLDED BACK AT THE ENDS OF THE SLEEVES AND FACED WITH VELVET.
8. LINING STITCHED TO SLEEVE ENDS.
9. BUTTONHOLES CUT AND OVER-SEWN.
10. STRIPS OF HEAVY SILVER BRAID ⅛" DEEP SEWN ON TOP TO RESEMBLE BUTTONHOLE STITCH.

TURN CUFF UNDER ON FOLD LINE TO FACE THE SLEEVE AND JOIN THE LINING.

SHOULDER SEAM TO HERE

FACE POCKET FLAP WITH PINK TAFFETA CUT ON THE CROSS.

UNDER SLEEVE   TOP SLEEVE

CUT SLEEVE LINING TO HERE ONLY.

VELVET UNDER CUFF   VELVET TOP CUFF
FOLD   FOLD

TURN BACK THE ENDS OF THE SLEEVES TO FORM THE CUFFS AND MEET THE DOTTED LINE.

A CARACO JACKET C1775-85

IN BROCADE WITH A SLATE BLUE BACKGROUND AND A DESIGN OF FLOWERS, LEAVES AND BERRIES IN SILVER GREY. IT IS LINED THROUGHOUT WITH SAFFRON YELLOW FINE GLAZED WOOL CUT ON THE SAME GRAIN.

METHOD USED IN ASSEMBLING JACKET.
1. BROCADE JACKET STITCHED TOGETHER.
2. SAFFRON YELLOW WOOL LINING STITCHED TOGETHER.
3. PLACE LINING INSIDE JACKET WRONG SIDES TOGETHER AND EDGE STITCH THE CENTRE FRONT BODICE AND SKIRT AND THE ENDS OF THE SLEEVES.
4. TURN THE BROCADE OVER THE LINING AT THE NECK EDGE AND AROUND THE HEM ¾" DEEP.
5. HEM STITCH THESE TURNINGS.
6. PLEAT UP ¾" WIDE SILVER GREY RIBBON INTO ⅛" TUCKS APPROXIMATELY ⅜" APART.
7. MOUNT THE RIBBON TRIMMING ON THE NECK AND SLEEVES. PASS A CORD THROUGH THE NECK SEAM TO TIE AT THE CENTRE FRONT.

A BAR IS WORKED HERE ON THE RIGHT SIDE OF THE JACKET TO HOLD THE PLEAT FIRMLY AND TAKE THE STRAIN FROM THE SEAM. A SMALL PIECE OF YELLOW WOOL IS ALSO STITCHED OVER THE LINING AT THIS POINT ON THE WRONG SIDE TO TAKE THE WEIGHT OF THE PLEAT.

CENTRE FRONT

THE FRONT FASTENS EDGE TO EDGE WITH HOOKS AND EYES
PIECES OF TAPE 13" LONG ARE STITCHED INSIDE THE JACKET ON BOTH FRONTS TO TIE ROUND THE WAIST.

THE PLEATS IN THE SKIRTS FALL LOOSELY AND ARE NOT PRESSED INTO POSITION.

CENTRE BACK

YELLOW BRAID LOOPS 5" LONG [10" DOUBLED OVER] ARE ATTACHED BELOW THE SIDE SEAMS INSIDE THE JACKET AT THE BACK. THESE MAY HAVE BEEN USED TO HANG THE JACKET ON PEGS WHEN NOT BEING WORN, OR MAY HAVE BEEN TIED ROUND THE WAIST WITH THE FRONT TAPES TO TAKE THE WEIGHT OF THE PLEATS.

THE BROCADED SILK DATES FROM THE LATE 1760'S. THE CARACO WAS PROBABLY CUT FROM A SACK DRESS WHICH HAD BEEN COMPLETELY UNPICKED.

SLEEVE

LOOPS OF BRAID ⅜" WIDE AND 2¼" LONG [4½" DOUBLED OVER] ARE STITCHED INSIDE THE JACKET AT THE CENTRE FRONT. THESE MAY HAVE BEEN PINNED TO THE PETTICOAT TO KEEP THE FRONT IN POSITION.

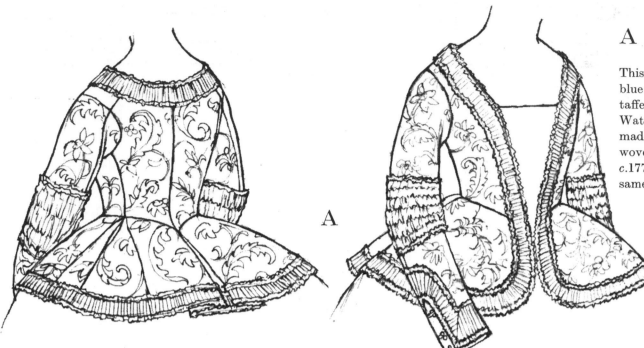

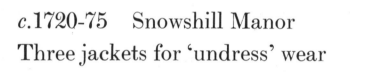

A   *c.*1720-40

This jacket is in saffron yellow woven silk patterned with green, white, orange, navy blue and pale blue flowers and leaves. It would have been worn over a stomacher. The bodice is lined with white taffeta. The fabric dates from *c.*1711-15 and the style resembles some of the jackets in paintings by Watteau. The cut follows the lines of the riding habit *c.*1730-50 (page 24). The jacket may have been made up from pieces left over from a dress, a little later than the date when the material was woven. The white gauze trimmings appear to have been added to renovate the jacket, probably in *c.*1770-80, and the bottom parts of the sleeves, which are detachable, may have been put in at the same time.

C   *c.*1760-70

This jacket is in pale rose pink and silver shot silk with a pattern of deep pink flowers over deep blue and deep green stripes. The cut of this jacket resembles that of the caraco jacket *c.*1775-85 (page 24). The fabric is dated *c.*1760-70 and, as the cuffs are pleated, it is possible that the jacket was made for an older lady who preferred this easier style to the winged cuffs of the 1760's, which were usually cut to shape without pleats at the elbows.

*c.*1720-75   Snowshill Manor
Three jackets for 'undress' wear

Jacket bodices and petticoats were worn throughout the eighteenth century for 'undress' wear, a contemporary term used to describe clothes that fell short of the full dress worn for formal occasions. The petticoats were plain or quilted during the first half of the eighteenth century. From *c.*1750 the plain variety was generally flounced round the hem, becoming more popular than the quilted type by *c.*1775. Gauze or lawn handkerchiefs could have filled in the necklines of the jackets and lawn ruffles would have been tacked to the ends of the elbow length sleeves.

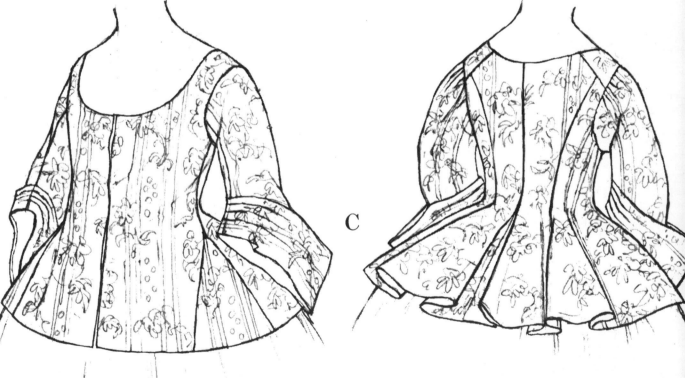

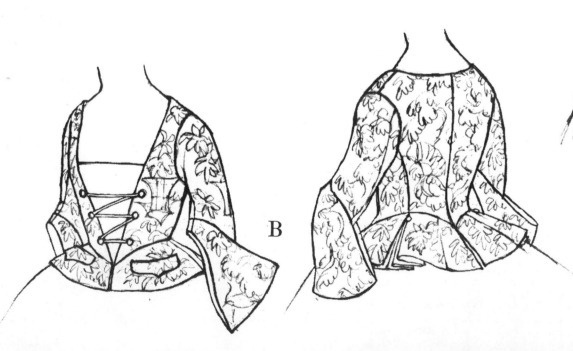

B   *c.*1735-40

This jacket is in bright red brocaded silk with a design of flowers in leaf green, deep green, navy blue, royal blue, pale blue, turquoise, maroon and silver. The bodice and skirt are both lined with pale blue taffeta. The sleeves are lined with white linen. Three buttons are stitched on either side of the front for laces to fasten the jacket over a stomacher. The cuffs, bodice fronts and skirt are all interlined with a stiff, brown, felted fabric.

A · A JACKET C 1720-40

IN SAFFRON YELLOW WOVEN SILK WITH A PATTERN OF GREEN,
WHITE, ORANGE, NAVY BLUE AND PALE BLUE FLOWERS AND
LEAVES.

THE BODICE IS DECORATED WITH A RUCHED STRIP OF
WHITE GAUZE 2½" DEEP WITH HEAVY WOVEN THREADS
RUNNING THROUGH IT ⅛" APART. ORANGE AND LEMON
STRIPED RIBBON ¼" WIDE IS
RUCHED AND STITCHED TO BOTH
EDGES. THE WHOLE STRIP IS
THEN MOUNTED ONTO THE
BODICE. IT OVERLAPS BY ¼"
AT THE CENTRE BACK NECK
AND DOWN THE FRONT
BODICE, GRADUALLY
INCREASING TO A 1"
OVERLAP ROUND THE
HEM. THIS IS MARKED
BY THE DOTTED LINE.
ALL THE GAUZE TRIMMINGS
WERE PROBABLY ADDED IN
C 1770 TO RENOVATE THE
JACKET.

LEAVE OPEN TO
HERE FROM THE
WAIST SEAM

THE LOWER SLEEVE IS DECORATED
AT THE WRIST WITH A RUCHED STRIP
OF WHITE GAUZE 2" DEEP TRIMMED
WITH RIBBON.

SHOULDER
SEAM TO
HERE

SMALL TUCK
TAKEN UNDER
THE ARM

UNDER
SLEEVE

TOP
SLEEVE

UNDER
SLEEVE

TOP
SLEEVE

LEAVE
OPEN
FOR 4½"
AT THE
WRIST
AND FASTEN

ROUND CUFF

WITH HOOKS AND EYES. THE BODICE
AND SLEEVES ARE LINED WITH FINE
WHITE SILK TAFFETA CUT ON THE
SAME GRAIN AS THE PATTERNED
SILK. THE SKIRTS OF THE JACKET ARE
NOT LINED. THE BOTTOM OF THE LINING
IS CAUGHT TO THE WAIST SEAM AND
CONCEALS ALL THE RAW EDGES. THE
LINING AND THE BODICE ARE EDGE
STITCHED TOGETHER AROUND THE NECK AND DOWN THE FRONT. THE ROUND
CUFF ON THE UPPER SLEEVE IS CUT IN WHITE GAUZE, AND GATHERING
THREADS RUN ON THE DOTTED LINES. ORANGE AND LEMON STRIPED RIBBON
¼" WIDE IS STITCHED FLAT TO BOTH EDGES. THE GATHERING THREADS ARE
PULLED UP AND THE CUFF IS MOUNTED ONTO THE BOTTOM OF THE SLEEVE
ALLOWING ½" TO HANG LOOSE AT THE EDGE. THE LOWER SLEEVE IS
MADE UP SEPARATELY FROM THE UPPER SLEEVE AND COULD BE
DETACHED. IT IS LINED WITH HEAVY WHITE LINEN. THE EDGE OF THE
UPPER SLEEVE IS FITTED TO THE DOTTED LINE ON THE LOWER SLEEVE.

B · A JACKET C 1735-40

TWO ¼" BONES, ONE
ON EITHER SIDE OF
THE CENTRE BACK,
IN WHITE COTTON
CASINGS.

THE BODICE IS
INTERLINED FROM
THE FRONT EDGE
TO THE DOTTED LINE

CENTRE BACK

FRONT

FOLD THIS PIECE BACK
AND CATCH TO THE
FRONT SKIRT
PLEATS

THESE PLEATS
ARE CAUGHT
TO HOLD THEM
IN POSITION

THESE PLEATS ARE
LEFT TO HANG LOOSELY

THE POCKET FLAP IS CUT
ON THE CROSS. IT IS FOR
DECORATION ONLY

TOP
SLEEVE

UNDER
SLEEVE

THREE ⅛" TUCKS ARE
MADE TO SHAPE THE
SLEEVE HEAD. THE CUFFS
ARE MADE UP WITH THE
INTERLINING AND THEN
FACED WITH SILK. THE
DOTTED LINE INDICATES
THE POSITION OF THE
SLEEVE WHEN
STITCHING ON THE
CUFF.

THE JACKET IS MADE OF BRIGHT RED BROCADED SILK WITH
A DESIGN OF FLOWERS IN LEAF GREEN, DEEP GREEN, NAVY-
BLUE, ROYAL BLUE, PALE BLUE AND TURQUOISE, MAROON AND SILVER
THREAD.

THE BODICE AND SKIRTS ARE LINED WITH PALE BLUE SILK
WHILE THE SLEEVES ARE LINED WITH WHITE LINEN.

THE POCKET FLAPS, THE CUFFS, THE BODICE FRONT AND THE
SKIRTS OF THE JACKET ARE ALL INTERLINED WITH A FIRM
FELTED SUBSTANCE WHICH CLOSELY RESEMBLES STIFF BROWN
BLOTTING PAPER.

C · A JACKET C 1760-70

IN PALE ROSE PINK AND SILVER WOVEN SILK WITH A PATTERN OF
DEEP PINK FLOWERS OVER DEEP BLUE AND GREEN STRIPES. BOTH
BODICE AND SLEEVES ARE LINED THROUGHOUT WITH FINE
UNBLEACHED LINEN.

SHOULDER SEAM TO HERE

BACK   FRONT

SLEEVE

= FITTING LINE FOR CUFF

THE SLEEVE IS MADE
UP SEPARATELY FROM
THE LINING. THE TWO
LAYERS ARE STITCHED
EDGE TO EDGE AT THE
ELBOW WITH TINY
STITCHES. THE SLEEVES
ARE THEN FITTED INTO
THE ARMHOLES
ALLOWING SLIGHT
GATHERING OVER THE
SLEEVE HEAD.

SLEEVE   SLEEVE

FOLD

THE CUFF IS FACED WITH UNBLEACHED
COTTON. THE SILK AND THE LINING ARE EDGE
STITCHED TOGETHER. THE COMPLETED CUFF IS
BACK STITCHED TO THE SLEEVE ON THE FITTING
LINE AND THEN PLEATED UP.

SLEEVE SEAM TO HERE

FIRST MAKE UP THE BODICE LINING
AND THEN THE PINK SILK BODICE.
FIT THE TWO TOGETHER, WRONG SIDES
FACING EACH OTHER AND TAKE IN
THE DART AT THE SIDE. FIT THE
GUSSET IN THE SLASH MADE
BELOW THIS DART. STITCH
THE BODICE AND THE
LINING EDGE TO EDGE
ROUND THE NECKLINE,
THE FRONT AND THE HEM.

THE GUSSET IS
BACK STITCHED
IN FROM THE
RIGHT SIDE.

CENTRE BACK

FOLD

CENTRE FRONT

GUSSET

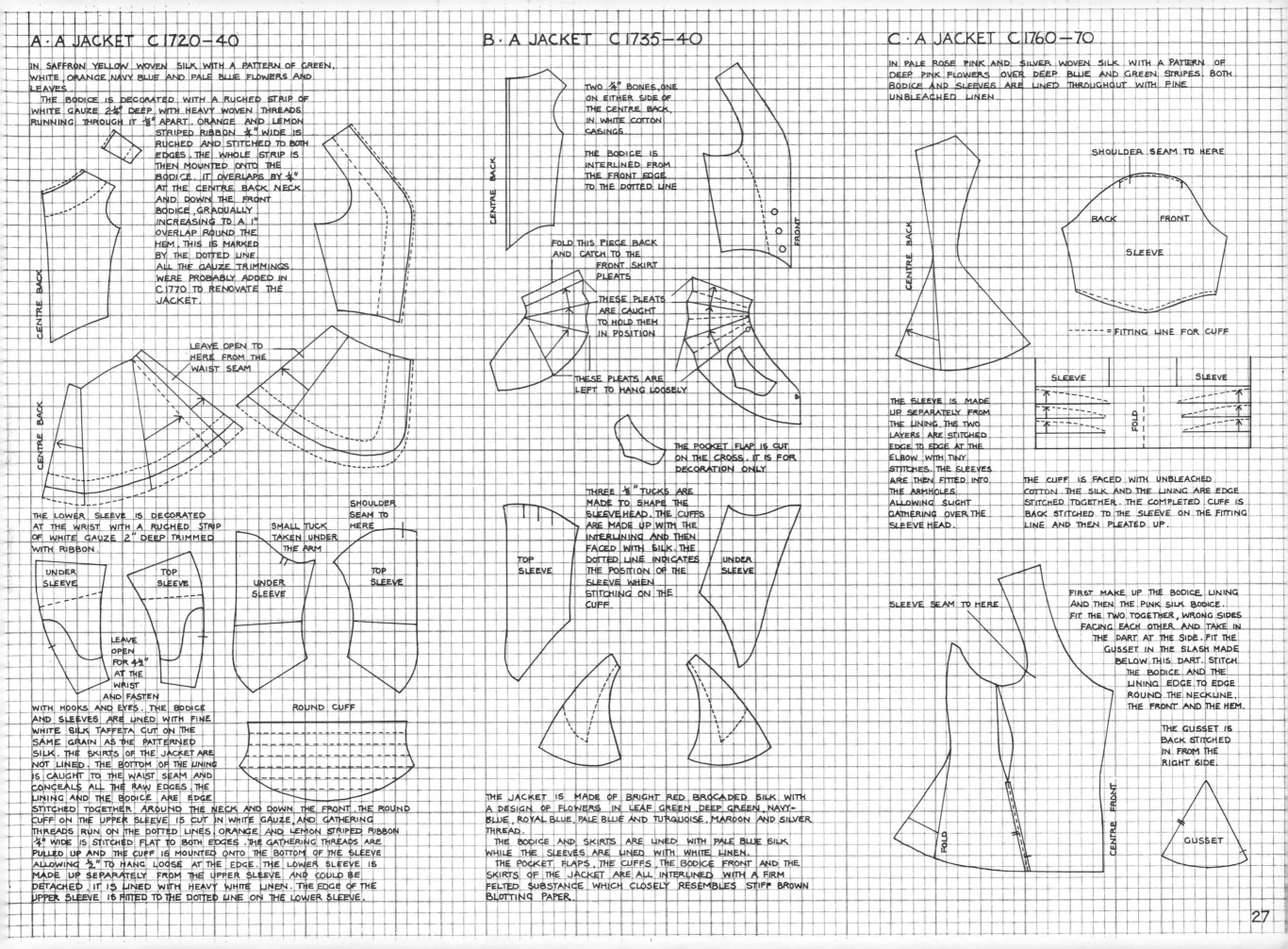

27

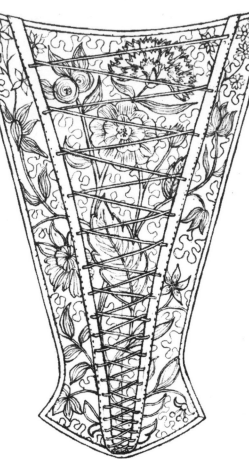

c.1700-50   Snowshill Manor

A stomacher with a boned foundation, in pale ivory silk embroidered in silver thread and deep green, leaf green, wine, brown, lemon and beige silk. The backing is made of two layers of fine, unbleached canvas with narrow whalebones stitched firmly between them. The edge of the stomacher is bound with ivory silk ribbon.

c.1745-55   Snowshill Manor

A detail of the pet-en-l'air (page 29) showing the white linen lining which laces up at the back to make the bodice fit more closely.

c.1725-50   Snowshill Manor

A hanging pocket in heavy white cotton and wool mixture with a woven stripe, backed with white linen. The embroidery is carried out in chain stitch in dark green, acid yellow, golden yellow, navy blue, bright pink, maroon, leaf green and pale pink fine wool. Hanging pockets were tied round the waist with tapes and were reached through openings left in both gown and petticoat. They were worn during most of the eighteenth century, being replaced by handbags known as 'Ridicules' or 'Indispensibles', at the end of the 1790's.

c.1750-75   The Victoria and Albert Museum

A stomacher with alternate rows of 1¼″ wide white-bordered, rose pink ribbon and silver and white thread lace 1½″ wide, pleated and mounted on white muslin.

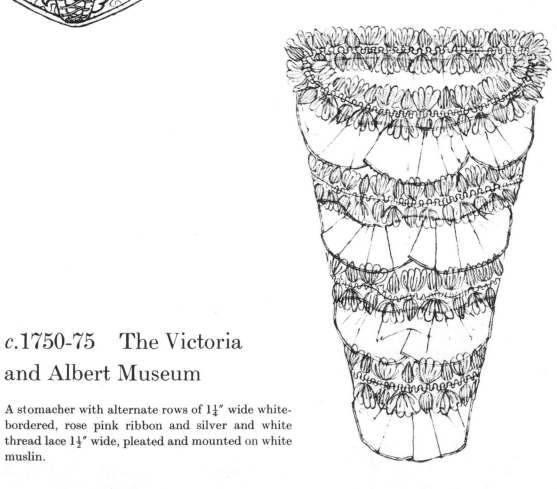

A HANGING POCKET C1725-50

IN WHITE HEAVY COTTON AND WOOL
MIXTURE WITH A WOVEN STRIPE. THE
POCKET IS BACKED
WITH WHITE LINEN.
THE EMBROIDERY
IS CARRIED OUT
IN CHAIN STITCH
AND SATIN STITCH.
LONG TAPES
ARE ATTACHED
AT THE TOP TO
TIE ROUND
THE WAIST.

SLASH OPEN AND BIND.

A STOMACHER WITH A BONED FOUNDATION C1700-50

IN IVORY HEAVY SILK EMBROIDERED
WITH SPRAYS OF FLOWERS AND LEAVES.
THE ⅛" BONES
ARE STITCHED
BETWEEN TWO
LAYERS OF FINE
CANVAS. THE
EMBROIDERED
IVORY SILK PANEL
IS THEN MOUNTED
ON TOP AND THE
EDGES ARE BOUND
WITH SILK OF THE
SAME COLOUR.

CENTRE FRONT

A STOMACHER TRIMMED WITH LACE AND RIBBON C1750-75

THE ALTERNATE ROWS OF 1¼" WIDE
ROSE PINK RIBBON AND 1½" WIDE
SILVER AND WHITE
THREAD LACE ARE
MOUNTED ON A
WHITE MUSLIN
FOUNDATION THIS
STOMACHER IS NOT
BONED. IT WOULD
HAVE BEEN PINNED
UNDER THE FRONT
OF A DRESS OR OVER
A CORSET TO HOLD
IT IN POSITION.

A PET-EN-L'AIR C1745-55

IN IVORY SILK WITH A BROCADED PATTERN OF SPRAYS
OF FLOWERS IN GREEN, PINK, YELLOW OCHRE, PALE
BLUE AND WHITE. THE PET-EN-L'AIR IS LINED WITH
WHITE LINEN. THE SILK AND THE LINING ARE MADE UP
AS ONE AS FAR AS THE CENTRE BACK. THERE THEY
ARE WORKED SEPARATELY. THE
LINING HAVING A LACED PANEL
FOR 7½". THE SILK IS PLEATED
UP AND STITCHED AT THE TOP
OF THE LINING. A FEW CATCH
STITCHES HOLD THE LINING TO
THE SILK AT THE WAIST. THE
LACED PANEL AT THE BACK IS
TO PULL THE BODICE IN AND
MAKE IT FIT MORE CLOSELY.

CENTRE BACK

CENTRE BACK

THE LINING IS PLEATED UP WITH
THE SILK AS ONE LAYER OF
MATERIAL FOLLOW THE DIRECTION
OF THE ARROWS ON THE SILK
TO FORM THE PLEATS.

LINING

FRONT

C.B.

PANEL OF BROCADE
TO COVER THE TOP
OF THE PLEATS AT
THE CENTRE BACK.

AN EYE IS SEWN TO EACH SHOULDER ON THE
FOLD UNDER THE ROBINGS. THEY MAY HAVE
BEEN USED TO SECURE A FINE LAWN
HANDKERCHIEF WHICH COULD HAVE BEEN
WORN AT THE NECK.

THE TABBED FALSE
FRONT IS STITCHED
ON THE DOTTED LINE TO
THE EDGE OF THE
PET-EN-L'AIR THE
BOTTOM TWO TABS ARE
STITCHED TOGETHER
FOR 1" FROM THE SIDE
TO THE BALANCE MARK
THE FRONT FASTENS
EDGE TO EDGE WITH
HOOKS AND EYES.

CENTRE FRONT

THE TUCKS ON
THE SLEEVE FIT
IN THIS CURVE

SHOULDER
SEAM TO
THIS
POINT

BACK

MAKE SMALL TUCKS OVER
THE SLEEVE-HEAD.

SLEEVE

THE DOTTED
LINE ON THE
SLEEVE INDICATES
THE STITCHING LINE
OF THE FLOUNCE THE
SEAM OF THE FLOUNCE
MEETS THE SLEEVE SEAM.

THE DOTTED LINE ON THE
FLOUNCE INDICATES A LINE
OF GATHERING STITCHES.

CENTRE BACK

SLASH OPEN ON
THE DOTTED LINE.
FOLD BACK THE
EDGES AND HEM
TO NEATEN AS AN
OPENING FOR THE
HANGING POCKETS

BACK

FLOUNCE

29

*c.*1745-55   Snowshill Manor

A pet-en-l'air, sometimes called a French jacket, in ivory silk with a brocaded pattern of pink, green, yellow ochre, white and pale blue sprays of flowers. The lining is in white linen and laces up at the back to make the dress fit more closely to the figure. The pleats at the back are only half-lined to avoid a bulky appearance at the top. The front tabs fasten with concealed hooks and eyes. The pet-en-l'air would have been worn with a petticoat which could have been plain or made in matching fabric, over boned stays and a dome-shaped hoop. A gauze or muslin handkerchief could have been worn at the neck with the long ends held in position by the tabs.

*c.*1745-60   Snowshill Manor

A white quilted satin jacket with a hood and matching petticoat. The white ruffles of the chemise would have shown below the flounce at the end of the sleeve. This suit would probably have been worn for travelling. The satin was backed with fine wool and silk before the quilting was carried out. At the hem of the petticoat wadding was used only under the leaves and petals of the flowers, giving a raised effect to the design. The bodice lining is in white linen. The false front fastens edge to edge with hooks and eyes. A handkerchief could have been worn at the neck. The skirt would have been supported by a dome-shaped hoop-petticoat. (See page 70).

A QUILTED JACKET WITH A HOOD AND MATCHING PETTICOAT   C 1745-60

IN WHITE SATIN QUILTED OVER WOOL AND BACKED WITH WHITE SILK. THE WOOL WADDING
IS UNDER ALL THE SKIRT EXCEPT THE PART NEAR THE HEM, WHERE IT IS ONLY USED TO
GIVE THE RAISED PETAL SHAPES OF THE FLOWERS.
 THE BODICE OF THE JACKET, THE FALSE FRONT AND THE SLEEVES ARE LINED WITH
WHITE LINEN. THE BODICE LINING IS MADE UP FIRST AND THE ¼" BONES ARE PUT INTO
THE ⅜" WIDE CASINGS. THE QUILTED JACKET IS THEN STITCHED TOGETHER AND MOUNTED
ON TOP OF THE LINING. THE FALSE FRONT IS CUT IN LINEN AND COVERED WITH QUILTED
SATIN. IT IS BONED UNDER THE HOOKS AND EYES TO KEEP IT FIRM.
 THE PETTICOAT PLEATS INTO 26½". IT IS MOUNTED ONTO A ¾" WIDE RIBBON BAND WHICH
IS DOUBLED OVER THE RAW EDGES, AND TIES AT THE CENTRE BACK.

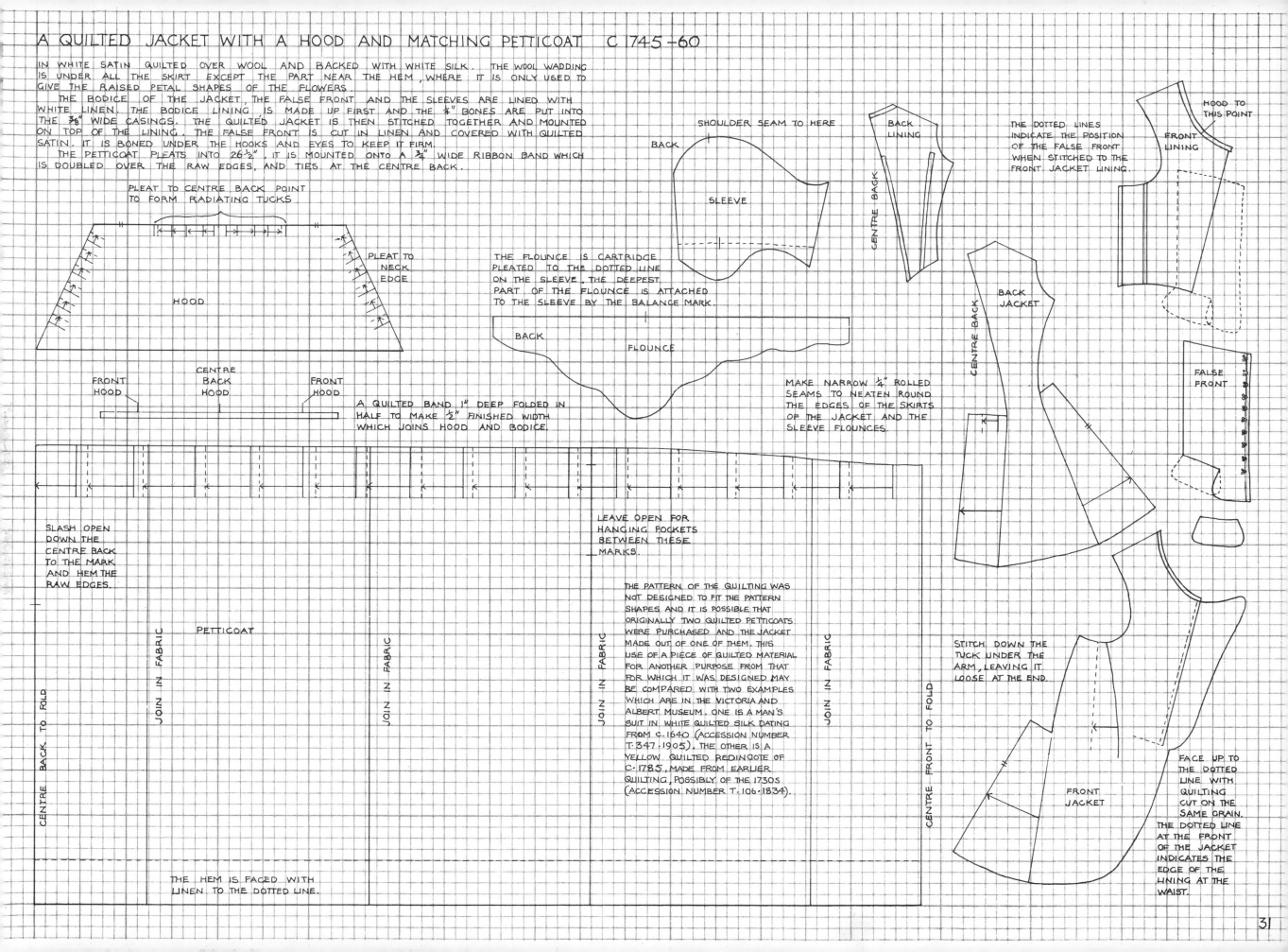

PLEAT TO CENTRE BACK POINT
TO FORM RADIATING TUCKS

PLEAT TO NECK EDGE

HOOD

FRONT HOOD   CENTRE BACK HOOD   FRONT HOOD

A QUILTED BAND 1" DEEP FOLDED IN
HALF TO MAKE ½" FINISHED WIDTH
WHICH JOINS HOOD AND BODICE.

SLASH OPEN DOWN THE CENTRE BACK TO THE MARK AND HEM THE RAW EDGES.

CENTRE BACK TO FOLD

JOIN IN FABRIC

PETTICOAT

JOIN IN FABRIC

LEAVE OPEN FOR HANGING POCKETS BETWEEN THESE MARKS.

THE PATTERN OF THE QUILTING WAS
NOT DESIGNED TO FIT THE PATTERN
SHAPES AND IT IS POSSIBLE THAT
ORIGINALLY TWO QUILTED PETTICOATS
WERE PURCHASED AND THE JACKET
MADE OUT OF ONE OF THEM. THIS
USE OF A PIECE OF QUILTED MATERIAL
FOR ANOTHER PURPOSE FROM THAT
FOR WHICH IT WAS DESIGNED MAY
BE COMPARED WITH TWO EXAMPLES
WHICH ARE IN THE VICTORIA AND
ALBERT MUSEUM. ONE IS A MAN'S
SUIT IN WHITE QUILTED SILK DATING
FROM C.1640 (ACCESSION NUMBER
T.347.1905). THE OTHER IS A
YELLOW QUILTED REDINGOTE OF
C.1785, MADE FROM EARLIER
QUILTING, POSSIBLY OF THE 1730s
(ACCESSION NUMBER T.106.1834).

JOIN IN FABRIC

JOIN IN FABRIC

CENTRE FRONT TO FOLD

THE HEM IS FACED WITH LINEN TO THE DOTTED LINE.

SHOULDER SEAM TO HERE

BACK

SLEEVE

THE FLOUNCE IS CARTRIDGE
PLEATED TO THE DOTTED LINE
ON THE SLEEVE. THE DEEPEST
PART OF THE FLOUNCE IS ATTACHED
TO THE SLEEVE BY THE BALANCE MARK.

BACK

FLOUNCE

MAKE NARROW ¼" ROLLED
SEAMS TO NEATEN ROUND
THE EDGES OF THE SKIRTS
OF THE JACKET AND THE
SLEEVE FLOUNCES.

BACK LINING

CENTRE BACK

THE DOTTED LINES
INDICATE THE POSITION
OF THE FALSE FRONT
WHEN STITCHED TO THE
FRONT JACKET LINING.

HOOD TO THIS POINT

FRONT LINING

BACK JACKET

CENTRE BACK

FALSE FRONT

STITCH DOWN THE
TUCK UNDER THE
ARM, LEAVING IT
LOOSE AT THE END.

FRONT JACKET

FACE UP TO
THE DOTTED
LINE WITH
QUILTING
CUT ON THE
SAME GRAIN.
THE DOTTED LINE
AT THE FRONT
OF THE JACKET
INDICATES THE
EDGE OF THE
LINING AT THE
WAIST.

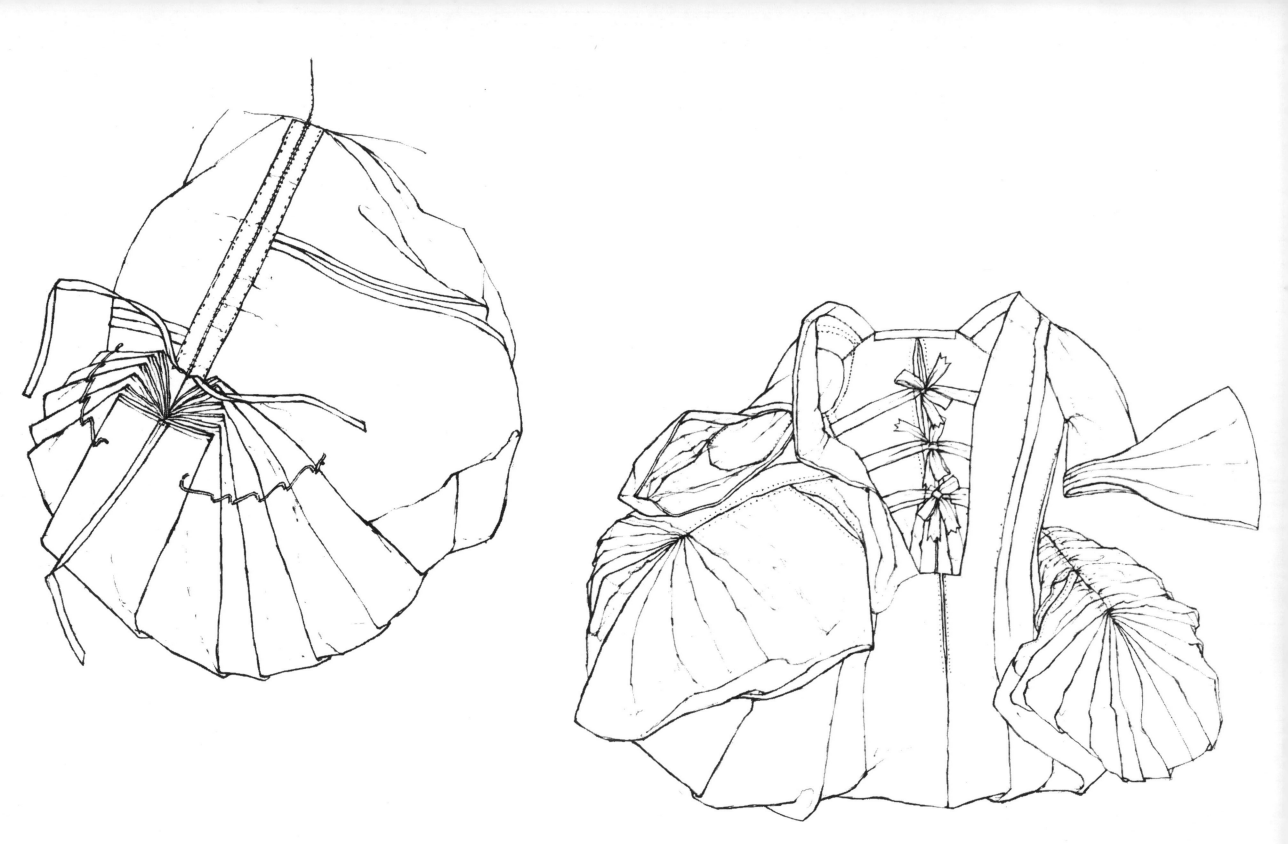

*c.*1745-55   The Victoria and Albert Museum

Inside the wide hip-piece of the pale beige and silver brocaded silk sack dress (page 34), showing the casings with the ribbons running through them. Double threads catch all the pleats together and hold them in position.

A detail of the pale beige and silver brocaded silk sack dress (page 34) showing one of the wide hip-pieces gathered up. The other side is left smooth to show the openings through which the hanging pockets are reached. The ribbon-ties at the back are to adjust the bodice to fit the figure under the pleats.

IN BROCADE WITH A PALE BEIGE BACKGROUND AND A
FORMAL DESIGN OF FLOWERS AND LEAVES IN SILVER.
THE BODICE AND SLEEVES ARE LINED WITH WHITE
LINEN. THE BODICE LINING IS MADE UP FIRST OVER THE
CORSET, AND THEN THE BROCADE IS MOUNTED ON TOP AND
STITCHED DOWN. INSIDE THE WIDE HIP PIECES OF THE
SKIRT ARE CASINGS WITH WHITE SILK RIBBON INSIDE TO
PULL THE FABRIC UP [SEE THE DRAWING]. THESE MAY HAVE
BEEN ADDED WHEN THE VERY WIDE HOOPS WENT OUT
OF FASHION EXCEPT FOR COURT WEAR IN C.1760, OR
PERHAPS TO ENABLE THE GOWN TO BE WORN OVER A
NARROWER HOOP AS AN ALTERNATIVE STYLE WHEN
THE GOWN WAS FIRST MADE.

CENTRE
BACK

STRIP OF BROCADE FOR NEATENING
THE PLEATS.

BACK
BODICE
LINING

THE BROCADE STRIP
LAPS OVER THE LINING
FOR ½" AT THE BACK

FRONT
BODICE
LINING

THE FRONT OF THE
SACK DRESS WOULD
HAVE FASTENED WITH
HOOKS OR RIBBONS
FROM THE BODICE
LINING OVER THE
STOMACHER OR
THE CORSET.

MATCH TO BALANCE MARKS ON SLEEVE

PANEL OF
BROCADE
TO FILL IN
THE CUFF

FOLD

THE CUFF IS FACED
WITH PALE BEIGE
SILK TO MATCH THE
BROCADE. IT IS
STIFFENED WITH
A WHITE FELTED
FABRIC CLOSELY
RESEMBLING
STIFF BLOTTING
PAPER.

SLEEVE

THE DOTTED LINE OVER THE
SLEEVE INDICATES THE
POSITION OF THE FRONT
PLEAT. THE CUFF IS MADE
UP COMPLETELY AND
STITCHED TO THE
SLEEVE. THE DOTTED
LINE MARKS THE TOP
OF THE CUFF.

THE TOP OF THE
CUFF MEETS THE
DOTTED LINE

JOIN OF CUFF
TO HERE

THE DOTTED LINES ON THE BODICE
LINING PIECES INDICATE THE STITCHING
LINES FOR THE SLEEVE AND FOR THE
TUCK MADE IN THE BROCADE ON THE
BACK BODICE. THE 1" WIDE RIBBONS TIE
AT THE CENTRE BACK UNDER THE PLEAT. THEY ARE ATTACHED AT
BOTH SIDE SEAM AND CENTRE BACK TO HOLD THEM FIRMLY

FIT TO DOTTED LINE ON SLEEVE

FIT TO DOTTED LINE

UNDER   TOP
CUFF   CUFF

FOLD

A PANEL OF BROCADE
IS STITCHED INSIDE
THE CUFF AND TO THE
THE SLEEVE
BETWEEN THE
BALANCE MARKS
TO NEATEN IT.

THE PLEATS ARE STITCHED LOOSELY
INSIDE TO HOLD THEM IN POSITION
[SEE THE DRAWING].

OPEN HERE FOR HANGING POCKETS

FRONT SKIRT
OPEN TO HERE

CENTRE BACK

JOIN IN FABRIC

JOIN IN FABRIC

JOIN IN FABRIC

JOIN IN FABRIC

CENTRE FRONT

THE HEM IS LINED AS FAR
AS THE DOTTED LINE WITH
SILK TO MATCH THE COLOUR
OF THE BROCADE.

c.1745-55 The Victoria and Albert Museum

A sack dress in pale beige stiff silk with a brocaded design of flowers and leaves in silver thread. It has a closed front and a wide skirt to be worn over an oblong hoop petticoat. After c.1750 it is more usual to find the sack worn as an open gown with a petticoat. Casings are stitched inside the wide hip pieces of the skirt, through which run white silk ribbons to pull the fabric up. These may have been added when the very wide hoops went out of fashion except for court wear in c.1760, or, more probably, put in when the gown was made, to enable it to be worn over a narrower hoop as an alternative style. The ruffles from the chemise show at the end of the sleeve. The front would have been fastened, probably with hooks, over the corset or a stomacher. The latter might have been embroidered, or decorated with a ladder of ribbon bows known as 'échelles'. A white lawn tucker with a lace edge could have bordered the neckline.

c.1770-5 Snowshill Manor

A cherry and white striped brocade sack dress [the French 'Robe à la Française'] with a matching petticoat and a buttoned 'compere' or false front. It would have been worn over pocket hoops which were tied round the waist and fitted over each hip. The design on the white stripe of the fabric is one of curving sprays of pink roses with deep green leaves. Treble flounces finish the sleeves. Ruffles of white embroidered lawn, cambric or lace would have been worn underneath them, tacked to the end of the sleeve so that they could be removed for laundering. The sleeve flounces and the furbelows [the strips of pleated material which decorate gown and petticoat] are all edged with cherry red braid. Sleeves during the eighteenth century were usually cut across the grain of the fabric so that the stripes run round the arm, instead of down from shoulder to elbow as they do in this example. A tucker could have bordered the neckline.

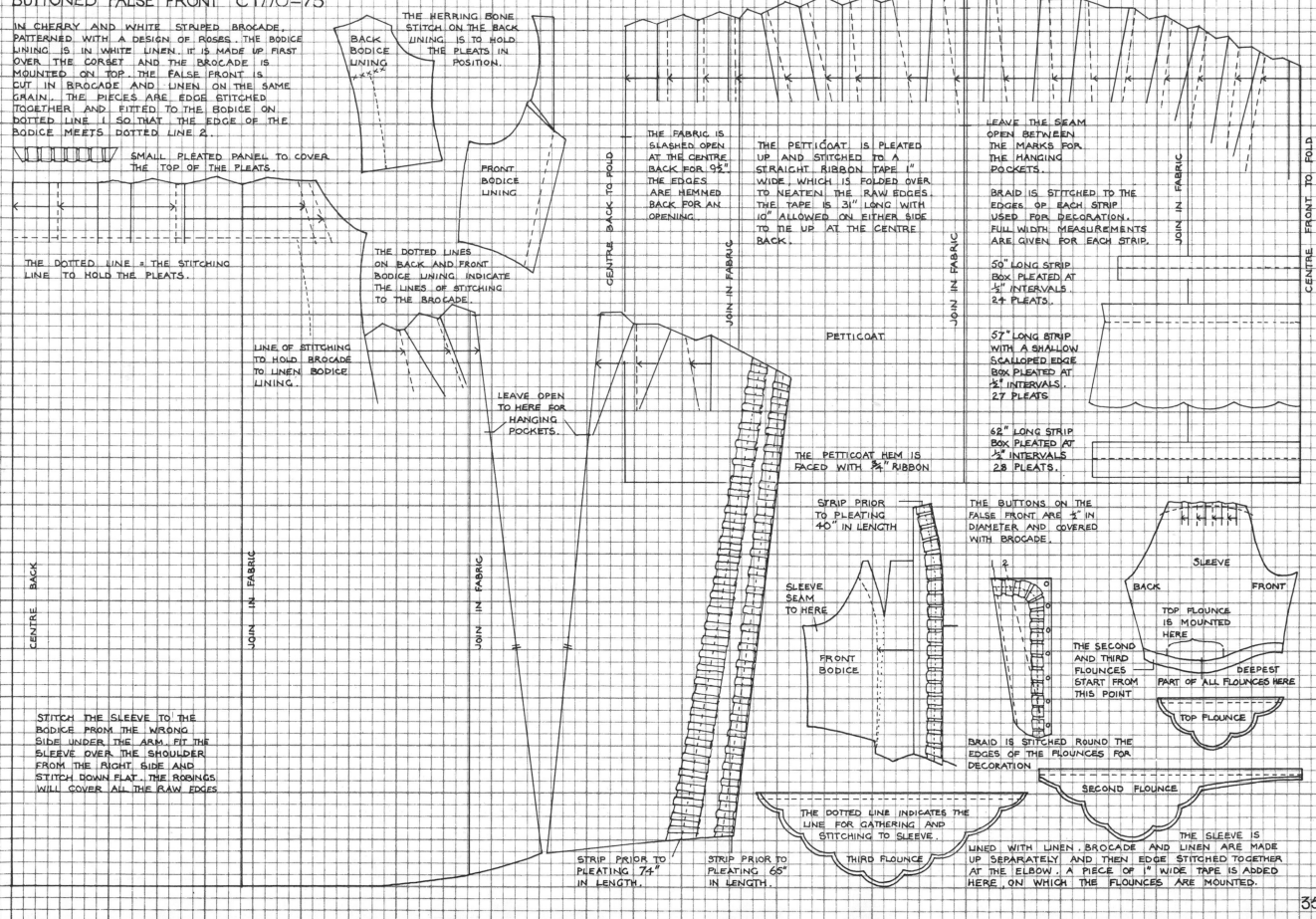

A SACK DRESS [THE FRENCH ROBE A LA FRANCAISE] WORN AS AN OPEN GOWN WITH A MATCHING PETTICOAT AND A COMPERE OR BUTTONED FALSE FRONT C 1770-75

IN CHERRY AND WHITE STRIPED BROCADE, PATTERNED WITH A DESIGN OF ROSES. THE BODICE LINING IS IN WHITE LINEN. IT IS MADE UP FIRST OVER THE CORSET AND THE BROCADE IS MOUNTED ON TOP. THE FALSE FRONT IS CUT IN BROCADE AND LINEN ON THE SAME GRAIN. THE PIECES ARE EDGE STITCHED TOGETHER AND FITTED TO THE BODICE ON DOTTED LINE 1 SO THAT THE EDGE OF THE BODICE MEETS DOTTED LINE 2.

SMALL PLEATED PANEL TO COVER THE TOP OF THE PLEATS.

THE DOTTED LINE = THE STITCHING LINE TO HOLD THE PLEATS.

THE HERRING BONE STITCH ON THE BACK LINING IS TO HOLD THE PLEATS IN POSITION.

BACK BODICE LINING

FRONT BODICE LINING

THE DOTTED LINES ON BACK AND FRONT BODICE LINING INDICATE THE LINES OF STITCHING TO THE BROCADE.

LINE OF STITCHING TO HOLD BROCADE TO LINEN BODICE LINING.

LEAVE OPEN TO HERE FOR HANGING POCKETS.

CENTRE BACK TO FOLD

JOIN IN FABRIC

THE FABRIC IS SLASHED OPEN AT THE CENTRE BACK FOR 9½". THE EDGES ARE HEMMED BACK FOR AN OPENING.

THE PETTICOAT IS PLEATED UP AND STITCHED TO A STRAIGHT RIBBON TAPE 1" WIDE WHICH IS FOLDED OVER TO NEATEN THE RAW EDGES. THE TAPE IS 31" LONG WITH 10" ALLOWED ON EITHER SIDE TO TIE UP AT THE CENTRE BACK.

PETTICOAT

THE PETTICOAT HEM IS FACED WITH ¾" RIBBON

JOIN IN FABRIC

LEAVE THE SEAM OPEN BETWEEN THE MARKS FOR THE HANGING POCKETS.

BRAID IS STITCHED TO THE EDGES OF EACH STRIP USED FOR DECORATION. FULL WIDTH MEASUREMENTS ARE GIVEN FOR EACH STRIP.

50" LONG STRIP BOX PLEATED AT ½" INTERVALS. 24 PLEATS.

57" LONG STRIP WITH A SHALLOW SCALLOPED EDGE BOX PLEATED AT ½" INTERVALS. 27 PLEATS

62" LONG STRIP BOX PLEATED AT ½" INTERVALS. 28 PLEATS.

JOIN IN FABRIC

CENTRE FRONT TO FOLD

STRIP PRIOR TO PLEATING 40" IN LENGTH

THE BUTTONS ON THE FALSE FRONT ARE ½" IN DIAMETER AND COVERED WITH BROCADE.

SLEEVE SEAM TO HERE

FRONT BODICE

CENTRE BACK

JOIN IN FABRIC

STITCH THE SLEEVE TO THE BODICE FROM THE WRONG SIDE UNDER THE ARM. FIT THE SLEEVE OVER THE SHOULDER FROM THE RIGHT SIDE AND STITCH DOWN FLAT. THE ROBINGS WILL COVER ALL THE RAW EDGES

STRIP PRIOR TO PLEATING 74" IN LENGTH.

STRIP PRIOR TO PLEATING 65" IN LENGTH.

THE DOTTED LINE INDICATES THE LINE FOR GATHERING AND STITCHING TO SLEEVE.

THIRD FLOUNCE

SLEEVE
BACK   FRONT

TOP FLOUNCE IS MOUNTED HERE

THE SECOND AND THIRD FLOUNCES START FROM THIS POINT

DEEPEST PART OF ALL FLOUNCES HERE

TOP FLOUNCE

BRAID IS STITCHED ROUND THE EDGES OF THE FLOUNCES FOR DECORATION

SECOND FLOUNCE

THE SLEEVE IS LINED WITH LINEN. BROCADE AND LINEN ARE MADE UP SEPARATELY AND THEN EDGE STITCHED TOGETHER AT THE ELBOW. A PIECE OF 1" WIDE TAPE IS ADDED HERE ON WHICH THE FLOUNCES ARE MOUNTED.

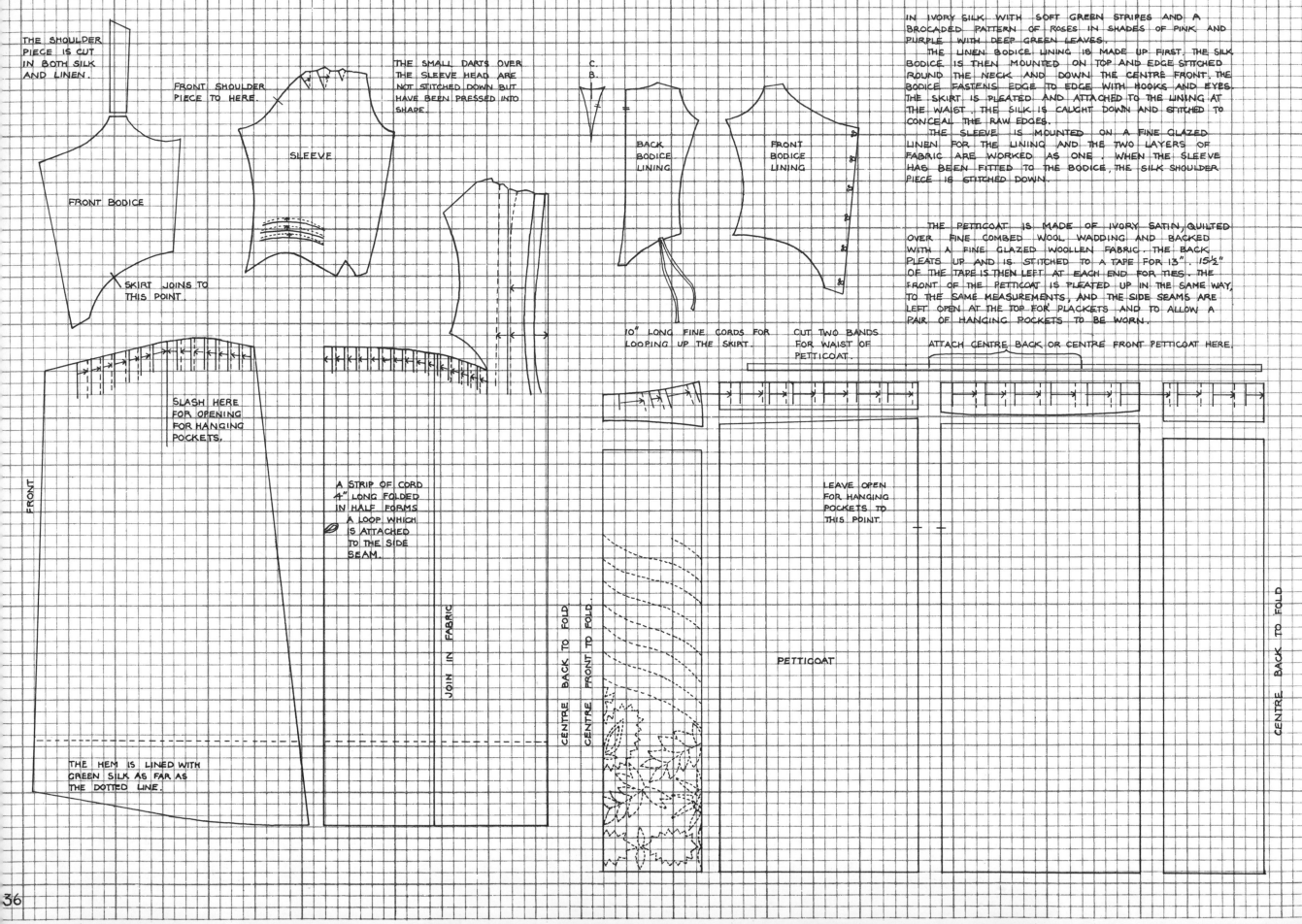

THE SHOULDER
PIECE IS CUT
IN BOTH SILK
AND LINEN.

FRONT SHOULDER
PIECE TO HERE.

THE SMALL DARTS OVER
THE SLEEVE HEAD ARE
NOT STITCHED DOWN BUT
HAVE BEEN PRESSED INTO
SHAPE.

C.
B.

SLEEVE

BACK
BODICE
LINING

FRONT
BODICE
LINING

FRONT BODICE

SKIRT JOINS TO
THIS POINT.

IN IVORY SILK WITH SOFT GREEN STRIPES AND A
BROCADED PATTERN OF ROSES IN SHADES OF PINK AND
PURPLE WITH DEEP GREEN LEAVES.
THE LINEN BODICE LINING IS MADE UP FIRST. THE SILK
BODICE IS THEN MOUNTED ON TOP AND EDGE STITCHED
ROUND THE NECK AND DOWN THE CENTRE FRONT. THE
BODICE FASTENS EDGE TO EDGE WITH HOOKS AND EYES.
THE SKIRT IS PLEATED AND ATTACHED TO THE LINING AT
THE WAIST. THE SILK IS CAUGHT DOWN AND STITCHED TO
CONCEAL THE RAW EDGES.
THE SLEEVE IS MOUNTED ON A FINE GLAZED
LINEN FOR THE LINING AND THE TWO LAYERS OF
FABRIC ARE WORKED AS ONE. WHEN THE SLEEVE
HAS BEEN FITTED TO THE BODICE, THE SILK SHOULDER
PIECE IS STITCHED DOWN.

THE PETTICOAT IS MADE OF IVORY SATIN, QUILTED
OVER FINE COMBED WOOL WADDING AND BACKED
WITH A FINE GLAZED WOOLLEN FABRIC. THE BACK
PLEATS UP AND IS STITCHED TO A TAPE FOR 13". 15½"
OF THE TAPE IS THEN LEFT AT EACH END FOR TIES. THE
FRONT OF THE PETTICOAT IS PLEATED UP IN THE SAME WAY,
TO THE SAME MEASUREMENTS, AND THE SIDE SEAMS ARE
LEFT OPEN AT THE TOP FOR PLACKETS AND TO ALLOW A
PAIR OF HANGING POCKETS TO BE WORN.

10" LONG FINE CORDS FOR
LOOPING UP THE SKIRT.

CUT TWO BANDS
FOR WAIST OF
PETTICOAT.

ATTACH CENTRE BACK OR CENTRE FRONT PETTICOAT HERE.

SLASH HERE
FOR OPENING
FOR HANGING
POCKETS.

FRONT

A STRIP OF CORD
4" LONG FOLDED
IN HALF FORMS
A LOOP WHICH
IS ATTACHED
TO THE SIDE
SEAM.

LEAVE OPEN
FOR HANGING
POCKETS TO
THIS POINT.

JOIN IN FABRIC

CENTRE BACK TO FOLD

CENTRE FRONT TO FOLD

PETTICOAT

CENTRE BACK TO FOLD

THE HEM IS LINED WITH
GREEN SILK AS FAR AS
THE DOTTED LINE.

c.1770-80 The Gallery of English Costume

A polonaise in ivory silk with soft green stripes and a brocaded pattern of roses in shades of pink and purple with deep green leaves. The back is cut en fourreau' with a curved waist seam to accommodate a false rump, which was a bustle pad stuffed with cork. The dress fastens edge to edge at the centre front with hooks and eyes. Fine cords are stitched to the waist seam at the back of the bodice, on the inside. These are passed through the loops at the side seams of the skirt and tied to pull up the fabric. The polonaise is shown over an ivory satin, quilted petticoat, which is made of one layer of satin backed with finely combed wool wadding and lined with a light-weight glazed woollen fabric. White lawn ruffles or round cuffs would have been worn at the ends of the sleeves. A detail of one of the brocaded rose motifs on the fabric is also shown.

c.1770-85 Snowshill Manor

A polonaise in cream silk decorated with pinked, box-pleated strips of the same fabric. Small artificial flowers made of flossed silk are stitched on top. There are covered buttons on the right side of the dress at the back, with long ribbon tapes attached on the wrong side for looping up the skirt. The sleeves would have been worn with single or double detachable lawn ruffles or with ruched round cuffs either in gauze or the same fabric as the dress. Round cuffs, to which short frills could be added, were very fashionable from c.1775–80. Short ruffles were popular from c.1780 onwards. The polonaise is shown over a short ankle-revealing petticoat, which could be either plain or decorated with a flounce round the hem. The dress would have been worn over a boned corset and a false rump or bustle pad.

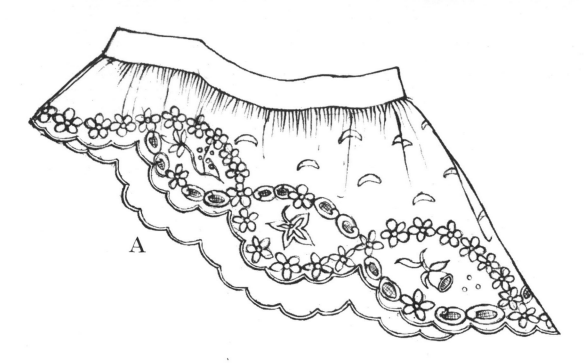

A

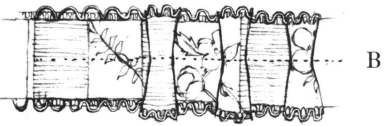

B

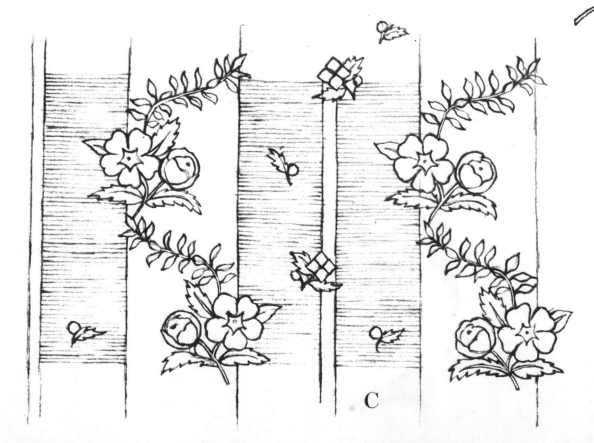

C

D

Snowshill Manor

A **c.1760-80** A detail of one of the white embroidered lawn ruffles shown with the cream silk polonaise (page 37). These ruffles could also have been worn with the cherry red and white striped sack dress (page 34).

B **c.1770-5** A detail of the braid trimmings on the cherry red and white striped sack dress (page 34).

C **c.1770-5** A detail of the cherry red and white striped brocaded silk used for the sack dress on page 34. The cherry red stripe is finely ribbed with small rosebuds scattered over it and has a satin stripe of the same colour running down the centre. On the white stripe is a curving pattern of pink roses and deep green leaves.

D **c.1770-85** A detail of the cream silk polonaise (page 37) showing the bodice construction and the fabric. The silk has fine, raised thread stripes $\frac{1}{16}''$ apart. Small lemon spots are woven on the stripes. There is a small flower motif woven at intervals all over the fabric. The flowers are in rose pink and blue with deep green and brown leaves. Each motif is approximately $1'' \times 1\frac{3}{4}''$ in size.

A POLONAISE WITH DETACHABLE EMBROIDERED LAWN RUFFLES C 1770-85

IN PALE CREAM BROCADED SILK PATTERNED WITH TINY FLOWERS. THE DRESS BELONGED TO MISS MASSEY OF CLANORALD, COUNTY LIMERICK.

EACH PIECE OF THE BODICE IS LINED WITH WHITE LINEN AND MADE UP SEPARATELY. THE BONES, WHICH ARE ¼" WIDE, ARE SET IN THEIR CASINGS ON THE INSIDE OF THE LINING SO THAT THEY DO NOT SHOW. ALL THE PIECES OF BODICE ARE THEN SEWN TOGETHER WHEN THEY ARE COMPLETE.

AT THE BACK OF THE SKIRT THE FABRIC IS FOLDED DOWN IN A GENTLE SLOPE BEFORE PLEATING. WHEN THE SKIRT IS PLEATED UP AND ATTACHED TO THE BODICE THIS PIECE IS LEFT, AS IT HELPS TO WAD OUT THE BACK PLEATS. A BUTTON IS SEWN ON THE RIGHT SIDE OF THE CENTRE BACK PANEL OF THE BODICE. UNDER IT, ON THE INSIDE OF THE DRESS, ARE TWO LONG TAPES ½" WIDE. THEY HAVE BEEN CUT, BUT ORIGINALLY THEY MUST HAVE BEEN APPROXIMATELY 30" LONG. THESE TAPES ARE SECURED ROUND THE BUTTON, THUS LOOPING UP THE SKIRT.

THE TRIMMING DOWN THE CENTRE FRONT SKIRT IS MADE FROM A STRAIGHT STRIP 1"x 65". THE EDGES ARE TURNED UNDER ¼" AND NARROW BRAID IS STITCHED ON TOP. THE STRIP IS THEN BOX PLEATED AND THE OBLONG PIECES WADDED WITH WOOL. SMALL ARTIFICIAL FLOWERS MADE OF FLOSSED SILK ARE STITCHED ON TOP.

THE EMBROIDERY ON THE WHITE LAWN RUFFLES IS ALL IN WHITE. THE RUFFLES ARE GATHERED AND STITCHED TO THE BANDS.

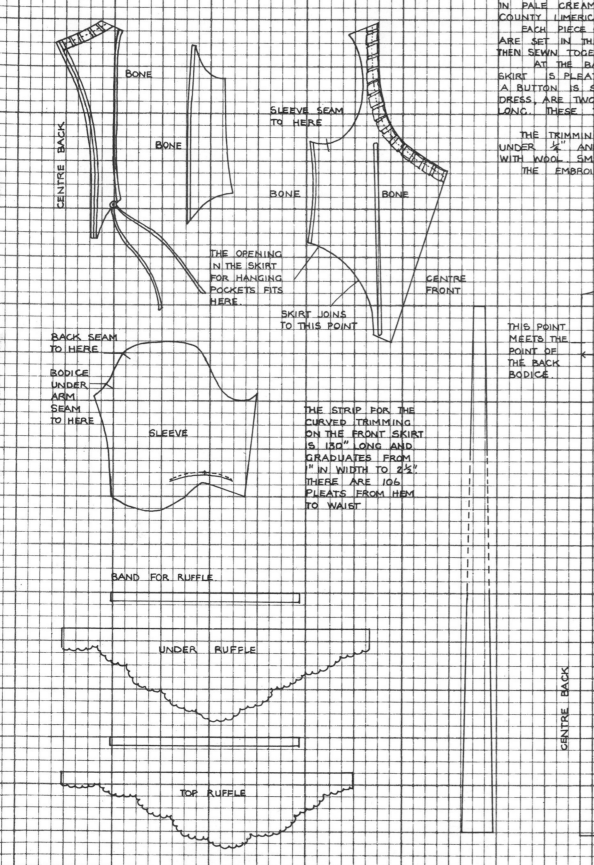

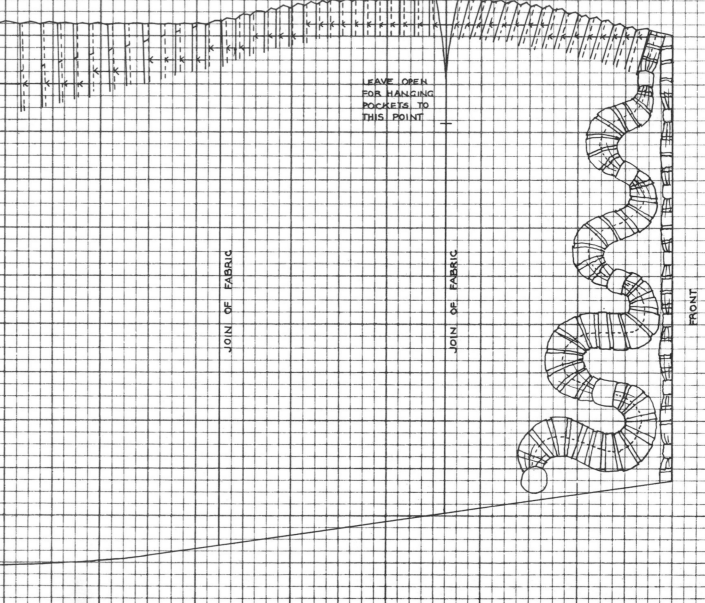

A detail of the scalloped and pleated strips.

A detail of the fabric.

c.1775-85   Snowshill Manor

An open gown and matching petticoat in terracotta and blue shot silk taffeta giving the effect of purple. The front fastens edge to edge with concealed hooks and eyes. Short embroidered lawn ruffles or round cuffs, either in gauze or of the same fabric as the dress, would have been tacked to the ends of the sleeves. The round cuffs were up to about 6″ deep and ruched all over. The ones shown in the drawing were taken from an engraving in *The Lady's Magazine*. The dress is decorated with strips of taffeta pinked in scallop shapes and box-pleated. The overskirt is open in front and has a trained skirt which could be worn 'retroussé dans les poches'. This method of hitching up the overskirt for walking or dancing, by pulling the front corners through the pocket holes, was frequently used. It gave a similar effect to the polonaise style of looping up the skirt with buttons and cords. A handkerchief could be worn to fill in the neckline for undress wear. The gown would have been worn over a stiffly boned corset and a false rump or bustle pad.

c.1780-90   The Gallery of English Costume

A gown in pale pink, stiff silk with a woven striped design of tiny orange and bright pink crescent shapes. The gown has a front fall opening, the front portion of the skirt being pleated into a band that ties round the waist, the bodice then fastening over it by means of lacing. The neckline is edged with a falling vandyked collar and a buffon or handkerchief of white lawn or gauze would have been tucked inside it. Short detachable ruffles of white lawn or gauze were tacked to the ends of the sleeves. The gown was worn over stays and a false rump or bustle pad, which was tied round the waist.

AN OPEN GOWN AND MATCHING PETTICOAT C1775-85

IN TERRA-COTTA AND BLUE SHOT TAFFETA GIVING THE EFFECT OF PURPLE.
THE BODICE AND SLEEVES ARE LINED WITH WHITE LINEN. THE LINING IS MADE UP FIRST
AND THE BONES ARE INSERTED IN THE CASINGS WHICH ARE ON THE OUTSIDE. THE TAFFETA
IS MOUNTED ON TOP OF THE LINING AND THE SEAMS ARE ALL BACK STITCHED WORKING
FROM THE RIGHT SIDE OF THE BODICE. THE BONES ARE CONCEALED BETWEEN THE
TAFFETA AND THE LINEN. A TUCK IS MADE IN THE CENTRE BACK PANEL, TAFFETA AND LINING
TOGETHER. THE OVERSKIRT IS SEAMED TOGETHER AND THE LARGE TUCK MADE AT THE
FRONT BEFORE THE DECORATIONS ARE MOUNTED. THE OVERSKIRT IS THEN PLEATED UP AND
SEWN TO THE BODICE.
A STRIP OF TAFFETA 2"x85" IS PINKED AND BOX PLEATED FOR THE DECORATION ON THE
FRONT EDGE OF THE SKIRT. A STRIP OF TAFFETA 2" x 93" IS USED FOR THE OTHER STRAIGHT
PIECE OF DECORATION. THE CURVED STRIP GRADES FROM 2" WIDE AT THE WAIST TO 2½" AT
THE HEM. AND IT IS 100" LONG. ALL THESE STRIPS ARE CUT ON THE STRAIGHT GRAIN. THE
BUTTONS ON THE CURVED STRIP ARE MADE OF CARDBOARD AND COVERED WITH TAFFETA.
THE LINEN LINING AND THE TAFFETA OF THE SLEEVE ARE MADE UP AS ONE LAYER OF
MATERIAL. THE SLEEVE IS STITCHED IN FROM THE WRONG SIDE UNDER THE ARM TO X AND XX.
FROM THERE THE TOP OF THE SLEEVE IS STITCHED FLAT ONTO THE LINEN SHOULDER BAND. THE
STRIP OF TRIMMING COVERS ALL THE RAW EDGES.
A STRAIGHT STRIP OF TAFFETA 9"x194" IS PINKED AND BOX PLEATED TO FORM A DECORATION
FOR THE HEM OF THE PETTICOAT. THE TOP IS THEN PLEATED UP AND FOLDED OVER TO FORM
THE SLOPE AT FRONT AND BACK. BOTH FRONT AND BACK MEASURE 14½" WHEN PLEATED
THEY ARE STITCHED TO ½" DEEP TAPES, LEAVING 6" AT EACH END TO TIE AT THE SIDES.
A STRIP OF TAFFETA 1½" x 80" PINKED IN SCALLOPED SHAPES IS BOX PLEATED TO FORM
THE DECORATION FOR THE NECKLINE.

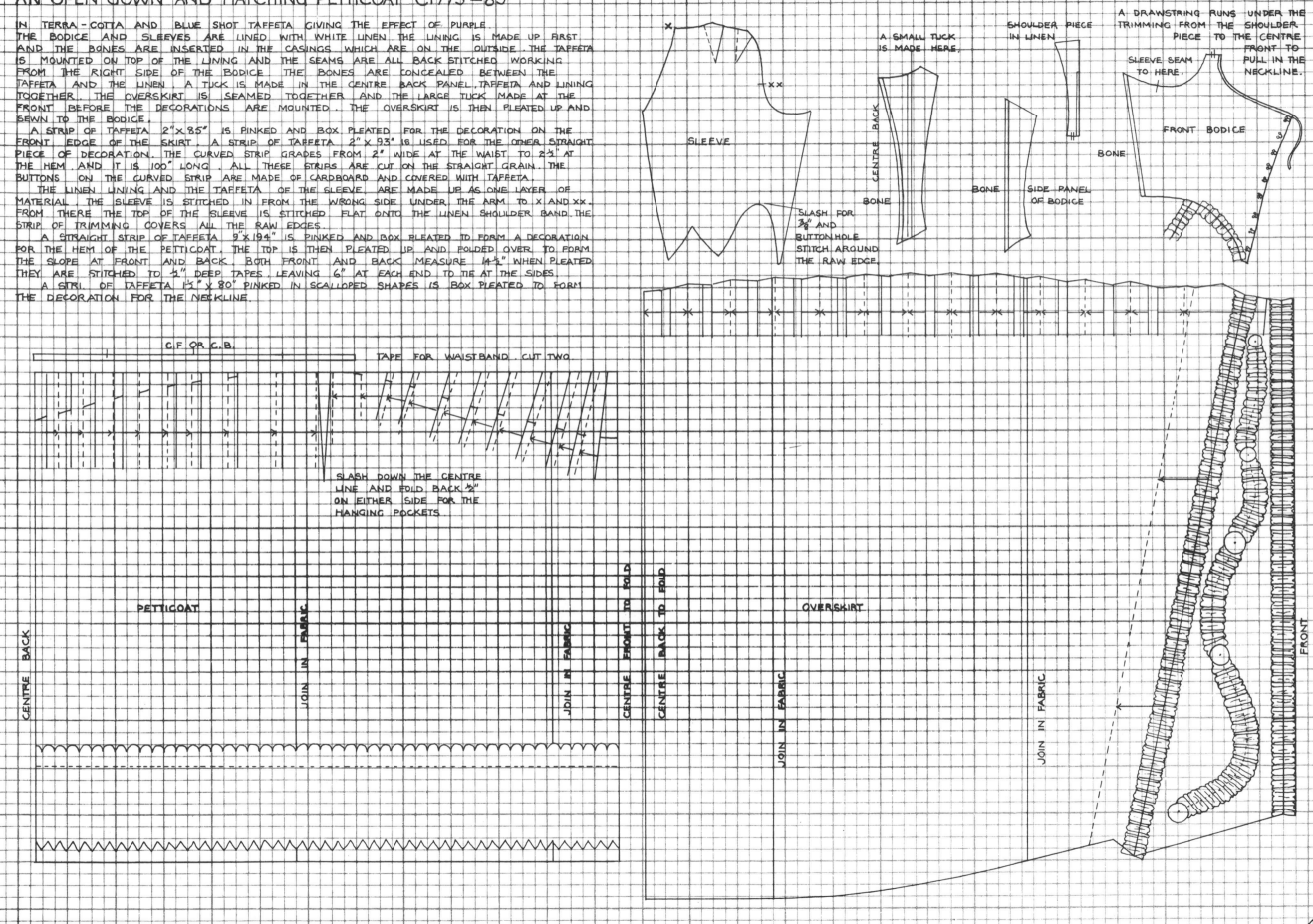

SLEEVE

A SMALL TUCK IS MADE HERE.

SHOULDER PIECE IN LINEN

A DRAWSTRING RUNS UNDER THE TRIMMING FROM THE SHOULDER PIECE TO THE CENTRE FRONT TO SLEEVE SEAM. PULL IN THE NECKLINE.

CENTRE BACK

BONE

BONE

SIDE PANEL OF BODICE

FRONT BODICE

BONE

SLASH FOR 3/8" AND BUTTONHOLE STITCH AROUND THE RAW EDGE.

C.F OR C.B.

TAPE FOR WAISTBAND. CUT TWO

SLASH DOWN THE CENTRE LINE AND FOLD BACK ½" ON EITHER SIDE FOR THE HANGING POCKETS

CENTRE BACK

PETTICOAT

JOIN IN FABRIC

CENTRE FRONT TO FOLD

CENTRE BACK TO FOLD

JOIN IN FABRIC

OVERSKIRT

JOIN IN FABRIC

JOIN IN FABRIC

FRONT

A GOWN WITH A FRONT FALL OPENING AND A VANDYKED COLLAR   C 1780-90

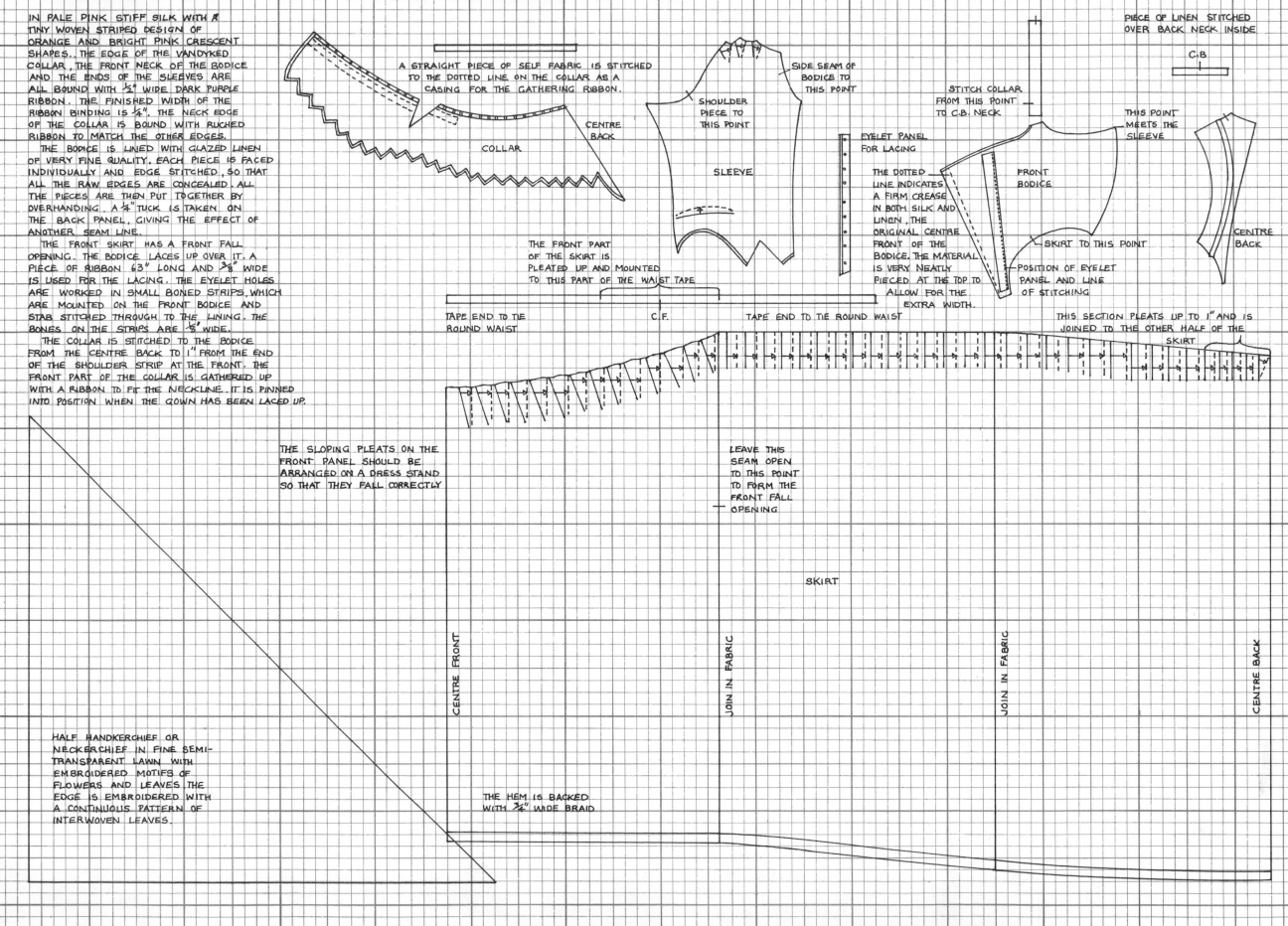

IN PALE PINK STIFF SILK WITH A TINY WOVEN STRIPED DESIGN OF ORANGE AND BRIGHT PINK CRESCENT SHAPES. THE EDGE OF THE VANDYKED COLLAR, THE FRONT NECK OF THE BODICE AND THE ENDS OF THE SLEEVES ARE ALL BOUND WITH ½" WIDE DARK PURPLE RIBBON. THE FINISHED WIDTH OF THE RIBBON BINDING IS ¼". THE NECK EDGE OF THE COLLAR IS BOUND WITH RUCHED RIBBON TO MATCH THE OTHER EDGES.

THE BODICE IS LINED WITH GLAZED LINEN OF VERY FINE QUALITY. EACH PIECE IS FACED INDIVIDUALLY AND EDGE STITCHED, SO THAT ALL THE RAW EDGES ARE CONCEALED. ALL THE PIECES ARE THEN PUT TOGETHER BY OVERHANDING. A ¼" TUCK IS TAKEN ON THE BACK PANEL, GIVING THE EFFECT OF ANOTHER SEAM LINE.

THE FRONT SKIRT HAS A FRONT FALL OPENING. THE BODICE LACES UP OVER IT. A PIECE OF RIBBON 63" LONG AND ⅜" WIDE IS USED FOR THE LACING. THE EYELET HOLES ARE WORKED IN SMALL BONED STRIPS, WHICH ARE MOUNTED ON THE FRONT BODICE AND STAB STITCHED THROUGH TO THE LINING. THE BONES ON THE STRIPS ARE ⅛" WIDE.

THE COLLAR IS STITCHED TO THE BODICE FROM THE CENTRE BACK TO 1" FROM THE END OF THE SHOULDER STRIP AT THE FRONT. THE FRONT PART OF THE COLLAR IS GATHERED UP WITH A RIBBON TO FIT THE NECKLINE. IT IS PINNED INTO POSITION WHEN THE GOWN HAS BEEN LACED UP.

A STRAIGHT PIECE OF SELF FABRIC IS STITCHED TO THE DOTTED LINE ON THE COLLAR AS A CASING FOR THE GATHERING RIBBON.

COLLAR

CENTRE BACK

SHOULDER PIECE TO THIS POINT

SIDE SEAM OF BODICE TO THIS POINT

SLEEVE

PIECE OF LINEN STITCHED OVER BACK NECK INSIDE

C.B

STITCH COLLAR FROM THIS POINT TO C.B. NECK

THIS POINT MEETS THE SLEEVE

EYELET PANEL FOR LACING

THE DOTTED LINE INDICATES A FIRM CREASE IN BOTH SILK AND LINEN, THE ORIGINAL CENTRE FRONT OF THE BODICE. THE MATERIAL IS VERY NEATLY PIECED AT THE TOP TO ALLOW FOR THE EXTRA WIDTH.

FRONT BODICE

SKIRT TO THIS POINT

POSITION OF EYELET PANEL AND LINE OF STITCHING

CENTRE BACK

THE FRONT PART OF THE SKIRT IS PLEATED UP AND MOUNTED TO THIS PART OF THE WAIST TAPE

TAPE END TO TIE ROUND WAIST

C.F.

TAPE END TO TIE ROUND WAIST

THIS SECTION PLEATS UP TO 1" AND IS JOINED TO THE OTHER HALF OF THE SKIRT

THE SLOPING PLEATS ON THE FRONT PANEL SHOULD BE ARRANGED ON A DRESS STAND SO THAT THEY FALL CORRECTLY

LEAVE THIS SEAM OPEN TO THIS POINT TO FORM THE FRONT FALL OPENING

SKIRT

CENTRE FRONT

JOIN IN FABRIC

JOIN IN FABRIC

CENTRE BACK

HALF HANDKERCHIEF OR NECKERCHIEF IN FINE SEMI-TRANSPARENT LAWN WITH EMBROIDERED MOTIFS OF FLOWERS AND LEAVES. THE EDGE IS EMBROIDERED WITH A CONTINUOUS PATTERN OF INTERWOVEN LEAVES.

THE HEM IS BACKED WITH ¾" WIDE BRAID

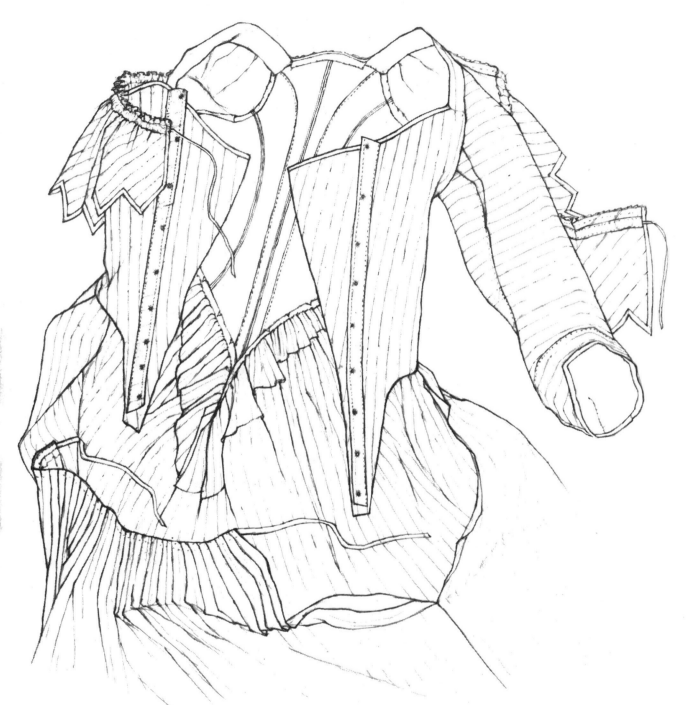

A detail of the tan-coloured, looped-cord braid which trims the front of the robe.

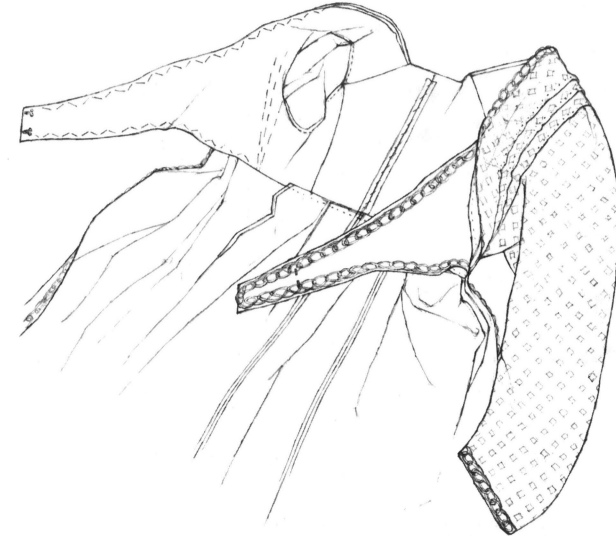

*c.*1780-90   The Gallery of English Costume

A detail of the gown in pale pink stiff silk (page 40) showing the front fall opening and the boned strips on the front bodice with worked eyelet holes for lacing.

*c.*1795-1803   The Victoria and Albert Museum

A detail of the cream silk robe (page 44) showing the seams and stitching lines and the raised diamond pattern on the fabric. The diamonds are $\frac{3}{16}''$ wide and placed $\frac{1}{2}''$ apart.

c.1795-1800   Snowshill Manor

A half robe in slate blue striped brocade. This would have been worn over a white muslin round gown for morning occasions, as shown in a fashion plate in *The Lady's Monthly Museum* of 1799. Small loops from the inside of the bodice fasten over buttons on the right side of the garment to give the neckline shape. This half robe has been altered from a gown of *c.*1780 and is interesting as an example of a transitional style. A small bustle pad would have been worn under the muslin gown at the back.

c.1795-1803   The Victoria and Albert Museum

A robe in cream silk with a raised diamond pattern and decorated with tan-coloured, looped-cord braid ¼″ wide. The front part of the bodice is made of plain cream-coloured satin and edged with braid. At the end of the eighteenth century the robe was worn for day and evening occasions but by *c.*1803 it was used for evening wear only. The robe was always trained and showed the skirt of the round gown at the front, which was often embroidered. The neckline would have been filled in either with a neckerchief or by the bodice of the round gown for day wear. This dress could have been worn over short stays and a small bustle pad, although both were frequently discarded at this date.

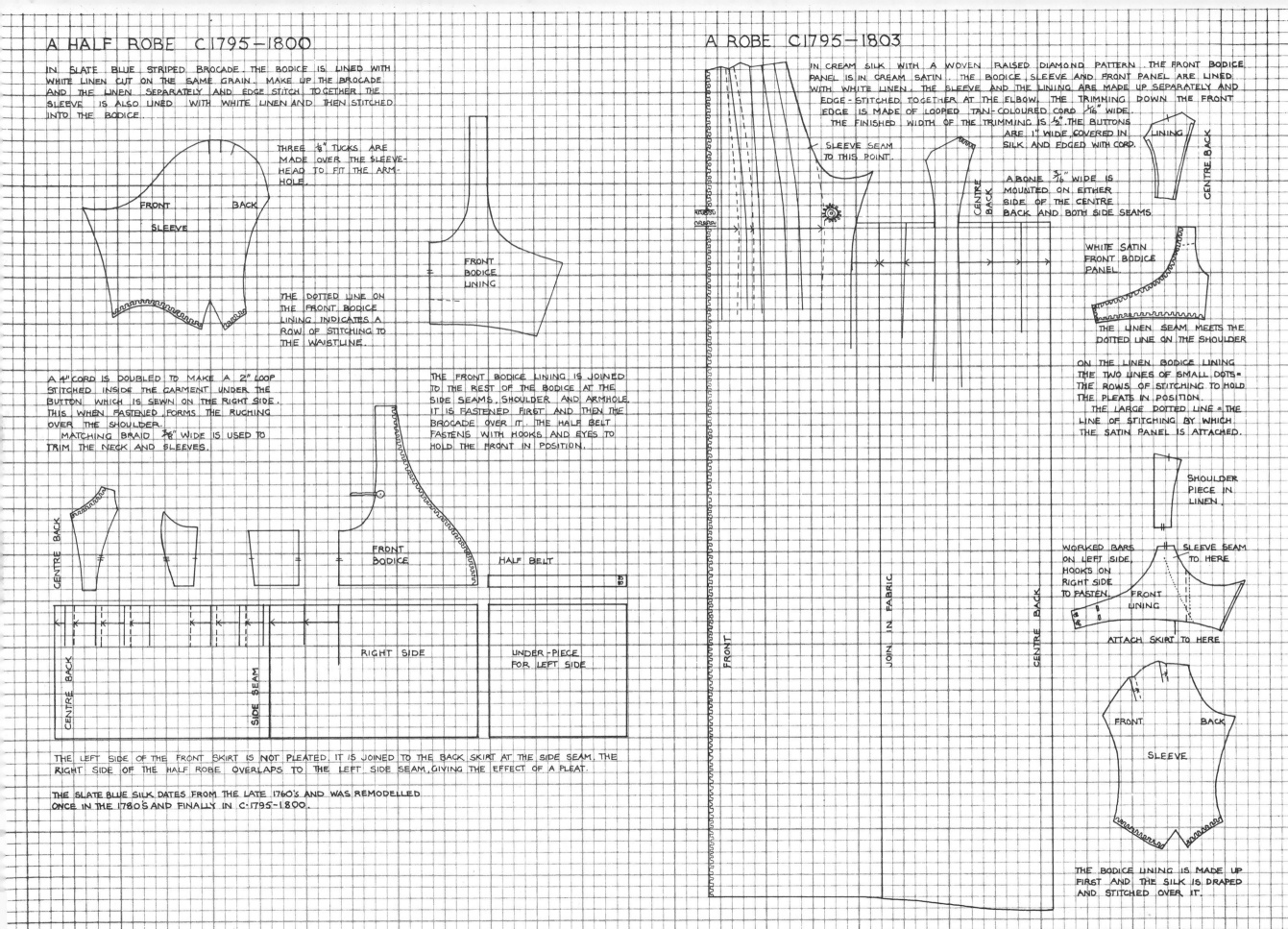

A HALF ROBE C1795-1800

IN SLATE BLUE STRIPED BROCADE. THE BODICE IS LINED WITH WHITE LINEN CUT ON THE SAME GRAIN. MAKE UP THE BROCADE AND THE LINEN SEPARATELY AND EDGE STITCH TOGETHER. THE SLEEVE IS ALSO LINED WITH WHITE LINEN AND THEN STITCHED INTO THE BODICE.

THREE ⅛" TUCKS ARE MADE OVER THE SLEEVE-HEAD TO FIT THE ARM-HOLE.

THE DOTTED LINE ON THE FRONT BODICE LINING INDICATES A ROW OF STITCHING TO THE WAISTLINE.

A 4" CORD IS DOUBLED TO MAKE A 2" LOOP STITCHED INSIDE THE GARMENT UNDER THE BUTTON WHICH IS SEWN ON THE RIGHT SIDE. THIS WHEN FASTENED FORMS THE RUCHING OVER THE SHOULDER.
MATCHING BRAID ⅜" WIDE IS USED TO TRIM THE NECK AND SLEEVES.

THE FRONT BODICE LINING IS JOINED TO THE REST OF THE BODICE AT THE SIDE SEAMS, SHOULDER AND ARMHOLE. IT IS FASTENED FIRST AND THEN THE BROCADE OVER IT. THE HALF BELT FASTENS WITH HOOKS AND EYES TO HOLD THE FRONT IN POSITION.

FRONT / BACK
SLEEVE

FRONT BODICE LINING

CENTRE BACK

FRONT BODICE

HALF BELT

RIGHT SIDE

UNDER-PIECE FOR LEFT SIDE

CENTRE BACK

SIDE SEAM

THE LEFT SIDE OF THE FRONT SKIRT IS NOT PLEATED. IT IS JOINED TO THE BACK SKIRT AT THE SIDE SEAM. THE RIGHT SIDE OF THE HALF ROBE OVERLAPS TO THE LEFT SIDE SEAM, GIVING THE EFFECT OF A PLEAT.

THE SLATE BLUE SILK DATES FROM THE LATE 1760's AND WAS REMODELLED ONCE IN THE 1780's AND FINALLY IN C·1795-1800.

A ROBE C1795-1803

IN CREAM SILK WITH A WOVEN RAISED DIAMOND PATTERN THE FRONT BODICE PANEL IS IN CREAM SATIN. THE BODICE, SLEEVE AND FRONT PANEL ARE LINED WITH WHITE LINEN. THE SLEEVE AND THE LINING ARE MADE UP SEPARATELY AND EDGE-STITCHED TOGETHER AT THE ELBOW. THE TRIMMING DOWN THE FRONT EDGE IS MADE OF LOOPED TAN-COLOURED CORD ⁵⁄₁₆" WIDE. THE FINISHED WIDTH OF THE TRIMMING IS ½". THE BUTTONS ARE 1" WIDE, COVERED IN SILK AND EDGED WITH CORD.

SLEEVE SEAM TO THIS POINT.

A BONE ³⁄₁₆" WIDE IS MOUNTED ON EITHER SIDE OF THE CENTRE BACK AND BOTH SIDE SEAMS

CENTRE BACK

LINING

WHITE SATIN FRONT BODICE PANEL

THE LINEN SEAM MEETS THE DOTTED LINE ON THE SHOULDER

ON THE LINEN BODICE LINING THE TWO LINES OF SMALL DOTS= THE ROWS OF STITCHING TO HOLD THE PLEATS IN POSITION.
THE LARGE DOTTED LINE = THE LINE OF STITCHING BY WHICH THE SATIN PANEL IS ATTACHED.

SHOULDER PIECE IN LINEN.

WORKED BARS ON LEFT SIDE, HOOKS ON RIGHT SIDE TO FASTEN.

SLEEVE SEAM TO HERE

FRONT LINING

ATTACH SKIRT TO HERE

FRONT

JOIN IN FABRIC

CENTRE BACK

FRONT / BACK
SLEEVE

THE BODICE LINING IS MADE UP FIRST AND THE SILK IS DRAPED AND STITCHED OVER IT.

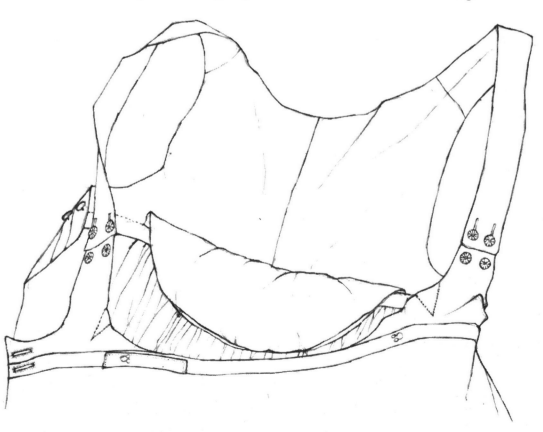

A detail of the back of the jacket showing the position of the seams and lines of stitching.

c.1795-1810   Salisbury Museum

A riding habit in pale blue, soft worsted woollen cloth. It would have been worn with a fine white linen or lawn habit shirt. The skirt is so long that it would have to be held up or carried over the arm until on horseback. There are tapes and tabs inside, which, when tied up, permit the habit to be worn for walking. The jacket is lined with white silk. An article in *The Lady's Monthly Museum* of September 1808 says that 'Habits are very appropriate for travelling costume and are at this period constructed with more than usual grace'.

Inside the skirt of the riding habit, showing the taffeta bodice which holds it up and the little bustle pad of taffeta, wadded with wool, stitched to the back.

RIDING HABIT C 1795-1810

IN PALE BLUE SOFT WOOLLEN WORSTED CLOTH. THE JACKET IS LINED WITH FINE WHITE SILK. THE LINING IS CUT ON THE SAME GRAIN AS THE JACKET AND REACHES RIGHT TO THE EDGE OF THE GARMENT WHERE IT IS STITCHED TO THE WOOL. THE SKIRT IS SEWN TO A SMALL BODICE THIS IS MADE OF BLUE AND GREY SHOT TAFFETA LINED WITH WHITE COTTON. THE LINING AND THE BODICE ARE CUT TO THE SAME PATTERN, MADE UP SEPARATELY AND THEN EDGE STITCHED TOGETHER. THE SKIRT IS MADE UP AND STITCHED TO THE WOOLLEN BAND. THE TOP OF THIS BAND IS THEN MOUNTED ON THE BODICE AND STITCHED TO THE DOTTED LINE SHOWN ON THE PATTERN. THE LINING IS THEN STITCHED TO THE CARTRIDGE PLEATS AT THE BACK AND TO THE BAND AT THE FRONT TO HOLD IT SECURELY. THE BOTTOM OF THE BODICE IS LEVEL WITH THE BOTTOM OF THE WAISTBAND.

THE JACKET FASTENS WITH FLAT BUTTONS ½" IN DIAMETER, COVERED IN BLUE WOOL. THERE ARE ALSO TWO BUTTONS AT THE SIDE BACK OVER THE BASQUE FOR DECORATION. JACKET AND SKIRT ARE HELD TOGETHER FIRMLY AT THE FRONT WITH TWO SMALL HOOKS AND EYES.

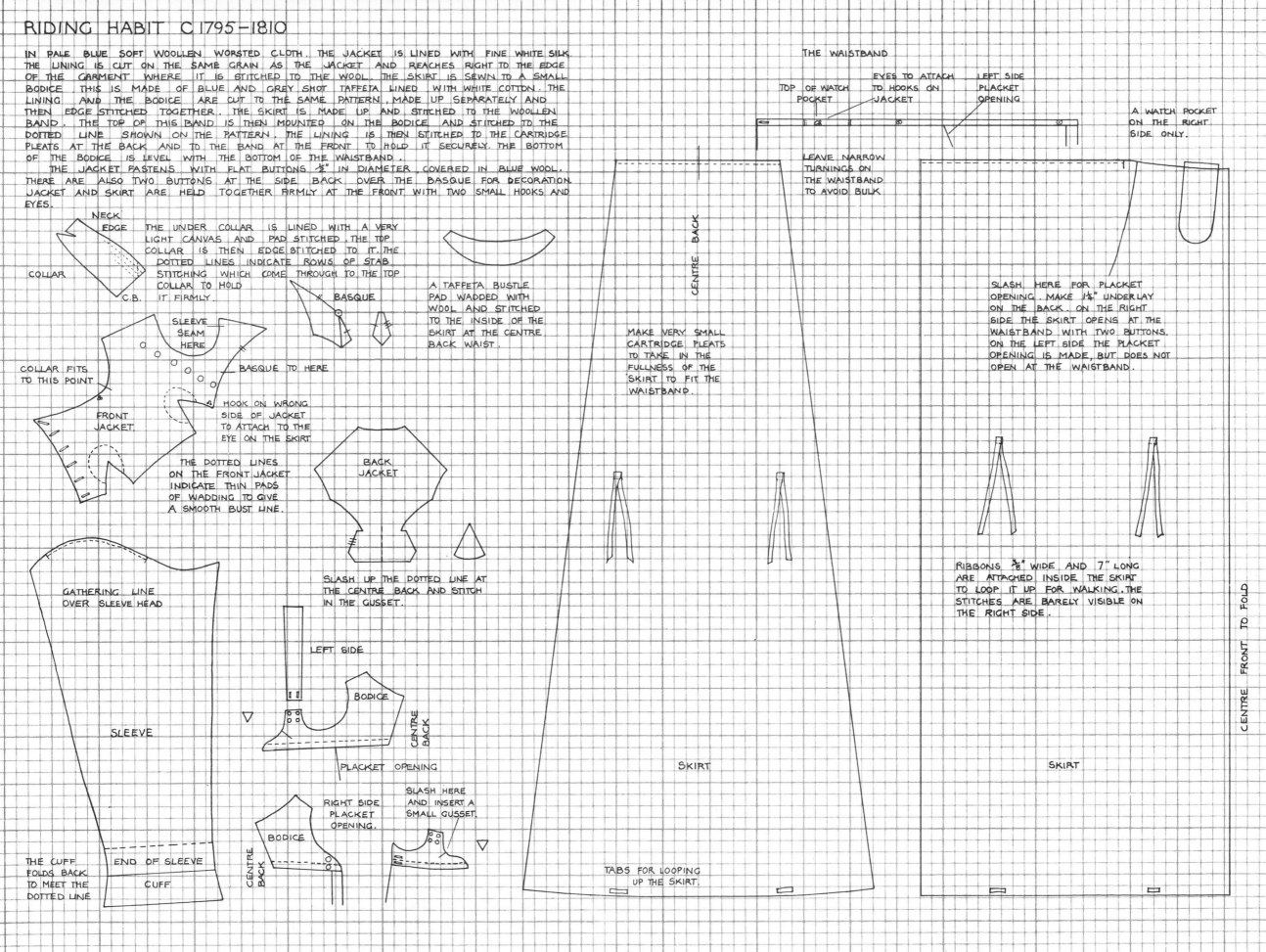

NECK
EDGE THE UNDER COLLAR IS LINED WITH A VERY LIGHT CANVAS AND PAD STITCHED. THE TOP COLLAR IS THEN EDGE STITCHED TO IT. THE DOTTED LINES INDICATE ROWS OF STAB STITCHING WHICH COME THROUGH TO THE TOP COLLAR TO HOLD IT FIRMLY.

COLLAR

C.B.

SLEEVE SEAM HERE

COLLAR FITS TO THIS POINT

FRONT JACKET

BASQUE

BASQUE TO HERE

HOOK ON WRONG SIDE OF JACKET TO ATTACH TO THE EYE ON THE SKIRT

THE DOTTED LINES ON THE FRONT JACKET INDICATE THIN PADS OF WADDING TO GIVE A SMOOTH BUST LINE.

BACK JACKET

A TAFFETA BUSTLE PAD WADDED WITH WOOL AND STITCHED TO THE INSIDE OF THE SKIRT AT THE CENTRE BACK WAIST.

SLASH UP THE DOTTED LINE AT THE CENTRE BACK AND STITCH IN THE GUSSET.

GATHERING LINE OVER SLEEVE HEAD

SLEEVE

THE CUFF FOLDS BACK TO MEET THE DOTTED LINE

END OF SLEEVE

CUFF

LEFT SIDE

BODICE

CENTRE BACK

PLACKET OPENING

RIGHT SIDE PLACKET OPENING.

BODICE

CENTRE BACK

SLASH HERE AND INSERT A SMALL GUSSET.

THE WAISTBAND

TOP OF WATCH POCKET

EYES TO ATTACH TO HOOKS ON JACKET

LEFT SIDE PLACKET OPENING

A WATCH POCKET ON THE RIGHT SIDE ONLY.

LEAVE NARROW TURNINGS ON THE WAISTBAND TO AVOID BULK

CENTRE BACK

MAKE VERY SMALL CARTRIDGE PLEATS TO TAKE IN THE FULLNESS OF THE SKIRT TO FIT THE WAISTBAND.

SLASH HERE FOR PLACKET OPENING. MAKE 1½" UNDERLAY ON THE BACK. ON THE RIGHT SIDE THE SKIRT OPENS AT THE WAISTBAND WITH TWO BUTTONS. ON THE LEFT SIDE THE PLACKET OPENING IS MADE, BUT DOES NOT OPEN AT THE WAISTBAND.

RIBBONS ⅝" WIDE AND 7" LONG ARE ATTACHED INSIDE THE SKIRT TO LOOP IT UP FOR WALKING. THE STITCHES ARE BARELY VISIBLE ON THE RIGHT SIDE.

SKIRT

TABS FOR LOOPING UP THE SKIRT.

SKIRT

CENTRE FRONT TO FOLD

*c.*1798-1805   Salisbury Museum

A morning dress in white cotton with a small, regular, geometric pattern printed in dark purple. It has a trained skirt and a high stomacher-front opening. There are two strings inside the dress at the centre-back waist which would have secured a small bustle pad, as well as tying round the waist to help hold the dress in position. A fine lawn or cambric chemisette or habit shirt, with a frill at the neck, could have been worn under the dress to fill in the neckline. The long sleeves could be removed and the dress worn with short sleeves only. The dress may have been worn with long stays, although the high stomacher front provides a certain amount of support without them.

*c.*1806-9   The Victoria and Albert Museum

A frock in white muslin embroidered with stylised flowers, in thick white cotton and silver thread. The design is carried out in chain stitch and satin stitch, with tiny gold sequins on the leaves and petals. The frock fastens at the back with buttons and strings. It closely resembles fashion plates and descriptions of evening dresses in *La Belle Assemblée* for 1807 and there are examples of the same style in plain muslin for day wear in the same magazine, as well as *The Lady's Monthly Museum*, between 1806 and 1809. One, in *La Belle Assemblée* of September 1808, which is described as a morning negligee, is worn with a Gipsy straw hat, a large, half-square scarf and 'it is necessary to observe that with this dress it is more consistent and decorous to cover the bosom either with a shirt of French net or wrought muslin'. The gown could have been worn with or without a corset and probably over a light petticoat.

MORNING DRESS C.1798—1805

IN WHITE COTTON WITH A SMALL REGULAR GEOMETRIC PATTERN PRINTED IN DARK PURPLE.
THE BODICE IS LINED WITH FINE WHITE LINEN.
THE LINING IS MADE UP FIRST. THE PRINTED
COTTON BODICE IS MOUNTED ON TOP AND
EDGE STITCHED TO THE LINEN ROUND THE
NECK AND AT THE BOTTOM OF THE BODICE.
THE PANEL AT THE FRONT IS LEFT IN PLAIN
LINEN AND HEMMED ROUND THE EDGES. C.B.
THE SHORT COTTON SLEEVE AND LINEN
UNDER SLEEVE ARE THEN MADE UP
AND ATTACHED TO THE ARMHOLE
WITH ONE ROW OF STITCHING.

A FROCK C.1806—1809

IN WHITE MUSLIN EMBROIDERED WITH STYLISED FLOWERS IN
THICK WHITE COTTON AND SILVER THREAD. THE DESIGN IS
CARRIED OUT IN CHAIN STITCH AND SATIN STITCH. TINY
GOLD SEQUINS ARE STITCHED ON THE LEAVES AND PETALS.
THE BODICE IS JOINED TOGETHER AND GATHERING THREADS
PUT THROUGH TOP AND BOTTOM SEAMS. THE BODICE IS STITCHED
TO THE ASSEMBLED NECKBAND
PIECES. SKIRT AND BODICE ARE
THEN JOINED TO THE WAISTBAND.

GATHER OVER
SLEEVE HEAD

FRONT   BACK

BACK NECK-BAND

SHOULDER
BAND

FRONT NECK-BAND

CENTRE
FRONT
TO FOLD

BACK BODICE

BODICE HERE

BACK BODICE AND
SHOULDER PIECE.
THE BACK BODICE
LINING IS CUT
ON THE STRAIGHT
GRAIN.

FRONT BODICE

LINEN

THE SKIRT IS JOINED
TO THE DOTTED LINES
ON FRONT AND BACK
BODICE PIECES. THE
PRINTED COTTON IS
STITCHED ON THE
LINING AS FAR
AS THIS LINE

FRONT BODICE

CENTRE
FRONT TO   GATHERING TO HERE
FOLD

EASE ONTO
WAISTBAND

FOLD THE WAISTBAND ON THE DOTTED LINE

GATHER INTO 1"

A 1¾ YARD LONG TAPE PASSES ROUND
THE WAIST THROUGH THIS CASING AND
TIES AT THE CENTRE BACK.

WAISTBAND.

FOLD THIS
PIECE BACK
TO FORM A
FACING

FOLD
UNDER

ATTACH TO BODICE
SHOULDER SEAM.

TO SEAM ON SIDE BACK
PANEL OF BODICE

LINEN UNDER
SLEEVE

THE LONG SLEEVE CUT
ON THE CROSS IS SEWN
TO THE DOTTED LINE

TO SEAM ON SIDE
BACK PANEL OF
BODICE

MAKE SMALL
TUCKS TO FIT
SLEEVE INTO
ARMHOLE

ATTACH TO LINEN
UNDERSLEEVE AND
SHOULDER SEAM

SHORT SLEEVE IN
PRINTED COTTON

SKIRT

GATHER UP
TO FIT 1½"

CENTRE
FRONT
TO
FOLD

SKIRT

LEAVE OPEN
TO THIS POINT

TWO TAPES 19½" LONG
TO TIE ROUND THE WAIST
AND ONE TAPE 32" LONG
WITH ONE 4¼" LONG, TO
ATTACH A BUSTLE PAD
ARE STITCHED TO THE
CENTRE BACK WAIST.

FOLD IN HALF ON
DOTTED LINE FOR
SHORT SLEEVE
BAND.

DETACHABLE
UNDER SLEEVE
IN PRINTED COTTON.
THE SEAM MEETS
THE SEAM OF THE
LINEN UNDER-
SLEEVE TO WHICH
IT IS ATTACHED

CENTRE
FRONT
TO
FOLD

JOIN IN FABRIC

CENTRE BACK

FOLD IN
HALF ON
DOTTED LINE TO FORM TOP OF
FRONT BODICE

TAKE A PIECE OF COTTON
AND MAKE ROWS OF
1⁄16" TUCKS THEN CUT OUT
THE BODICE THE TWO
SMALL BANDS ARE
FOLDED IN HALF ON THE
DOTTED LINES TO FORM
THE EDGES OF THE FRONT
BODICE.

GATHER
INTO 3"

C.F.

GATHER
INTO 3"

FIT
THIS
EDGE
OF THE
BODICE
TO THE
WAIST BAND

SMALL BANDS OF
TAPE TO LOOP UP
TRAIN

CENTRE BACK TO FOLD.

49

A · C 1800-25

A WHITE CAMBRIC CHEMISETTE WITH THREE MUSHROOM PLEATED FRILLS FORMING THE COLLAR. THESE FRILLS ARE MADE OF STRIPS OF CAMBRIC CUT ON THE STRAIGHT GRAIN, 1½" DEEP AT THE CENTRE FRONT WIDENING TO 2¼" AT THE CENTRE BACK AND 90" LONG. THEY ARE MUSHROOM PLEATED ONTO ⅛" WIDE TAPES AND THEN STITCHED TO THE NECK BAND WHICH IS A CROSSWAY PIECE 15¾" LONG. THE TOP FRILL IS RIGHT ON THE EDGE OF THE BAND AND THE BOTTOM ONE IS ALMOST ON THE NECK SEAM.

MAKE SMALL TUCKS ON THE SHOULDER TO FIT THE BACK

THE NECK FASTENS WITH ¼" CORDS 9" LONG.

CENTRE FRONT

CENTRE BACK TO FOLD.

NECK BAND

AN 18" LONG TAPE [36" FULL WIDTH] IS ATTACHED AT THE CENTRE BACK AND PASSES THROUGH THE HEMS TO TIE AT THE CENTRE FRONT.

B · C 1800-25

A CHEMISETTE IN WHITE LAWN WITH A FINELY TUCKED FRONT. BOTH NECK FRILLS ARE CUT ON THE STRAIGHT GRAIN, WIDENING FROM 1½" DEEP AT THE CENTRE FRONT TO 2¼" AT THE CENTRE BACK AND 66" LONG. MAKE ⅛" TUCKS ON EACH LINE ON THE FRONT. THIS WILL DRAW THE NECK IN TO 5¼" AND THE SHOULDER TO 5". THE PLEATS ARE CAUGHT DOWN INVISIBLY ON THE DOTTED LINE.

THE NECK FASTENS WITH ⅛" CORD 9" LONG

CENTRE BACK TO FOLD.

A ¼" WIDE TAPE 15" LONG [30" FULL WIDTH] IS ATTACHED AT THE CENTRE BACK AND PASSES THROUGH THE HEMS TO TIE AT THE CENTRE FRONT.

NECK BAND FOR FRILLS.

C · C 1823-28

A CHEMISETTE IN WHITE LAWN WITH AN EMBROIDERED COLLAR. THE EDGES OF THE COLLAR ARE ROLLED AND FINISHED VERY NEATLY AS THE COLLAR IS MADE FROM A SINGLE LAYER OF FABRIC. THE FRILL IS CUT ON THE STRAIGHT GRAIN WIDENING FROM 1½" AT THE CENTRE FRONT TO 2¼" AT THE CENTRE BACK. IT IS 36" LONG [72" FULL WIDTH].

CENTRE BACK TO FOLD

CENTRE FRONT

C.B. FOLD

A DESIGN OF WHITE LEAVES AND FLOWERS IS EMBROIDERED ON THE COLLAR

THE FRILL IS THEN GATHERED UP AND ATTACHED TO THE COLLAR. THE EDGE IS PINKED AND BUTTONHOLE STITCHED.

D · C 1828-35

A WHITE CAMBRIC CHEMISETTE WITH A DOUBLE COLLAR. BOTH COLLARS ARE FORMED FROM A SINGLE LAYER OF CAMBRIC AND ARE NOT FACED. THE FRILL FOR THE TOP COLLAR IS CUT ON THE STRAIGHT GRAIN AND IS 1¼" DEEP ALL THE WAY ROUND. IT IS 60" LONG [120" FULL WIDTH].

CENTRE FRONT

5" TAPE TO JOIN TO THE FRONT PANEL

CENTRE BACK TO FOLD.

CENTRE BACK TO FOLD

CENTRE BACK TO FOLD

UNDER COLLAR

THE FRILL FOR THE BOTTOM COLLAR IS CUT ON THE STRAIGHT GRAIN AND WIDENS FROM 1¾" AT THE CENTRE FRONT TO 3½" AT THE CENTRE BACK. IT IS 60" LONG [120" FULL WIDTH] THE FRILLS ARE STITCHED TO THE NARROW ROLLED HEMS OF BOTH COLLARS.

E · C 1830-35

A CHEMISETTE IN VERY FINE SOFT WHITE MUSLIN WITH WHITE EMBROIDERY ROUND THE NECK DESCENDING INTO A V-SHAPE AT THE CENTRE FRONT. TAPES MEASURING 12" IN LENGTH ARE ATTACHED AT THE SIDES OF FRONT AND BACK BODICE TO TIE UNDER THE ARM.

CENTRE FRONT TO FOLD

CENTRE BACK TO FOLD

A DRAWSTRING RUNS THROUGH THE HEM AT THE FRONT TO TIE WITH THE TAPES WHICH ARE ATTACHED TO THE BACK. THE EMBROIDERY REACHES TO THE DOTTED LINE ON THE FRONT BODICE.

F · C 1845-60

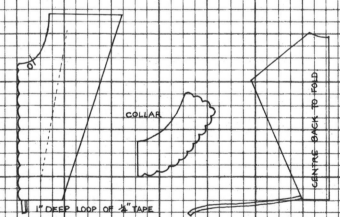

COLLAR

CENTRE BACK TO FOLD

1" DEEP LOOP OF ½" TAPE

A CHEMISETTE IN WHITE LAWN WITH FINE BRODERIE ANGLAISE WORK. THE EMBROIDERY REACHES TO THE DOTTED LINE ON THE FRONT BODICE. THE BRODERIE ANGLAISE COLLAR IS MADE FROM A SINGLE LAYER OF FABRIC. THE EMBROIDERY ON THE RIGHT SIDE OF THE FRONT BODICE IS STARTED 1" FROM THE EDGE SO THAT THE SCALLOPS OF THE LEFT SIDE DO NOT COVER IT. THE CHEMISETTE FASTENS LEFT OVER RIGHT WITH A LITTLE BUTTON AT THE NECK. 16" LONG TAPES ARE STITCHED ON EITHER SIDE OF THE BACK PANEL TO SLOT THROUGH LOOPS AT THE CENTRE FRONT AND TIE ROUND THE WAIST.

G · C 1845-60

A CHEMISETTE IN FINE WHITE MUSLIN WITH A CROCHETED LACE COLLAR. AT THE CENTRE FRONT THERE ARE FOUR FINE CORDED LINES IN THE WEAVE OF THE FABRIC

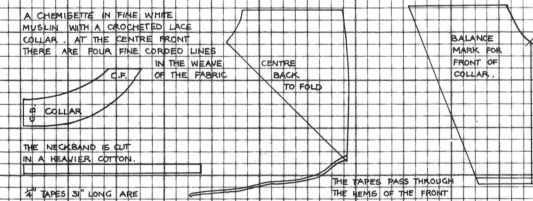

C.F.

CENTRE BACK TO FOLD

C.B. COLLAR

THE NECKBAND IS CUT IN A HEAVIER COTTON.

¼" TAPES 31" LONG ARE ATTACHED ON EITHER SIDE OF THE CENTRE BACK

BALANCE MARK FOR FRONT OF COLLAR.

CENTRE FRONT

THE TAPES PASS THROUGH THE HEMS OF THE FRONT PANELS AND TIE AT THE CENTRE FRONT.

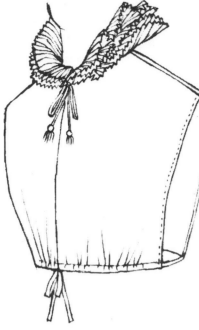

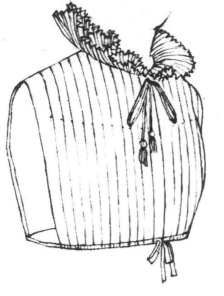

C c.1823-8
A white lawn chemisette with white embroidery on the collar. The edge of the collar is pinked and button-hole stitched.

D c.1828-35
A white cambric chemisette with finely pleated frills bordering the edges of the double collar.

A c.1800-25
A white cambric chemisette with a treble mushroom-pleated frill at the neck.

B c.1800-25
A white lawn chemisette with a finely tucked front and a double mushroom-pleated frill at the neck.

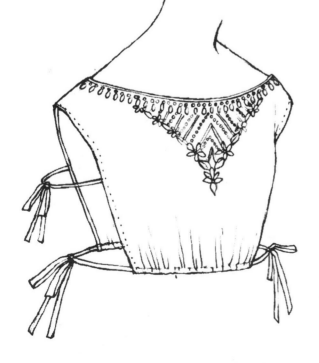

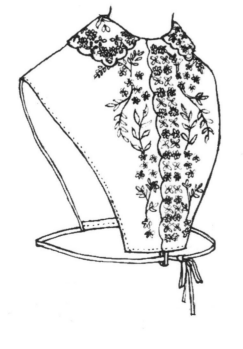

E c.1830-5
A chemisette in soft, fine, white muslin with white embroidery at the front, to be worn with the wide low necklines.

F c.1845-60
A white lawn chemisette with fine broderie anglaise work on the front and the collar.

G c.1845-60
A white muslin chemisette with a crocheted lace collar.

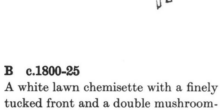

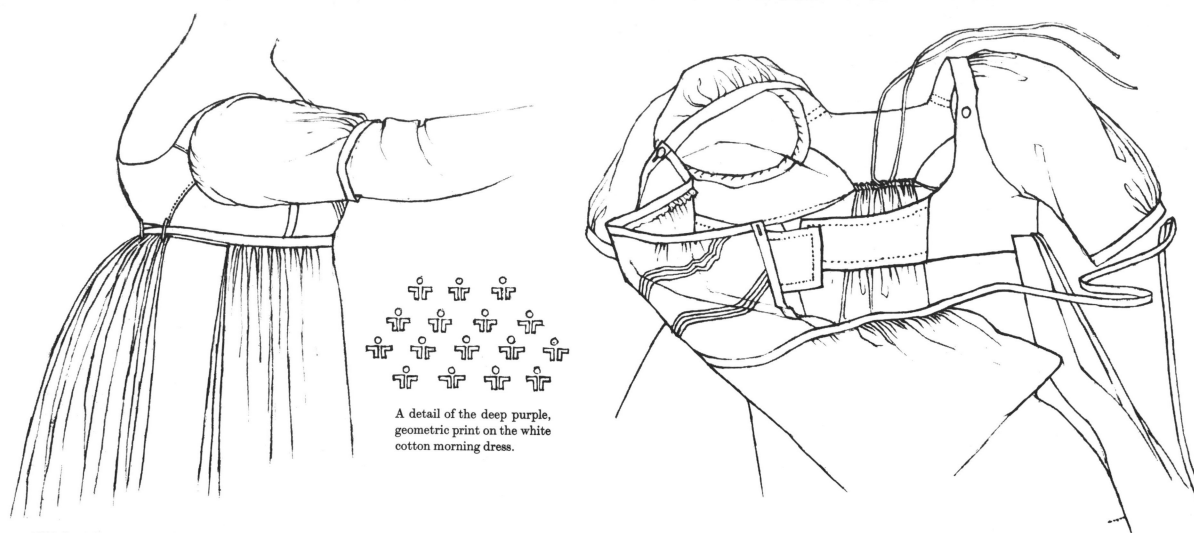

A detail of the deep purple, geometric print on the white cotton morning dress.

c.1798-1805 Salisbury Museum

A side view of the white cotton morning dress with a high stomacher front opening (page 48), to show the worked loops at the centre-back bodice. The narrow bands from the front waist pass through these loops and are held in position before being tied at the centre-front under the bodice.

A detail of the morning dress to show the linen under-pieces which are pinned under the bust before tying the waist bands and buttoning the high stomacher front in position. The two long strings at the back secured a bustle pad and helped to hold the dress in position.

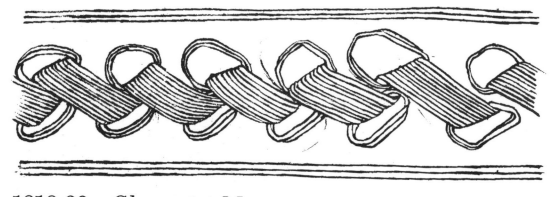

c.1818-23 Gloucester Museum

The strips of decorative piping on the deep blue silk pelisse (page 54) are made of satin cut on the cross. The oval shapes are cut out and the edges of the strips and the raw edges of these shapes are double-piped with satin. A long strip of 10-piped satin is twisted through the holes. All the piping is done with $\frac{1}{16}$" wide cord.

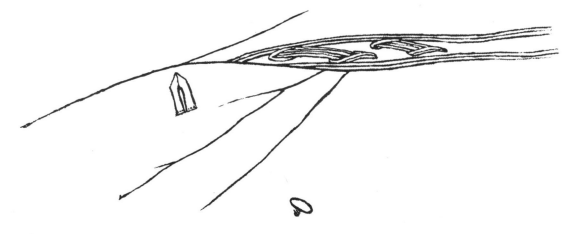

The pelisse is fastened down the centre-front with small tab buttonholes and buttons covered in blue silk.

A PELISSE C 1818-23

IN DEEP BLUE FINELY RIBBED SILK, LINED THROUGHOUT WITH FINE WHITE SILK. SATIN OF A MATCHING SHADE OF
BLUE IS USED TO MAKE THE BELT AND THE PIPING WHICH TRIMS THE PELISSE. THE BLUE SILK IS MADE
UP FIRST. THE PLEATS AT THE BACK ARE TAPED TO HOLD THEM FIRMLY. THE SATIN FOR THE FRONT TRIMMING,
THE EDGE OF THE COLLAR, THE MANCHERONS AND ALL THE STRIPS FOR PIPING ARE CUT ON THE CROSS. THE
SATIN FOR THE FRONT TRIMMING HAS THE OVAL SHAPES CUT OUT AND THE RAW EDGES TRIMMED WITH DOUBLE
PIPING. A LONG STRIP OF 10-PIPED SATIN APPROXIMATELY $\frac{7}{8}$" WIDE IS THEN TWISTED THROUGH THE HOLES. THE
TRIMMING IS THEN MOUNTED ONTO THE PELISSE DOWN THE FRONT AND ROUND THE HEM. THE SAME KIND OF TRIMMING IS
USED FOR THE END OF THE SLEEVE BUT THE STRIP IS PIPED WITH 8 INSTEAD OF 10 CORDS. THE MANCHERONS ARE
MOUNTED ON BLACK NET CUT ON THE SAME GRAIN AND THE HORSESHOE SHAPES ARE CUT OUT. THE RAW EDGES
ARE DOUBLE PIPED. THE 8 PIPED SATIN BANDS APPROXIMATELY $\frac{1}{2}$" WIDE ARE THEN STITCHED TO THE SLEEVE
HEAD. THE MANCHERON IS GATHERED ALONG THE EDGE AND ATTACHED TO THE $\frac{1}{8}$" WIDE DOUBLE PIPED SATIN
BAND. THE 8 PIPED BANDS ARE THEN TUCKED UNDER THE HORSESHOE SHAPES AND STITCHED THUS RUCHING UP THE
SILK. THE MANCHERON IS THEN FITTED TO THE SLEEVE AND STITCHED TO THE ARMHOLE AT THE SAME TIME. THE
SATIN BELT IS CUT ON THE STRAIGHT GRAIN, DOUBLE PIPED ON THE EDGES AND LINED WITH WHITE
SILK. ALL THE CORD USED FOR PIPING IS $\frac{1}{16}$" WIDE. SILK COVERED BUTTONS AND TABS UNDER THE
CENTRE FRONT PROVIDE A CONCEALED FASTENING FOR THE PELISSE.

THE EDGE OF THE COLLAR IS BOUND WITH
SATIN CUT ON THE CROSS AND A DOUBLE
ROW OF PIPING. THERE IS A SEAM AT THE
CENTRE BACK. BOTH TOP AND UNDER COLLAR
ARE CUT ON THE SAME GRAIN.

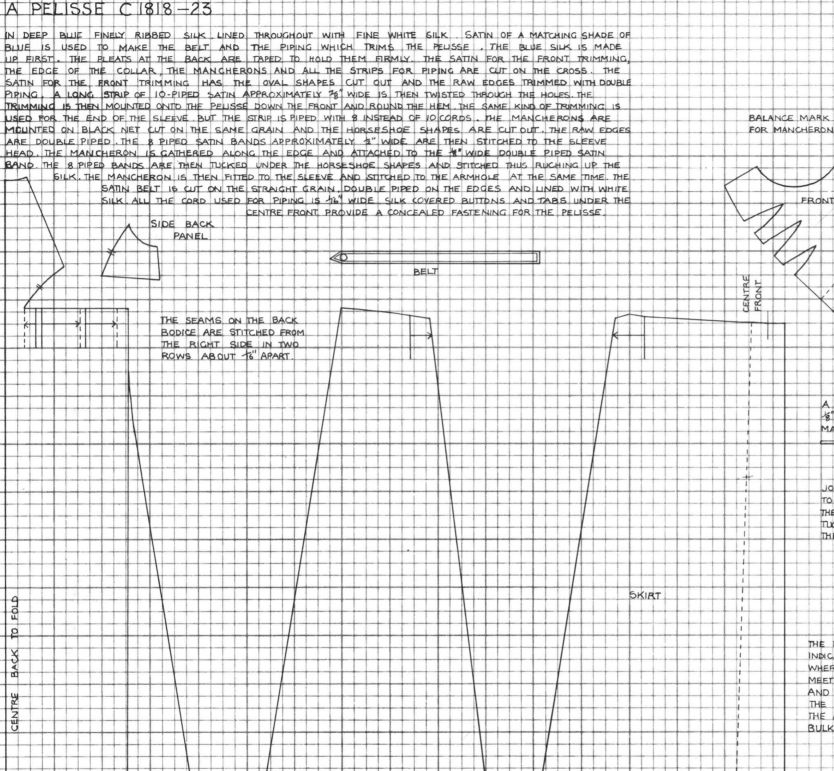

SIDE BACK
PANEL

BELT

THE SEAMS ON THE BACK
BODICE ARE STITCHED FROM
THE RIGHT SIDE IN TWO
ROWS ABOUT $\frac{1}{16}$" APART.

CENTRE BACK TO FOLD

SKIRT

SATIN TRIMMING
TO THE DOTTED LINE

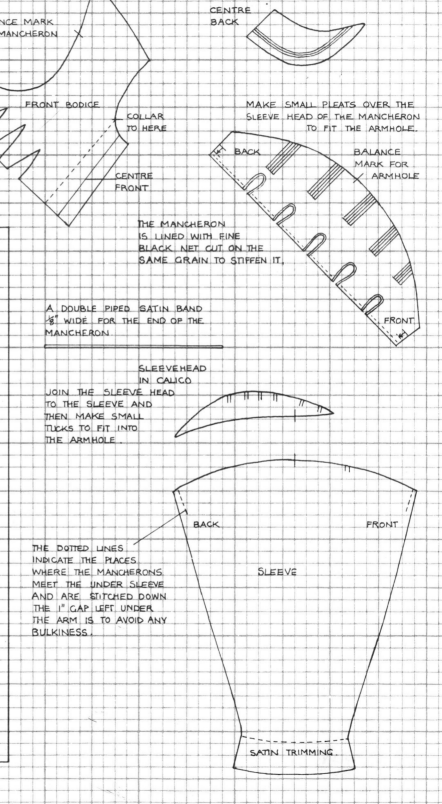

BALANCE MARK
FOR MANCHERON

CENTRE
BACK

FRONT BODICE

COLLAR
TO HERE

CENTRE
FRONT

MAKE SMALL PLEATS OVER THE
SLEEVE HEAD OF THE MANCHERON
TO FIT THE ARMHOLE.

BACK

BALANCE
MARK FOR
ARMHOLE

THE MANCHERON
IS LINED WITH FINE
BLACK NET CUT ON THE
SAME GRAIN TO STIFFEN IT.

FRONT

A DOUBLE PIPED SATIN BAND
$\frac{1}{8}$" WIDE FOR THE END OF THE
MANCHERON

SLEEVEHEAD
IN CALICO

JOIN THE SLEEVE HEAD
TO THE SLEEVE AND
THEN MAKE SMALL
TUCKS TO FIT INTO
THE ARMHOLE.

THE DOTTED LINES
INDICATE THE PLACES
WHERE THE MANCHERONS
MEET THE UNDER SLEEVE
AND ARE STITCHED DOWN
THE 1" GAP LEFT UNDER
THE ARM IS TO AVOID ANY
BULKINESS.

BACK

FRONT

SLEEVE

SATIN TRIMMING.

c.1818-23   Gloucester Museum

A pelisse in deep blue ribbed silk, lined throughout with fine white silk. The pelisse is decorated with satin piping in a matching shade of blue. This garment would have been worn over a dress for outdoor wear with a white muslin ruff showing over the collar. A bustle pad tied round the waist under the dress would have held out the skirt at the back.

c.1824-7   Salisbury Museum

A pelisse-robe, a development from the pelisse, in acid green silk, lined throughout with fine white silk. The hem is padded and a deep band of black, acid green and white flossed silk is set above it. The pelisse-robe would have been worn as a dress over a lightly-boned corset with a bustle pad tied round the waist at the back. A white cambric or lawn collar would have been worn at the neck. The one shown is taken from a fashion plate in *Journal des Dames et des Modes*, September 1824.

A PELISSE ROBE C1824 -27

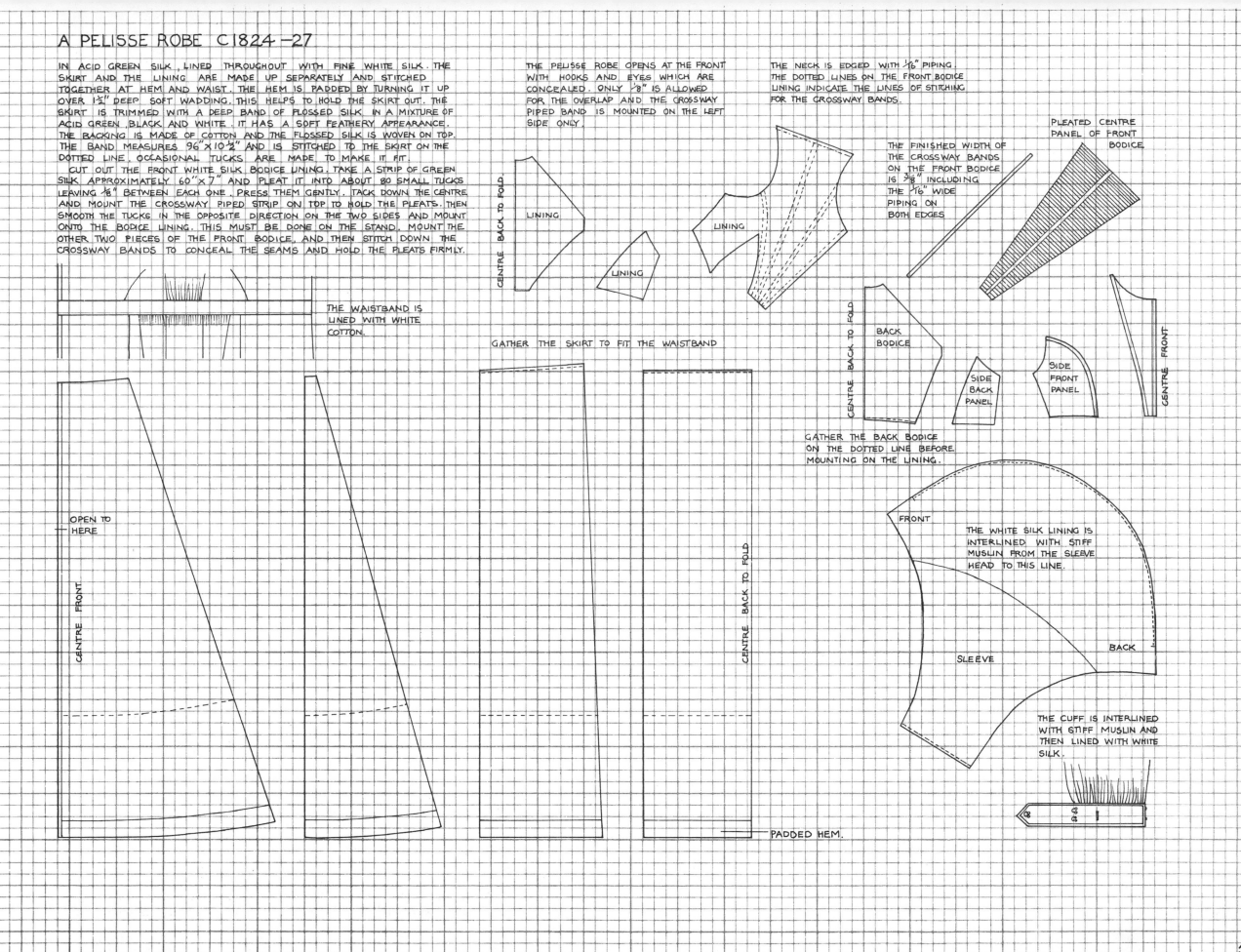

IN ACID GREEN SILK, LINED THROUGHOUT WITH FINE WHITE SILK. THE SKIRT AND THE LINING ARE MADE UP SEPARATELY AND STITCHED TOGETHER AT HEM AND WAIST. THE HEM IS PADDED BY TURNING IT UP OVER 1½" DEEP SOFT WADDING. THIS HELPS TO HOLD THE SKIRT OUT. THE SKIRT IS TRIMMED WITH A DEEP BAND OF FLOSSED SILK IN A MIXTURE OF ACID GREEN, BLACK AND WHITE. IT HAS A SOFT FEATHERY APPEARANCE. THE BACKING IS MADE OF COTTON AND THE FLOSSED SILK IS WOVEN ON TOP. THE BAND MEASURES 96"×10½" AND IS STITCHED TO THE SKIRT ON THE DOTTED LINE. OCCASIONAL TUCKS ARE MADE TO MAKE IT FIT.
CUT OUT THE FRONT WHITE SILK BODICE LINING. TAKE A STRIP OF GREEN SILK APPROXIMATELY 60"×7" AND PLEAT IT INTO ABOUT 80 SMALL TUCKS LEAVING ⅛" BETWEEN EACH ONE. PRESS THEM GENTLY. TACK DOWN THE CENTRE AND MOUNT THE CROSSWAY PIPED STRIP ON TOP TO HOLD THE PLEATS. THEN SMOOTH THE TUCKS IN THE OPPOSITE DIRECTION ON THE TWO SIDES AND MOUNT ONTO THE BODICE LINING. THIS MUST BE DONE ON THE STAND. MOUNT THE OTHER TWO PIECES OF THE FRONT BODICE, AND THEN STITCH DOWN THE CROSSWAY BANDS TO CONCEAL THE SEAMS AND HOLD THE PLEATS FIRMLY.

THE PELISSE ROBE OPENS AT THE FRONT WITH HOOKS AND EYES WHICH ARE CONCEALED. ONLY ⅛" IS ALLOWED FOR THE OVERLAP AND THE CROSSWAY PIPED BAND IS MOUNTED ON THE LEFT SIDE ONLY.

THE NECK IS EDGED WITH ⅟₁₆" PIPING. THE DOTTED LINES ON THE FRONT BODICE LINING INDICATE THE LINES OF STITCHING FOR THE CROSSWAY BANDS.

THE FINISHED WIDTH OF THE CROSSWAY BANDS ON THE FRONT BODICE IS ⅜" INCLUDING THE ⅟₁₆" WIDE PIPING ON BOTH EDGES

PLEATED CENTRE PANEL OF FRONT BODICE

LINING

LINING

LINING

CENTRE BACK TO FOLD

THE WAISTBAND IS LINED WITH WHITE COTTON.

GATHER THE SKIRT TO FIT THE WAISTBAND

BACK BODICE

CENTRE BACK TO FOLD

SIDE BACK PANEL

SIDE FRONT PANEL

CENTRE FRONT

GATHER THE BACK BODICE ON THE DOTTED LINE BEFORE MOUNTING ON THE LINING.

OPEN TO HERE

CENTRE FRONT

CENTRE BACK TO FOLD

FRONT

SLEEVE

BACK

THE WHITE SILK LINING IS INTERLINED WITH STIFF MUSLIN FROM THE SLEEVE HEAD TO THIS LINE.

THE CUFF IS INTERLINED WITH STIFF MUSLIN AND THEN LINED WITH WHITE SILK.

PADDED HEM.

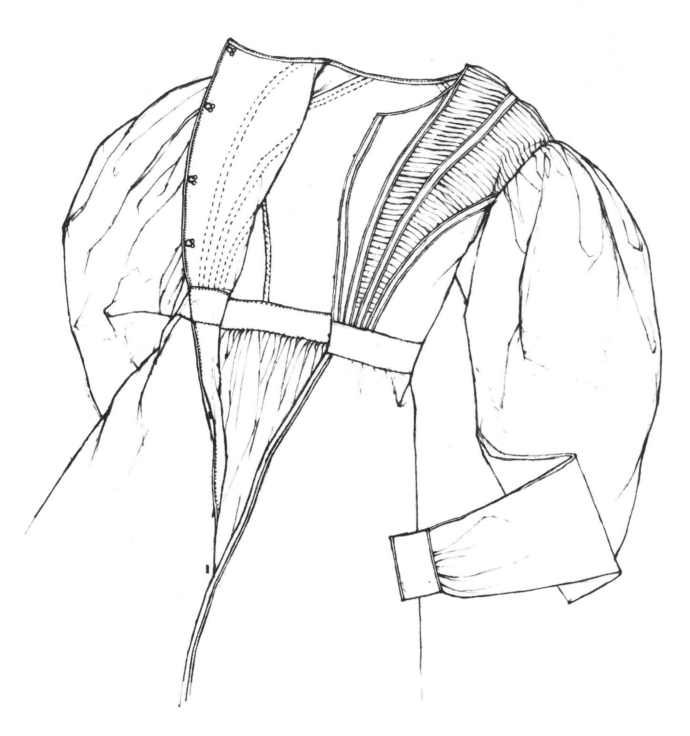

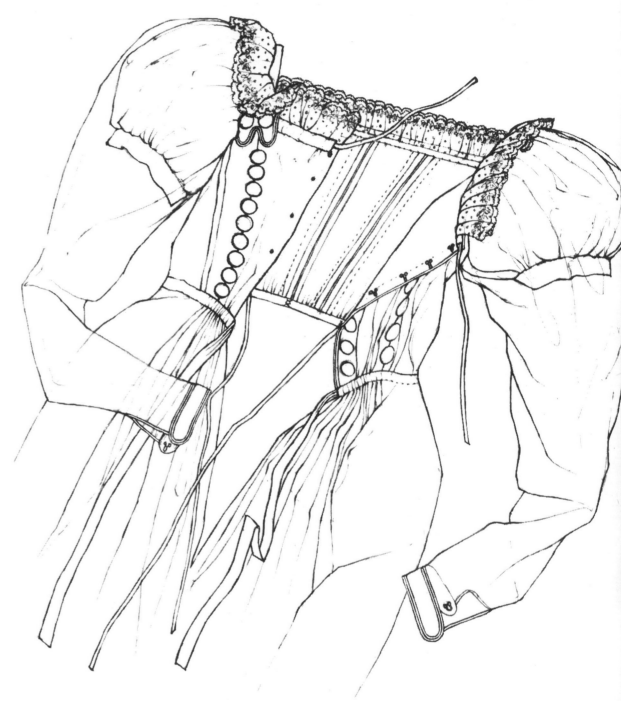

*c.*1824-7   Salisbury Museum

A detail of the pelisse-robe (page 54), showing the front opening and the panel of decorative pleats. The top of the sleeve is interlined with muslin to stiffen it.

*c.*1827-9   Snowshill Manor

A detail of the back of the evening dress in grey silk taffeta trimmed with pink gauze (page 58). The oversleeve is in transparent rose pink gauze. Both short sleeves and oversleeves have cuffs of matching pink satin, the cuffs of the oversleeves being piped with pale grey taffeta. The decorative buttons are covered in pink satin. The back fastens with hooks and eyes and is tied at the top with pink silk ribbons. The back of the bodice is trimmed with crossway strips of pink gauze and the front with pink satin fishtail shapes piped with grey, which are mounted on top of the pleated taffeta. Cream lace is sewn round the neck.

EVENING DRESS C1827-29

IN VERY PALE PINKISH GREY LIGHTWEIGHT SILK TAFFETA. THE
OVERSLEEVE IS IN TRANSPARENT ROSE PINK GAUZE. BOTH
SHORT SLEEVES AND OVERSLEEVES HAVE CUFFS OF MATCHING
PINK SATIN. THE CUFFS OF THE OVERSLEEVES ARE PIPED
WITH PALE GREY TAFFETA. THE DECORATIVE BUTTONS ARE
COVERED IN PINK SATIN. THE BACK FASTENS WITH HOOKS AND
EYES AND TIES AT THE TOP WITH PINK SILK RIBBONS. THE BACK
OF THE BODICE IS TRIMMED WITH STRIPS OF CROSSWAY PINK
GAUZE AND THE FRONT WITH PINK SATIN FISH-TAIL SHAPES,
PIPED WITH GREY, WHICH ARE MOUNTED ON TOP OF THE
PLEATED TAFFETA. AT THE HEM THERE ARE TWO BANDS OF
PINK SATIN LIGHTLY PADDED, DIVIDED BY DOUBLED STRIPS
OF GREY TAFFETA. ABOVE THESE BANDS ARE PINK SATIN
AND PINK GAUZE TRIMMINGS. THE SATIN FORMS TRIANGULAR
SHAPES FROM WHICH EMERGE PLEATED FANS OF DOUBLED
GAUZE. CREAM LACE IS SEWN ROUND THE NECK.
METHOD USED IN ASSEMBLING DRESS.
1. CUT THE CROSSWAY PIECE FOR THE FRONT BODICE AND PLEAT AS INDICATED
2. FOLD ON THE DOTTED LINE. FOLD AGAIN SO THAT THE 1½" WIDE STRIP HANGS OVER THE FRONT
3. STITCH A STRIP OF PINK RIBBON ⅜" WIDE × 13" ACROSS THE CENTRE FRONT TO HOLD THE NECK IN POSITION.
4. MOUNT THE FISH-TAIL SHAPED DECORATIVE PIECES AND STITCH.
5. MAKE UP BACK AND JOIN IT TO THE FRONT. EDGE STITCH THE FINE WHITE COTTON LINING [CUT TO THE SAME SHAPE] TO THE BACK.
6. PUT IN THE SHOULDER PIECES AND LINE THEM.
7. GATHER THE FRONT AND BACK WAIST OF BODICE AND SKIRT TO FIT THE WAIST MEASUREMENT.
8. WHEN THE BODICE IS JOINED TO THE SKIRT A STRIP OF PINK RIBBON ⅝" × 26" IS STITCHED INSIDE TO HOLD THE WAIST.
9. TAKE A PIECE OF RIBBON 60" LONG AND FOLD IN HALF. STITCH 6" ACROSS THE FRONT WAIST ON THE WRONG SIDE. THE LONG ENDS TIE
   ROUND THE WAIST TO HOLD THE DRESS IN POSITION.
10. PINK RIBBONS 1" × 19½" ARE STITCHED ON EITHER SIDE OF THE CENTRE BACK WAIST TO
    FASTEN THE DRESS.

THE CENTRE BACK OPENING IS PIPED ON THE RIGHT SIDE ONLY. EYELET HOLES ARE WORKED ON THE LEFT SIDE.
THE DECORATIVE BUTTONS ARE DOME SHAPED AND ⅝" IN DIAMETER. THEY ARE COVERED WITH PINK SATIN RIBBON.
THE LACE AT THE NECK IS 2½" DEEP AND IS STITCHED ½" UNDER THE BODICE AT FRONT AND BACK. IT IS FLATTENED
OVER THE SLEEVE ON THE SHOULDER AND STITCHED OUTSIDE. THERE IS AN UNDERLAY ON THE LEFT SIDE ONLY AT
THE CENTRE BACK. THE RIGHT SIDE HAS HOOKS UNDER THE CENTRE BACK. A 12" RIBBON ¼" WIDE IS SLOTTED
THROUGH A RIBBON CASING TO TIE AND PULL IN THE NECKLINE. IT IS ATTACHED TO THE NECKLINE AT X.

BACK

SLEEVE   BODICE

SHOULDER STRAP

FRONT

PINK
GAUZE
STRIP.
PLACE ON
TOP OF GREY
TAFFETA ONE.

GREY TAFFETA DECORATIVE
STRIP. FOLD ON THE
DOTTED LINE STITCH TO
BACK BODICE

CENTRE BACK

A ½" WIDE PADDED PINK SATIN
ROLL IS STITCHED TO THE
BACK NECK ON BOTH SIDES

FRONT BODICE IN
GREY TAFFETA.

CENTRE
FRONT

EACH PIECE
GATHERS INTO 1½"

C.
F.
GATHER
INTO 3"

FISHTAILS IN PINK SATIN
PIPED WITH GREY TAFFETA

GATHER ON THE DOTTED
LINE FOR THESE TWO
PANELS. THEY MEASURE
1½" BOTH TOGETHER
WHEN GATHERED UP.
THE REINFORCING
RIBBON HOLDS THE
GATHERING FIRM AS
THE BODICE IS ALSO
GATHERED HERE.

OPEN
TO HERE

FRONT   BACK

GATHER TO FIT BAND

FOLD LINE

BOTH SLEEVE SEAMS MATCH
BODICE SIDE SEAM.

2" DEEP SATIN RIBBON FOLDED IN HALF TO FORM A 1"
WIDE BAND FOR THE UNDERSLEEVE

TRIMMINGS FOR THE SKIRT.
TAKE A 2" × 5" STRIP OF
PINK SATIN RIBBON, FOLD
ON THE LINES AND STITCH.
TAKE A 20" × 8" CROSSWAY
STRIP OF GAUZE, FOLD IT
IN HALF LENGTH WAYS AND
PRESS. PLEAT IT FAN-WISE
AND STITCH UNDER THE
RIBBON. ELEVEN PAIRS
OF TRIANGLES ARE
STITCHED ROUND THE
HEM APPROXIMATELY
7" APART. THE APEX
OF THE TOP TRIANGLE
OF EACH PAIR IS 10"
FROM THE HEM.

THE DOTTED LINE
ROUND THE WAIST
INDICATES THE
STITCHING LINE OF
REINFORCING SATIN
RIBBON ON THE
WRONG SIDE

FOLD   FRONT
        SKIRT

CENTRE FRONT TO FOLD

BACK
SKIRT

CENTRE BACK TO FOLD

STRIPS OF
CROSSWAY
GREY TAFFETA
2½" WIDE
FOLDED IN
HALF AND
TURNED
UNDER THE
TOP ONE
SHOWS
FOR ½"
AND THE
BOTTOM
ONE FOR
⅛"

THE CUFF FOR THE
OVERSLEEVE IS
A ½" WIDE
BAND OF
PINK SATIN
RIBBON.
DOUBLE
PIPED
WITH
GREY
TAFFETA
AND
BACKED
WITH
WHITE
SILK.

GATHER OVER
SLEEVEHEAD

BACK

FRONT

PINK GAUZE
OVERSLEEVE.

ATTACH THE OVER-
SLEEVE TO THE
SHORT SLEEVE
ABOVE THE
CUFF ON THE
SEAM AT
THESE POINTS.

2" WIDE PINK SATIN RIBBON FOLDED
IN HALF AND LIGHTLY PADDED.

*c.*1827-9   Snowshill Manor

An evening dress in very pale, pinkish-grey, light-weight silk taffeta trimmed with rose pink gauze. At the hem there are two lightly padded bands of pink satin, divided by doubled strips of grey taffeta, above which are stitched pink satin and pink gauze trimmings. The satin forms triangular shapes from which emerge pleated fans of doubled gauze. The dress would have been worn over a lightly-boned corset with a small bustle pad tied round the waist to hold out the skirt at the back.

*c.*1827-9   Gloucester Museum

A wedding dress in ivory brocaded silk with Marie sleeves and a vandyked collar edged with blonde lace. The hem is padded and above it is a deep vandyked band of brocade cut on the cross, the edges of which are bound with satin. *The Lady's Monthly Museum* and *The World of Fashion* magazines of these years show several evening dresses which closely resemble this one. It would have been worn over a lightly boned corset and a bustle pad tied round the waist with tapes.

A WEDDING DRESS C 1827-29

IN IVORY SILK BROCADE WITH MARIE SLEEVES AND A VANDYKED COLLAR EDGED WITH BLOND LACE. THE BACK OF THE BODICE AND THE WAISTBAND ARE LINED WITH CALICO. THE NECK YOKE IS LINED WITH COTTON CUT ON THE SAME GRAIN. THE COLLAR IS STITCHED ON TOP. THE STRAPS WHICH TWIST ROUND THE COLLAR ARE MADE OF CROSSWAY STRIPS EDGED WITH 1/16" PIPING. THEY ARE 2 1/2" LONG AND 3/8" IS STITCHED UNDER THE COLLAR TO HOLD THEM IN POSITION. AT THE NECK THEY ARE CAUGHT BETWEEN THE COLLAR PIPING AND THE COLLAR. THE COLLAR IS FACED WITH STIFF MUSLIN AND A LACE FRILL IS STITCHED TO THE EDGE.

METHOD USED IN ASSEMBLING THE SLEEVE.
1. MOUNT THE TOP PART ON STIFF MUSLIN AND GATHER IT ON THE DOTTED LINES.
2. ATTACH THE PIPED BANDS AND JOIN THE SEAM.
3. MOUNT THE LOWER PART OF THE SLEEVE ON WHITE CAMBRIC AND JOIN THE SEAM.
4. GATHER THE BOTTOM SLEEVE TO FIT THE BAND AND NEATEN THE RAW EDGES WITH A STRIP OF TAPE AT THE BACK OF THE BAND. ATTACH THE TWO TAPES MEASURING 1/2" x 2 1/4" TO THE BANDS INSIDE THE SLEEVE TO HOLD THE BOTTOM PUFF OF THE SLEEVE IN POSITION.

THE CROSSWAY STRIP FOR THE VANDYKED FRILL MEASURES 16" x 164". THIS GOES ROUND THE WHOLE SKIRT. BIND THE TOP EDGES WITH 1/4" (FINISHED WIDTH) WADDED SATIN CROSSWAY STRIPS. ALLOW 1" FOR MAKING UP. BIND THE LOWER EDGE OF THE FRILL WITH 3/4" WIDE SATIN CROSSWAY STRIPS GIVING A FINISHED WIDTH OF 5/16" ON THE RIGHT SIDE. CATCH ALL THE POINTS TO THE DRESS.

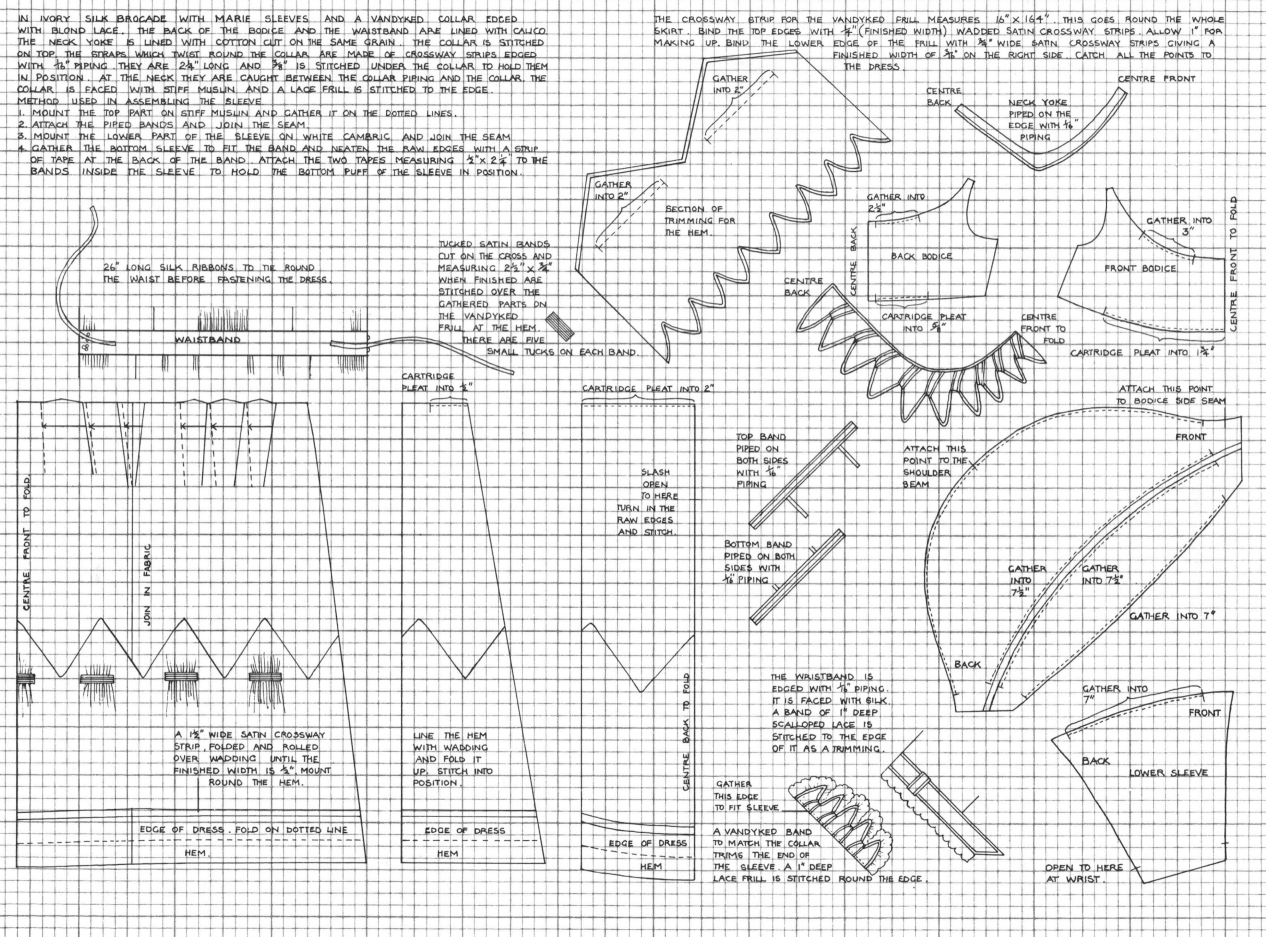

26" LONG SILK RIBBONS TO TIE ROUND THE WAIST BEFORE FASTENING THE DRESS.

WAISTBAND

TUCKED SATIN BANDS CUT ON THE CROSS AND MEASURING 2 1/2" x 3/8" WHEN FINISHED ARE STITCHED OVER THE GATHERED PARTS ON THE VANDYKED FRILL AT THE HEM. THERE ARE FIVE SMALL TUCKS ON EACH BAND.

CARTRIDGE PLEAT INTO 1/2"

CARTRIDGE PLEAT INTO 2"

CENTRE FRONT TO FOLD

CENTRE FRONT TO FOLD

JOIN IN FABRIC

A 1 1/2" WIDE SATIN CROSSWAY STRIP, FOLDED AND ROLLED OVER WADDING UNTIL THE FINISHED WIDTH IS 1/2". MOUNT ROUND THE HEM.

EDGE OF DRESS. FOLD ON DOTTED LINE
HEM.

LINE THE HEM WITH WADDING AND FOLD IT UP. STITCH INTO POSITION.

EDGE OF DRESS
HEM

SLASH OPEN TO HERE
TURN IN THE RAW EDGES AND STITCH.

CENTRE BACK TO FOLD

EDGE OF DRESS
HEM

TOP BAND PIPED ON BOTH SIDES WITH 1/16" PIPING

BOTTOM BAND PIPED ON BOTH SIDES WITH 1/16" PIPING

GATHER THIS EDGE TO FIT SLEEVE

A VANDYKED BAND TO MATCH THE COLLAR TRIMS THE END OF THE SLEEVE. A 1" DEEP LACE FRILL IS STITCHED ROUND THE EDGE.

THE WRISTBAND IS EDGED WITH 1/16" PIPING. IT IS FACED WITH SILK. A BAND OF 1" DEEP SCALLOPED LACE IS STITCHED TO THE EDGE OF IT AS A TRIMMING.

SECTION OF TRIMMING FOR THE HEM.

GATHER INTO 2"

GATHER INTO 2"

GATHER INTO 2 1/2"

CENTRE BACK

CENTRE BACK

BACK BODICE

CARTRIDGE PLEAT INTO 5/8"

CENTRE FRONT

NECK YOKE PIPED ON THE EDGE WITH 1/16" PIPING

GATHER INTO 3"

FRONT BODICE

CENTRE FRONT TO FOLD

CENTRE FRONT TO FOLD

CARTRIDGE PLEAT INTO 1 3/4"

ATTACH THIS POINT TO BODICE SIDE SEAM

ATTACH THIS POINT TO THE SHOULDER SEAM

FRONT

GATHER INTO 7 1/2"

GATHER INTO 7 1/2"

GATHER INTO 7"

BACK

GATHER INTO 7"

FRONT

BACK
LOWER SLEEVE

OPEN TO HERE AT WRIST.

c.1829-31 Snowshill Manor

An evening dress in lilac and white satin-striped cotton. The centre-front and centre-back bodice panels, the decorative apron, the cape-collar and beret sleeves are all in ivory satin. The cape-collar is divided on the shoulder. The satin has a silk surface with the reverse side in cotton. The embroidered net over the sleeves is decorated round the edge with a design of flowers and buds. The bodice panels and apron are decorated with crossed strips of lilac ribbon and ivory embroidered net. The dress would have been worn over a lightly-boned corset and a small bustle pad. The padded rolls which decorate the hem also help to hold the skirt out.

c.1830-6 Northampton Museum

A dinner dress in pale dove grey light-weight moiré taffeta, with gigot sleeves. The bodice is slightly pointed 'à la Marie Stuart'. The skirt is decorated with grey taffeta piping $\frac{1}{8}''$ wide, in a design of thistles and leaves. The dress would have been worn over a tightly-laced corset and a bustle made of gathered rows of stiffened material, tied round the waist with tapes. The skirt is lined with white glazed cotton to stiffen it. Many dresses of this style, but with less decoration, are shown for morning wear in *The Ladies' Cabinet of Fashions*, *The Ladies' Pocket Magazine* and *The World of Fashion* between 1830 and 1836.

AN EVENING DRESS WITH BERET SLEEVES C 1829-31

IN LILAC AND WHITE SATIN STRIPED COTTON. THE LILAC SATIN STRIPES ARE 1" WIDE. THE WHITE STRIPES ARE 2½" WIDE AND ARE SEMI-TRANSPARENT, THE MATERIAL RESEMBLING ORGANDIE. PRINTED ON THE WHITE STRIPES 1½" APART ARE SPRAYS OF FLOWERS IN LILAC, TAN, GOLD AND GREEN. SMALL DOTTED ⅛" CIRCLES ARE PRINTED BETWEEN THE FLOWERS. THE DECORATIVE APRON AND THE CENTRE FRONT AND CENTRE BACK BODICE PANELS ARE IN IVORY SATIN BOUND ROUND THE EDGES WITH 1/16 WIDE LILAC SATIN PIPING. ⅜" WIDE EMBROIDERED NET IS STITCHED ROUND THE EDGES OF THE APRON AND AT THE TOP OF THE BODICE PANELS. THE APRON IS TRIMMED WITH CROSSED STRIPS OF ½" WIDE LILAC SATIN RIBBON. THE BODICE IS TRIMMED IN THE SAME WAY, BUT THE RIBBON IS FOLDED TO ¼". THE SLEEVES ARE CUT IN IVORY SATIN AND WHITE STIFF GLAZED COTTON. THE TWO LAYERS ARE MADE UP AS ONE. THE BODICE IS GATHERED ON THE SHOULDERS AND THE NECK EDGE IS BOUND WITH ⅛" WIDE IVORY SATIN PIPING AND TRIMMED WITH ½" DEEP EMBROIDERED NET. WHEN THE SATIN PANELS ARE STITCHED TO THE BODICE A ⅜" UNDERLAP IS ALLOWED. THE DRESS OPENS AT THE BACK ON THE RIGHT SIDE WITH HOOKS AND EYES SEWN IMMEDIATELY UNDERNEATH THE SATIN BINDING ON THE BODICE. A STRAP IN IVORY SATIN PIPED WITH 1/16" WIDE LILAC SATIN IS STITCHED OVER THE SHOULDER TO CONCEAL THE GATHERS. THE WAISTBAND COVERS THE BOTTOM OF THE BODICE FOR 1". THE CAPE COLLAR IS IN IVORY SATIN FACED WITH IVORY ORGANDIE AND PIPED WITH 1/16" LILAC CROSSWAY SATIN. IT IS BORDERED ON THE OUTER EDGE ONLY WITH ½" DEEP IVORY EMBROIDERED NET. IT IS DETACHABLE AND FASTENS AT THE CENTRE FRONT, WHERE IT HAS OBVIOUSLY BEEN PINNED AS THERE ARE SEVERAL MARKS, ALLOWING AN OVERLAP OF ¼". A TAPE MEASURING 42" IS STITCHED TO THE CENTRE FRONT WAIST ON THE INSIDE FOR 3". THIS WOULD TIE ROUND THE WAIST TO HELP HOLD THE DRESS IN POSITION AND TO SECURE THE SMALL BUSTLE.

EASE A STRAIGHT STRIP OF EMBROIDERED NET 48" LONG TO THE CURVED EDGE OF THE OVERSLEEVE. GATHER THE COMPLETED SLEEVE AND STITCH TO THE ARMHOLE.   SECTION OF STRIP OF EMBROIDERED NET 48" LONG.

FRONT COLLAR

BACK COLLAR

YOKE OF COLLAR

CENTRE FRONT

CENTRE FRONT

IVORY NET OVER-SLEEVE

GATHER TO FIT ARMHOLE.

CENTRE BACK

CENTRE FRONT

CENTRE BACK

CENTRE BACK

GATHER INTO 2¾"

GATHER INTO 1¼"

FRONT AND BACK BODICE PANELS IN IVORY SATIN WITH LILAC RIBBON TRIMMINGS.

A STRIP OF IVORY SATIN PIPED WITH 1/16" WIDE LILAC SATIN FORMS THE SHOULDER STRAP TO HOLD THE GATHERS.

PANEL LINE

GATHER INTO 1¾" TO MEET FRONT UNDER THE SHOULDER BAND

PANEL LINE

THE WAISTBAND COVERS THE BOTTOM OF THE BODICE FOR 1".

BACK BODICE

FRONT BODICE.

GATHER INTO 2"

CROSSWAY IVORY SATIN ARMHOLE BAND WITH TWO ROWS OF 1/16" PIPING AT THE TOP. FOLD THE BAND ON

THIS POINT MEETS THE SHOULDER STRAP OF THE BODICE

IVORY SILK WAISTBAND BACKED WITH BRAID OF THE SAME WIDTH. IT FASTENS WITH HOOKS AND EYES ALLOWING AN OVERLAP OF ¼".

GATHER THE WAIST TO FIT THE BAND.

THE SEAM IS LEFT OPEN TO HERE.

IVORY SATIN APRON WITH LILAC RIBBON TRIMMINGS

THE DOTTED LINE FOR THE FACING. A ½" WIDE PADDED SATIN ROLL IS MOUNTED ON TOP.

GATHER SLEEVE ON THE DOTTED LINE

BERET SLEEVE

FRONT

CUT HERE AND BIND WITH THE CROSSWAY PIPED BAND FOR THE SLEEVE OPENING

BACK

CENTRE FRONT TO FOLD.

JOIN IN FABRIC

CENTRE BACK

ON TOP OF THE HEM ARE STITCHED THREE PADDED ROLLS FOR DECORATION AND TO HOLD OUT THE SKIRT. THE TOP AND BOTTOM ROLLS ARE IN WHITE SATIN CUT ON THE CROSS AND ARE ¾" FINISHED WIDTH. THE CENTRE ROLL IS IN LILAC SATIN ALSO CUT ON THE CROSS AND MEASURES ¼" FINISHED WIDTH.

APRON

THE NET OVERSLEEVE MEETS THESE TWO POINTS AND IS STITCHED OVER THE SLEEVE HEAD. THE ARMHOLES ARE EDGED WITH 1/16" IVORY SATIN PIPING.

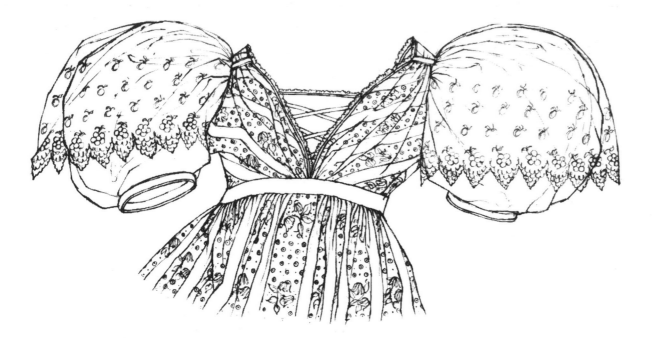

c.1829-31 Snowshill Manor

A detail of the front bodice of the lilac and white striped evening dress (page 60). The lilac satin stripes are 1″ wide. The white stripes are 2½″ wide and are semi-transparent, the material resembling organdie. Sprays of flowers in lilac, tan, gold and green are printed on the white stripes 1½″ apart, with a pattern of small dotted circles, ⅛″ in diameter, between them. The satin beret sleeves are lined with light-weight, stiffened, glazed cotton cut on the same grain.

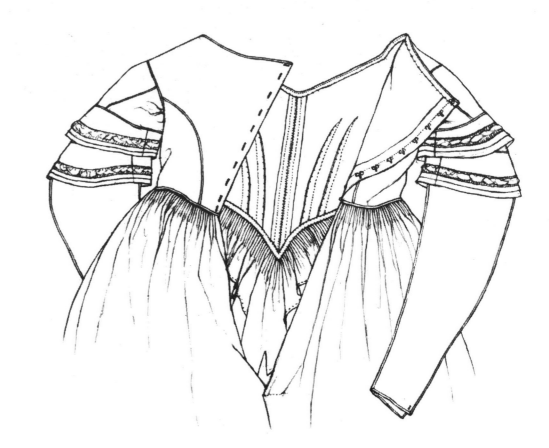

c.1839-45 The Gallery of English Costume

A detail of the construction of the bodice of the deep beige silk day dress (page 64) showing the waist piping and the cartridge-pleated skirt.

c.1837-41
Gloucester Museum

A detail of the inside of the morning dress (page 64) showing the flat pleats of the skirt attached to the linen waistband and stitched to the skirt between the piping and the bodice.

c.1830-6 Northampton Museum

A detail of the front of the bodice of the dove grey silk dinner dress (page 60), showing the pelerine collar trimmed round the edges with ⅛″ piping and then with grey, twisted cord braid. Lace is stitched round the neckline but a low-cut, embroidered lawn chemisette could have been worn instead. The sleeves are lined with white, glazed cotton cut on the same grain to stiffen them, and would have been supported by down-stuffed pads or whalebone hoops.

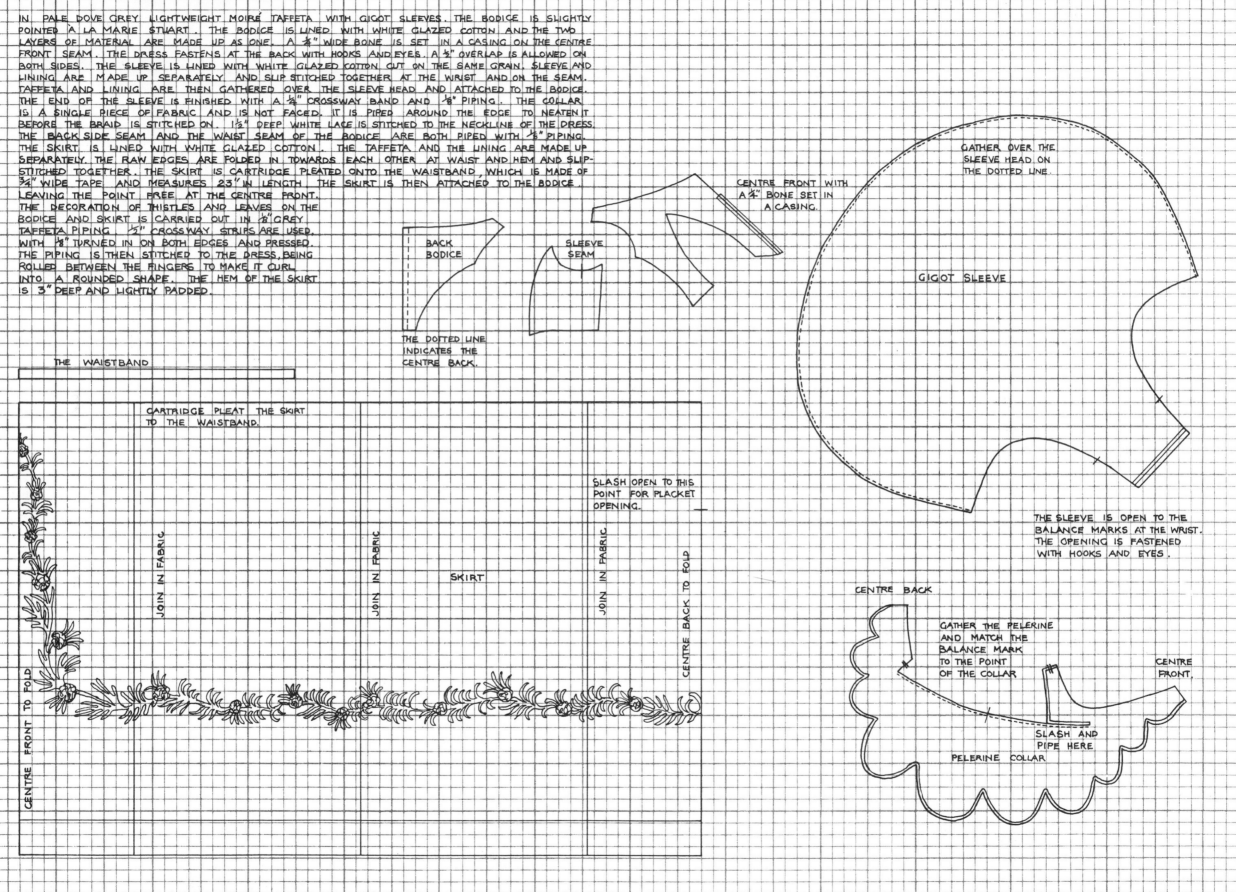

A DINNER DRESS C1830-36

IN PALE DOVE GREY LIGHTWEIGHT MOIRÉ TAFFETA WITH GIGOT SLEEVES. THE BODICE IS SLIGHTLY POINTED À LA MARIE STUART. THE BODICE IS LINED WITH WHITE GLAZED COTTON AND THE TWO LAYERS OF MATERIAL ARE MADE UP AS ONE. A ¼" WIDE BONE IS SET IN A CASING ON THE CENTRE FRONT SEAM. THE DRESS FASTENS AT THE BACK WITH HOOKS AND EYES. A ½" OVERLAP IS ALLOWED ON BOTH SIDES. THE SLEEVE IS LINED WITH WHITE GLAZED COTTON CUT ON THE SAME GRAIN. SLEEVE AND LINING ARE MADE UP SEPARATELY AND SLIP STITCHED TOGETHER AT THE WRIST AND ON THE SEAM. TAFFETA AND LINING ARE THEN GATHERED OVER THE SLEEVE HEAD AND ATTACHED TO THE BODICE. THE END OF THE SLEEVE IS FINISHED WITH A ½" CROSSWAY BAND AND ⅛" PIPING. THE COLLAR IS A SINGLE PIECE OF FABRIC AND IS NOT FACED. IT IS PIPED AROUND THE EDGE TO NEATEN IT BEFORE THE BRAID IS STITCHED ON. 1½" DEEP WHITE LACE IS STITCHED TO THE NECKLINE OF THE DRESS. THE BACK SIDE SEAM AND THE WAIST SEAM OF THE BODICE ARE BOTH PIPED WITH ⅛" PIPING. THE SKIRT IS LINED WITH WHITE GLAZED COTTON. THE TAFFETA AND THE LINING ARE MADE UP SEPARATELY. THE RAW EDGES ARE FOLDED IN TOWARDS EACH OTHER AT WAIST AND HEM AND SLIP-STITCHED TOGETHER. THE SKIRT IS CARTRIDGE PLEATED ONTO THE WAISTBAND, WHICH IS MADE OF ¾" WIDE TAPE AND MEASURES 23" IN LENGTH. THE SKIRT IS THEN ATTACHED TO THE BODICE LEAVING THE POINT FREE AT THE CENTRE FRONT.
THE DECORATION OF THISTLES AND LEAVES ON THE BODICE AND SKIRT IS CARRIED OUT IN ⅛" GREY TAFFETA PIPING. ½" CROSSWAY STRIPS ARE USED, WITH ⅛" TURNED IN ON BOTH EDGES AND PRESSED. THE PIPING IS THEN STITCHED TO THE DRESS, BEING ROLLED BETWEEN THE FINGERS TO MAKE IT CURL INTO A ROUNDED SHAPE. THE HEM OF THE SKIRT IS 3" DEEP AND LIGHTLY PADDED.

CENTRE FRONT WITH A ¼" BONE SET IN A CASING.

BACK BODICE

SLEEVE SEAM

THE DOTTED LINE INDICATES THE CENTRE BACK.

GATHER OVER THE SLEEVE HEAD ON THE DOTTED LINE.

GIGOT SLEEVE

THE SLEEVE IS OPEN TO THE BALANCE MARKS AT THE WRIST. THE OPENING IS FASTENED WITH HOOKS AND EYES.

THE WAISTBAND

CARTRIDGE PLEAT THE SKIRT TO THE WAISTBAND.

SLASH OPEN TO THIS POINT FOR PLACKET OPENING.

JOIN IN FABRIC.

JOIN IN FABRIC.

SKIRT

JOIN IN FABRIC.

CENTRE BACK TO FOLD

CENTRE FRONT TO FOLD

CENTRE BACK

GATHER THE PELERINE AND MATCH THE BALANCE MARK TO THE POINT OF THE COLLAR

CENTRE FRONT.

SLASH AND PIPE HERE

PELERINE COLLAR

c.1837-41   Gloucester Museum

A morning dress in brown silk with bishop sleeves. The bodice is trimmed with vandyked, crossway silk strips and a white lace collar or a white lawn chemisette would have been worn with it. The skirt is lined with brown glazed cotton which is very light but firmly woven and helps to hold the skirt out. The dress would have been worn over a lightly-boned demi-corset as it is for morning wear. For more formal occasions tightly-laced long corsets were worn. The skirt was supported at the back by a bustle made of stiff frills.

c.1839-45   The Gallery of English Costume

A day dress in a delicate shade of deep beige. The fabric is a silk and cashmere mixture with a soft glossy finish. The two-piece straight sleeves are decorated with double crossway pieces, which are trimmed with piping and bouillons. The neckline would have been edged with lace or worn with a chemisette. The bodice is decorated with flat, pleated folds of the same fabric as the dress, which descend from the shoulder to the centre-front. The dress would have been worn over a tightly-laced corset and several stiff petticoats, giving a dome-shaped silhouette to the skirt.

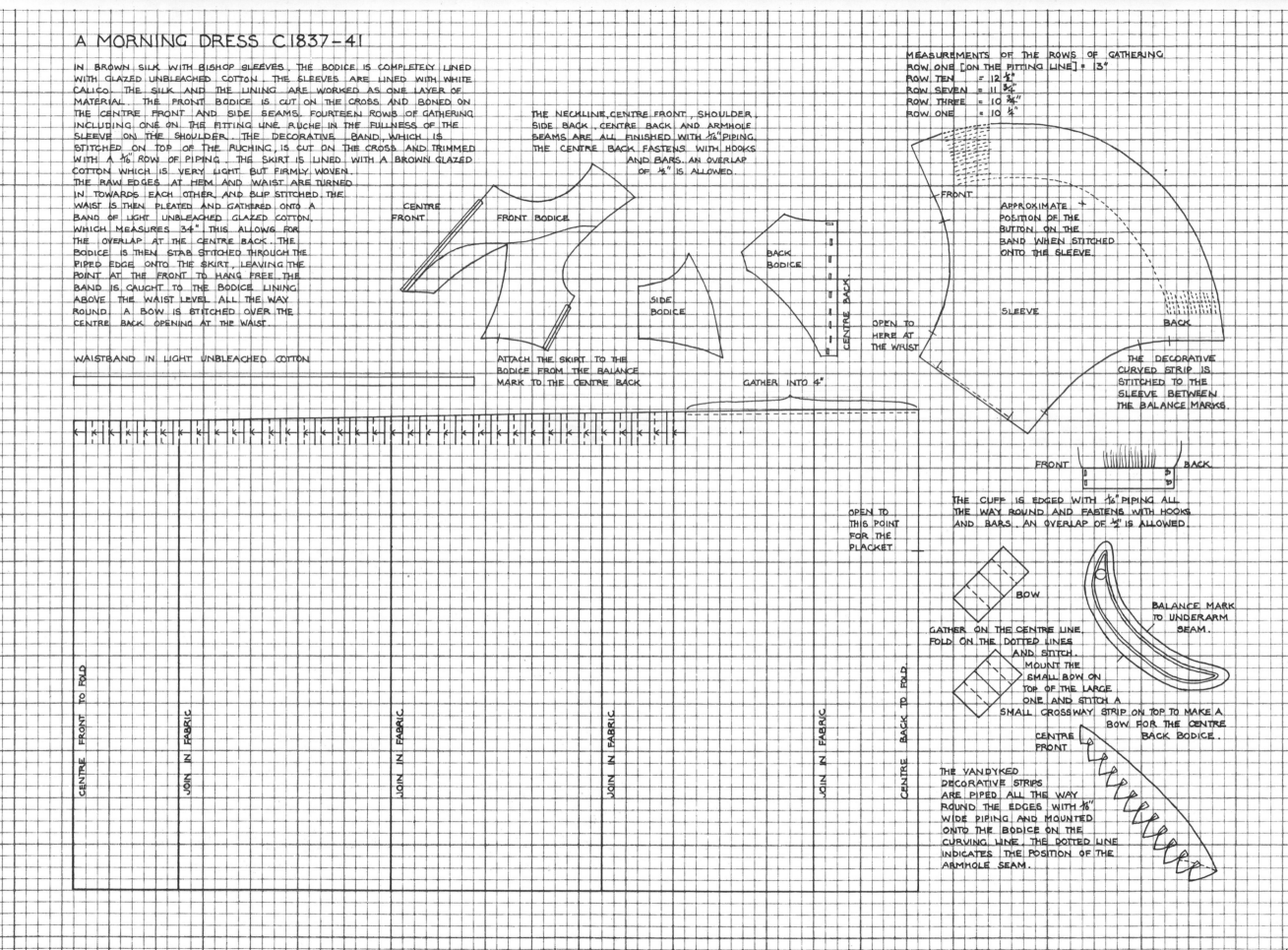

A MORNING DRESS C.1837-41

IN BROWN SILK WITH BISHOP SLEEVES. THE BODICE IS COMPLETELY LINED WITH GLAZED UNBLEACHED COTTON. THE SLEEVES ARE LINED WITH WHITE CALICO. THE SILK AND THE LINING ARE WORKED AS ONE LAYER OF MATERIAL. THE FRONT BODICE IS CUT ON THE CROSS AND BONED ON THE CENTRE FRONT AND SIDE SEAMS. FOURTEEN ROWS OF GATHERING INCLUDING ONE ON THE FITTING LINE RUCHE IN THE FULLNESS OF THE SLEEVE ON THE SHOULDER. THE DECORATIVE BAND, WHICH IS STITCHED ON TOP OF THE RUCHING, IS CUT ON THE CROSS AND TRIMMED WITH A 1/16" ROW OF PIPING. THE SKIRT IS LINED WITH A BROWN GLAZED COTTON WHICH IS VERY LIGHT BUT FIRMLY WOVEN. THE RAW EDGES AT HEM AND WAIST ARE TURNED IN TOWARDS EACH OTHER AND SLIP STITCHED. THE WAIST IS THEN PLEATED AND GATHERED ONTO A BAND OF LIGHT UNBLEACHED GLAZED COTTON, WHICH MEASURES 34". THIS ALLOWS FOR THE OVERLAP AT THE CENTRE BACK. THE BODICE IS THEN STAB STITCHED THROUGH THE PIPED EDGE ONTO THE SKIRT, LEAVING THE POINT AT THE FRONT TO HANG FREE. THE BAND IS CAUGHT TO THE BODICE LINING ABOVE THE WAIST LEVEL ALL THE WAY ROUND. A BOW IS STITCHED OVER THE CENTRE BACK OPENING AT THE WAIST.

WAISTBAND IN LIGHT UNBLEACHED COTTON

CENTRE FRONT

FRONT BODICE

SIDE BODICE

ATTACH THE SKIRT TO THE BODICE FROM THE BALANCE MARK TO THE CENTRE BACK

THE NECKLINE, CENTRE FRONT, SHOULDER, SIDE BACK, CENTRE BACK AND ARMHOLE SEAMS ARE ALL FINISHED WITH 1/16" PIPING. THE CENTRE BACK FASTENS WITH HOOKS AND BARS. AN OVERLAP OF 1/2" IS ALLOWED.

BACK BODICE

CENTRE BACK

OPEN TO HERE AT THE WRIST

GATHER INTO 4"

MEASUREMENTS OF THE ROWS OF GATHERING
ROW ONE [ON THE FITTING LINE] = 13"
ROW TEN = 12 1/2"
ROW SEVEN = 11 3/4"
ROW THREE = 10 3/4"
ROW ONE = 10 1/2"

FRONT

APPROXIMATE POSITION OF THE BUTTON ON THE BAND WHEN STITCHED ONTO THE SLEEVE.

SLEEVE

BACK

THE DECORATIVE CURVED STRIP IS STITCHED TO THE SLEEVE BETWEEN THE BALANCE MARKS.

FRONT   BACK

THE CUFF IS EDGED WITH 1/16" PIPING ALL THE WAY ROUND AND FASTENS WITH HOOKS AND BARS. AN OVERLAP OF 1/2" IS ALLOWED.

OPEN TO THIS POINT FOR THE PLACKET

BOW

GATHER ON THE CENTRE LINE. FOLD ON THE DOTTED LINES AND STITCH. MOUNT THE SMALL BOW ON TOP OF THE LARGE ONE AND STITCH A SMALL CROSSWAY STRIP ON TOP TO MAKE A BOW FOR THE CENTRE BACK BODICE.

BALANCE MARK TO UNDERARM SEAM.

CENTRE FRONT TO FOLD

JOIN IN FABRIC

JOIN IN FABRIC

JOIN IN FABRIC

JOIN IN FABRIC

CENTRE BACK TO FOLD

CENTRE FRONT

THE VANDYKED DECORATIVE STRIPS ARE PIPED ALL THE WAY ROUND THE EDGES WITH 1/16" WIDE PIPING AND MOUNTED ONTO THE BODICE ON THE CURVING LINE. THE DOTTED LINE INDICATES THE POSITION OF THE ARMHOLE SEAM.

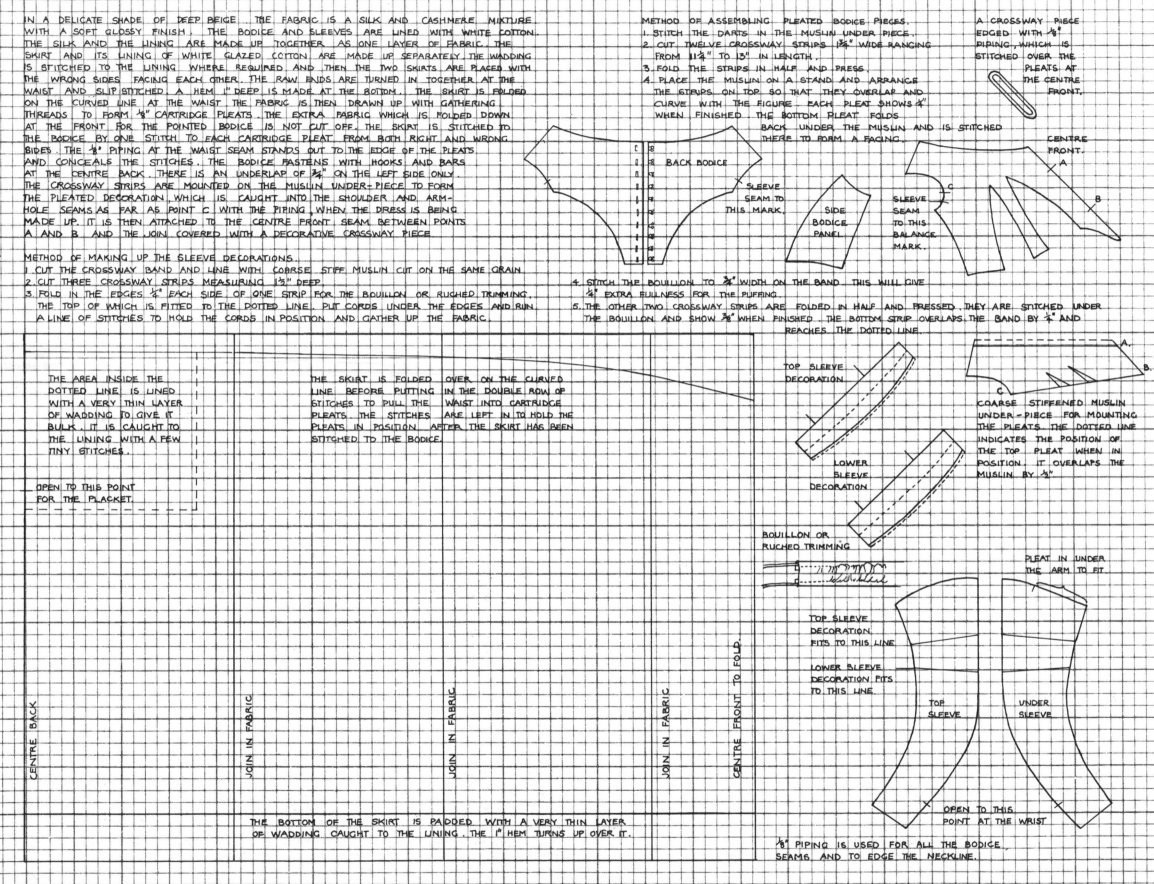

IN A DELICATE SHADE OF DEEP BEIGE. THE FABRIC IS A SILK AND CASHMERE MIXTURE WITH A SOFT GLOSSY FINISH. THE BODICE AND SLEEVES ARE LINED WITH WHITE COTTON. THE SILK AND THE LINING ARE MADE UP TOGETHER AS ONE LAYER OF FABRIC. THE SKIRT AND ITS LINING OF WHITE GLAZED COTTON ARE MADE UP SEPARATELY. THE WADDING IS STITCHED TO THE LINING WHERE REQUIRED AND THEN THE TWO SKIRTS ARE PLACED WITH THE WRONG SIDES FACING EACH OTHER. THE RAW ENDS ARE TURNED IN TOGETHER AT THE WAIST AND SLIP STITCHED. A HEM 1" DEEP IS MADE AT THE BOTTOM. THE SKIRT IS FOLDED ON THE CURVED LINE AT THE WAIST. THE FABRIC IS THEN DRAWN UP WITH GATHERING THREADS TO FORM 1/8" CARTRIDGE PLEATS. THE EXTRA FABRIC WHICH IS FOLDED DOWN AT THE FRONT FOR THE POINTED BODICE IS NOT CUT OFF. THE SKIRT IS STITCHED TO THE BODICE BY ONE STITCH TO EACH CARTRIDGE PLEAT FROM BOTH RIGHT AND WRONG SIDES. THE 1/8" PIPING AT THE WAIST SEAM STANDS OUT TO THE EDGE OF THE PLEATS AND CONCEALS THE STITCHES. THE BODICE FASTENS WITH HOOKS AND BARS AT THE CENTRE BACK. THERE IS AN UNDERLAP OF 3/4" ON THE LEFT SIDE ONLY. THE CROSSWAY STRIPS ARE MOUNTED ON THE MUSLIN UNDER-PIECE TO FORM THE PLEATED DECORATION, WHICH IS CAUGHT INTO THE SHOULDER AND ARMHOLE SEAMS AS FAR AS POINT C WITH THE PIPING, WHEN THE DRESS IS BEING MADE UP. IT IS THEN ATTACHED TO THE CENTRE FRONT SEAM BETWEEN POINTS A AND B AND THE JOIN COVERED WITH A DECORATIVE CROSSWAY PIECE.

METHOD OF MAKING UP THE SLEEVE DECORATIONS.
1. CUT THE CROSSWAY BAND AND LINE WITH COARSE STIFF MUSLIN CUT ON THE SAME GRAIN
2. CUT THREE CROSSWAY STRIPS MEASURING 1 1/2" DEEP.
3. FOLD IN THE EDGES 1/4" EACH SIDE OF ONE STRIP FOR THE BOUILLON OR RUCHED TRIMMING. THE TOP OF WHICH IS FITTED TO THE DOTTED LINE. PUT CORDS UNDER THE EDGES AND RUN A LINE OF STITCHES TO HOLD THE CORDS IN POSITION AND GATHER UP THE FABRIC.

METHOD OF ASSEMBLING PLEATED BODICE PIECES.
1. STITCH THE DARTS IN THE MUSLIN UNDER PIECE.
2. CUT TWELVE CROSSWAY STRIPS 1 3/4" WIDE RANGING FROM 11 3/4" TO 13" IN LENGTH.
3. FOLD THE STRIPS IN HALF AND PRESS.
4. PLACE THE MUSLIN ON A STAND AND ARRANGE THE STRIPS ON TOP SO THAT THEY OVERLAP AND CURVE WITH THE FIGURE. EACH PLEAT SHOWS 1/2" WHEN FINISHED. THE BOTTOM PLEAT FOLDS BACK UNDER THE MUSLIN AND IS STITCHED THERE TO FORM A FACING.

4. STITCH THE BOUILLON TO 3/4" WIDTH ON THE BAND. THIS WILL GIVE 1/4" EXTRA FULLNESS FOR THE PUFFING.
5. THE OTHER TWO CROSSWAY STRIPS ARE FOLDED IN HALF AND PRESSED. THEY ARE STITCHED UNDER THE BOUILLON AND SHOW 3/8" WHEN FINISHED. THE BOTTOM STRIP OVERLAPS THE BAND BY 1/4" AND REACHES THE DOTTED LINE.

A CROSSWAY PIECE EDGED WITH 1/8" PIPING, WHICH IS STITCHED OVER THE PLEATS AT THE CENTRE FRONT.

CENTRE FRONT.

BACK BODICE

SLEEVE SEAM TO THIS MARK.

SIDE BODICE PANEL

SLEEVE SEAM TO THIS BALANCE MARK.

THE AREA INSIDE THE DOTTED LINE IS LINED WITH A VERY THIN LAYER OF WADDING TO GIVE IT BULK. IT IS CAUGHT TO THE LINING WITH A FEW TINY STITCHES.

OPEN TO THIS POINT FOR THE PLACKET.

THE SKIRT IS FOLDED OVER ON THE CURVED LINE BEFORE PUTTING IN THE DOUBLE ROW OF STITCHES TO PULL THE WAIST INTO CARTRIDGE PLEATS. THE STITCHES ARE LEFT IN TO HOLD THE PLEATS IN POSITION AFTER THE SKIRT HAS BEEN STITCHED TO THE BODICE.

TOP SLEEVE DECORATION

LOWER SLEEVE DECORATION

BOUILLON OR RUCHED TRIMMING

COARSE STIFFENED MUSLIN UNDER-PIECE FOR MOUNTING THE PLEATS. THE DOTTED LINE INDICATES THE POSITION OF THE TOP PLEAT WHEN IN POSITION. IT OVERLAPS THE MUSLIN BY 1/2".

PLEAT IN UNDER THE ARM TO FIT

TOP SLEEVE DECORATION FITS TO THIS LINE

LOWER SLEEVE DECORATION FITS TO THIS LINE

TOP SLEEVE

UNDER SLEEVE

OPEN TO THIS POINT AT THE WRIST

CENTRE BACK

JOIN IN FABRIC

JOIN IN FABRIC

JOIN IN FABRIC

CENTRE FRONT TO FOLD.

THE BOTTOM OF THE SKIRT IS PADDED WITH A VERY THIN LAYER OF WADDING CAUGHT TO THE LINING. THE 1" HEM TURNS UP OVER IT.

1/8" PIPING IS USED FOR ALL THE BODICE SEAMS AND TO EDGE THE NECKLINE.

c.1852-6 The Victoria and Albert Museum

A day dress in white muslin printed with a geometric design in black and deep lilac. The skirt is trimmed with three flounces printed 'à disposition' and the pagoda sleeves and mancherons are trimmed with ¼″ wide white braid. The bodice has a gathered front 'à la vierge'. The waist seam, armhole seams and neckline are all edged with $\frac{1}{16}$″ wide piping. A narrow muslin or lace collar would have been worn at the neck, with detachable white muslin or broderie anglaise engageantes tacked to the undersleeves to show beneath the pagoda sleeves. The dress would have been worn over a lightly-boned corset with the skirt supported by numerous starched petticoats, flounced and re-inforced with rows of cording at the hem to stiffen them, as well as a horsehair petticoat. There is an identical dress to this one at Bethnal Green Museum, which suggests that this may be one of the **ready-made dresses** advertised at this time.

c.1856-60 The Victoria and Albert Museum

A wedding dress, made in the style of a day dress, in white silk, trimmed with white flossed-silk fringing. Small silk bobbles are stitched on top of the fringing on the bodice, at the sides of the skirt and on the sleeves. The jacket bodice is separate from the skirt and is cut with deep basques. The wide pagoda sleeves are open almost to the bodice to show the white muslin or lawn engageantes which would have been tacked to the armhole. The skirt is trimmed with three flounces. A small collar in fine worked muslin or lace would have been worn at the neck. This dress was worn over a lightly-boned corset and a dome-shaped steel wire (later watch-spring) cage petticoat – the 'Artificial Crinoline' – introduced in 1856 to replace the numerous petticoats.

An engageante, or false sleeve, in white cambric with broderie anglaise work, which would have been worn under a pagoda sleeve, is also shown. (c.1852–60 The London Museum).

67

DAY DRESS WITH PAGODA SLEEVES AND FLOUNCES PRINTED A DISPOSITION C 1852-56

IN WHITE MUSLIN WITH A GEOMETRIC DESIGN IN BLACK AND DEEP LILAC. A
SEPARATE BODICE WITH A LOW NECK IN WHITE CALICO FORMS THE BODICE LINING. THE
PRINTED MUSLIN IS GATHERED UP AND MOUNTED ON TOP. THE FOUR LINES OF
GATHERING STITCHES AT THE CENTRE FRONT WAIST AND THE TWO LINES AT THE
CENTRE BACK WAIST ARE LEFT IN TO HOLD THE GATHERS IN POSITION. THE MUSLIN
AND THE CALICO ARE JOINED TOGETHER AT THE SHOULDER SEAM. A CASING FOR A ¼"
BONE IS STITCHED ON THE CENTRE FRONT LINING AT THE WAIST. AN OVERLAP OF
¾" IS ALLOWED ON THE CENTRE BACK LINING, WHICH FASTENS WITH HOOKS AND
WORKED EYELET HOLES. THE BACK OF THE MUSLIN BODICE FASTENS WITH HOOKS AND
WORKED BARS WHICH ARE PLACED ⅜" FROM THE EDGE. THE NECKLINE, THE ARMHOLES
AND THE WAIST SEAM ARE ALL FINISHED WITH ⅛" PIPING. THE PAGODA SLEEVE AND
THE MANCHERON ARE DECORATED WITH ¾" WIDE WHITE BRAID TRIMMING. THE PAGODA
SLEEVE IS ATTACHED TO THE WHITE LINEN UNDER-SLEEVE ON THE DOTTED LINE, WITH
THE MANCHERON OVER IT CONCEALING THE STITCHES. THE SEAMS OF MANCHERON,
PAGODA SLEEVE, AND UNDER-SLEEVE ALL MEET. A WHITE MUSLIN OR LAWN ENGAGEANTE
WOULD HAVE BEEN TACKED TO THE UNDER-SLEEVE BENEATH THE PAGODA SLEEVE.

THE SKIRT IS GATHERED TO THE BODICE WITH TINY CARTRIDGE PLEATS. THE FINISHED
DEPTH OF EACH FLOUNCE IS 13¾" AND A NARROW ½" HEM IS MADE AT THE BOTTOM. THE
TOP OF EACH FLOUNCE IS TURNED DOWN OVER A 1/16" CORD AND SLIGHTLY GATHERED
OVER IT WITH SMALL RUNNING STITCHES. IT IS THEN STITCHED TO THE SKIRT ON ONE
OF THE DOTTED LINES. THE FABRIC FOR THE FLOUNCES, WHICH IS PRINTED A
DISPOSITION, IS 31" WIDE. THERE ARE 4½ WIDTHS IN THE TOP LAYER, 5 WIDTHS IN
THE MIDDLE LAYER AND 5½ WIDTHS IN THE BOTTOM LAYER. THESE ALLOWANCES
ARE FOR THE WHOLE SKIRT.

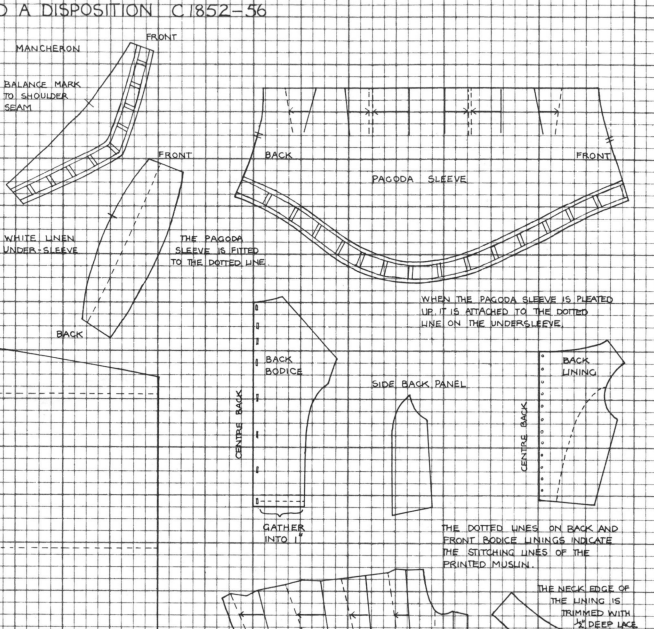

MANCHERON

BALANCE MARK
TO SHOULDER
SEAM

FRONT

BACK

FRONT

BACK

WHITE LINEN
UNDER-SLEEVE

FRONT

PAGODA SLEEVE

THE PAGODA
SLEEVE IS FITTED
TO THE DOTTED LINE.

BACK

WHEN THE PAGODA SLEEVE IS PLEATED
UP, IT IS ATTACHED TO THE DOTTED
LINE ON THE UNDERSLEEVE.

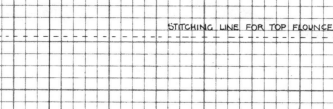

STITCHING LINE FOR TOP FLOUNCE

SLASH OPEN TO
THIS POINT FOR
THE PLACKET.

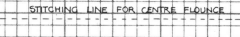

STITCHING LINE FOR CENTRE FLOUNCE

BACK
BODICE

SIDE BACK PANEL

BACK
LINING

CENTRE BACK

CENTRE BACK

GATHER
INTO 1"

THE DOTTED LINES ON BACK AND
FRONT BODICE LININGS INDICATE
THE STITCHING LINES OF THE
PRINTED MUSLIN.

THE NECK EDGE OF
THE LINING IS
TRIMMED WITH
½" DEEP LACE

SLEEVE
SEAMS TO
THIS POINT

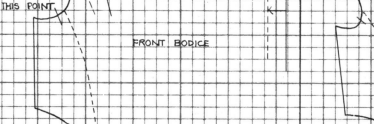

FRONT
LINING

STITCHING LINE FOR BOTTOM FLOUNCE

FRONT BODICE

¾" WIDE WHITE BRUSH BRAID
IS STITCHED UNDER THE HEM.

CENTRE BACK TO FOLD

JOIN IN FABRIC

JOIN IN FABRIC

CENTRE FRONT TO FOLD

CENTRE FRONT TO FOLD

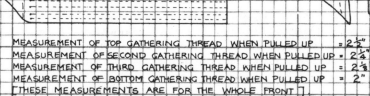

MEASUREMENT OF TOP GATHERING THREAD WHEN PULLED UP	= 2½"
MEASUREMENT OF SECOND GATHERING THREAD WHEN PULLED UP	= 2¼"
MEASUREMENT OF THIRD GATHERING THREAD WHEN PULLED UP	= 2⅛"
MEASUREMENT OF BOTTOM GATHERING THREAD WHEN PULLED UP	= 2"

[THESE MEASUREMENTS ARE FOR THE WHOLE FRONT]

A WEDDING DRESS C 1856-60

IN WHITE SILK, TRIMMED WITH WHITE FLOSSED SILK FRINGING. SMALL ½" SILK BOBBLES ARE STITCHED ON TOP OF THE FRINGING ON THE BODICE. AT THE SIDES OF THE SKIRT AND ON THE SLEEVES. THE WHOLE JACKET BODICE IS LINED WITH WHITE FIRMLY WOVEN COTTON. A PIECE OF SILK 5" DEEP FORMS THE HEM OF THE JACKET ALL THE WAY ROUND, WITH A SEAM AT THE CENTRE BACK. PADS OF COTTON WOOL COVERED WITH SILK ARE TACKED TO THE LINING ABOVE THE DARTS ON THE FRONT BODICE TO GIVE A SMOOTH SHAPE. THE JACKET FASTENS AT THE CENTRE FRONT WITH ½" ROUND PEARL GLOBE BUTTONS WITH GOLD IN THE CENTRE. THEY ARE DETACHABLE. WORKED HOLES ARE MADE IN THE BODICE FOR THE BUTTON-SHANKS TO PASS THROUGH AND BE CLIPPED. AN UNDERLAP OF ½" IS ALLOWED ON THE LEFT SIDE ONLY. THE SKIRT IS LINED WITH STIFF WHITE MUSLIN. A BAND OF PLAITED STRAW, 1" DEEP, ENCASED IN WHITE GLAZED COTTON CUT ON THE CROSS, IS STITCHED TO THE LINING 5" UP FROM THE HEM TO STIFFEN IT. THE SKIRT AND LINING ARE MADE UP INDIVIDUALLY AND JOINED AT WAIST AND HEM. THE STITCHING OF THE FLOUNCES COMES THROUGH TO THE LINING. THE SILK HEM TURNS UP OVER THE LINING. ALL THE FLOUNCES ARE CUT ON THE STRAIGHT GRAIN OF THE FABRIC AND EDGED WITH 2" DEEP FLOSSED SILK FRINGING.

TOP FLOUNCE MEASUREMENT = 10½" × 69" (138" FOR WHOLE SKIRT)
CENTRE FLOUNCE MEASUREMENT = 14" × 80½" (161" FOR WHOLE SKIRT)
BOTTOM FLOUNCE MEASUREMENT = 16" × 80½" (161" FOR WHOLE SKIRT)

C.F.

THE SLEEVE IS LINED WITH WHITE SILK. 1" WIDE WHITE SATIN RIBBON IS BOX-PLEATED AND STITCHED ALL THE WAY ROUND THE WIDE OPENING ON THE INSIDE UNDER THE FRINGING. THE DOTTED LINES INDICATE THE STITCHING LINES FOR THE WHITE SILK FRINGING. ONLY THE TOP 3½" OF THE SLEEVE SEAM IS JOINED AND THE REST HANGS FREE. THE PLEATS ARE CAUGHT DOWN AT THE SLEEVE HEAD WITH A FEW STITCHES.

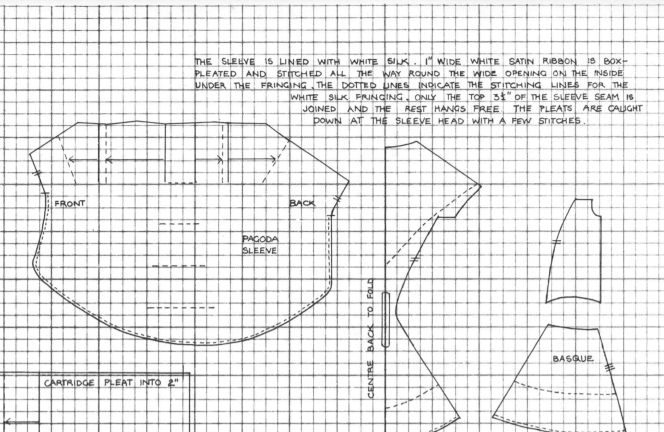

FRONT

BACK

PAGODA SLEEVE

CENTRE BACK TO FOLD

BASQUE

WAISTBAND.

CARTRIDGE PLEAT INTO 2"

LINE OF STITCHING FOR TOP FLOUNCE

LEAVE OPEN TO THIS POINT, CUTTING THROUGH THE FLOUNCE.

A SMALL DART IS MADE IN THE LINING AT THE CENTRE BACK. A SHORT BONE IN A COTTON CASING IS ATTACHED TO IT. THE DOTTED LINES ON BOTH FRONT AND BACK BODICE INDICATE THE STITCHING LINES FOR THE WHITE FLOSSED SILK FRINGING.

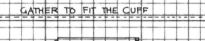

A NARROW HEM ⅛" WIDE IS MADE AT THE TOP OF THE ENGAGEANTE

LINE OF STITCHING FOR CENTRE FLOUNCE

AN ENGAGEANTE, OR FALSE SLEEVE, IN WHITE CAMBRIC WITH BRODERIE ANGLAISE WORK.

OPEN TO HERE

GATHER TO FIT THE CUFF

THE ARMHOLE SEAM IS PIPED

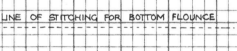

CUFF

LINE OF STITCHING FOR BOTTOM FLOUNCE

A BONE SET IN A WHITE COTTON CASING IS STITCHED TO THE SIDE SEAM

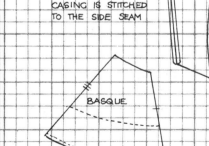

CENTRE FRONT

CENTRE FRONT TO FOLD.

JOIN IN FABRIC

JOIN IN FABRIC

CENTRE BACK

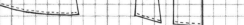

BASQUE

Additional material on the cut of early eighteenth-century dresses.

Author's note

The original intention of this book was to present a practical guide to cutting period costumes, working from perfect unaltered specimens in almost all cases, mainly for use in schools, colleges and the theatre. Much of the information proved useful for conservation work as well and I therefore recorded an increasing amount of detail on each pattern. Since 1965 I have examined over 500 other eighteenth-century dresses, taking patterns of some of them and noting alterations and remodelling on others. In the light of this evidence I am glad to have the opportunity of adding further information to two specimens recorded in 1962-3, in this revised edition.

c. 1720-50 A wrapping gown in cherry pink brocaded satin. Laing Art Gallery and Museum.

The gown (pages 22, 23) posed an interesting problem when first studied in 1962. The design of the silk was dated to *c.* 1707-14 by Natalie Rothstein and although there were some little joins in the skirt the gown did not appear to have been altered. There are very few specimens surviving from this period and in the light of evidence available at that time I decided to record it. Since taking patterns of a mantua of *c.* 1708-9 (see opposite) and two gowns of *c.* 1720-30 and *c.* 1740-2 at the London Museum (see folding patterns in *Women's Costumes 1600-1750*, Z. Halls, H.M.S.O. 1969), it is now obvious that this very expensive silk had been unpicked from its original form, which would have been similar to the mantua from Clive House (see opposite), pressed flat and completely remodelled as a gown with a fitted back and loose wrapover front. It may well have been used for maternity wear. The lines of joins, which were very neatly matched, have now been included in the pattern on page 23. The flamboyant design of the silk makes it seem likely that it would have been remodelled fairly soon after the date of weaving, probably in *c.* 1720, as it would otherwise have looked unfashionable, although the gown may have been worn at a later date by a provincial lady. Silks which have been remodelled at a later date are usually fairly close in style to the fashionable contemporary designs. The early eighteenth-century silks do not seem to have been reused for dresses very frequently until the late nineteenth century. (For further information on alterations to silks see *A Handbook of Costume*, J. Arnold, Macmillan 1972). The original mantua is likely to have been worn in fashionable circles, as the silk is of extremely fine quality. If the patterns on pages 23 and 71 are compared side by side, the method of alteration will be apparent. The sleeves have been recut, instead of being joined on as a T-shape in the mantua. The small joined pieces in the skirt have been taken from the side pieces of a trained mantua skirt. The bodice has been fitted at the sides.

c. 1745-60 White quilted satin jacket and petticoat, Snowshill Manor.

The jacket and petticoat on page 30 were given a date of *c.* 1745-55 when I took the pattern in 1962. This date might be extended to *c.* 1760; the height of the hood makes it difficult to visualise it being worn over the high piled hairstyles much after this. The simple shape of the flounced cuff would also indicate an early date. The front had been incorrectly stitched to the lining, probably in the nineteenth century, but fortunately the marks of the earlier stitching remained. These are the lines given in the pattern on page 31. When I made the drawing I had to visualise how the jacket would probably have looked with the 'compère', or false front, correctly positioned. Conservation work was carried out for the National Trust in 1970 by Karen Finch; the compère has been restored to its correct place and it is now possible to see that the jacket has a more cutaway appearance, consistent with the late 1770s and 1780s. Originally the hooded jacket may have had a straight edge-to-edge front and been cut away in a curved shape in the late 1770s. There are small pieces joined on at the centre front which allow for wider lapels. These may have been added at this date from the pieces cut away at the lower front, although it is difficult to tell from the stitching. The linen lining was probably put in at the same time, as the lines of boning indicate a later date than the early 1750s, but the sewing is not of the quality that might be expected in the 1770s. It is possible that the jacket was not used very much after the alteration, as the hood could not be enlarged.

The pattern of the quilting was not designed to fit the pattern shapes and it is possible that originally two quilted petticoats were purchased and the jacket made out of one of them.

c.1708-9   Clive House Museum

In March 1968 this mantua was sent to the Textile Department at the Victoria and Albert Museum, where Miss Natalie Rothstein was able to date the silk from which it was made to *c.*1708-9. The mantua proved to be of considerable interest, as although it had been taken in a little at the side seams and there were signs of restitching in places, it was otherwise a very rare and perfect specimen of the style which first began to appear for informal wear at the end of the seventeenth century. The gown is very simply made. It is constructed from two lengths of fabric which run straight over the shoulders from ground level at the front to the end of the short train at the back. These lengths are joined together at the centre back. Extra pieces are added at the sides, the joins being turned to the right side of the material to allow for looping up the train.

THE MANTUA IS MADE OF SAP GREEN BROCADED SILK, PATTERNED IN WHITE, TAN, PINK AND BRIGHT YELLOW WITH A GREENISH TINGE. IT IS ASSEMBLED VERY LOOSELY. THERE IS NO LINING, ONLY A RIBBON STITCHED ACROSS THE PLEATS AT THE BACK INSIDE THE BODICE, TO HOLD THEM IN POSITION. THE MANTUA IS CUT VERY SIMPLY, FROM TWO LENGTHS OF SILK RUNNING FROM THE FRONT, OVER THE SHOULDERS TO THE TRAIN AT THE BACK. PIECES ARE ADDED AT THE SIDE TO GIVE MORE FULLNESS TO THE SKIRT. PIECES ARE ALSO ADDED FOR THE SLEEVES, GIVING A T-SHAPE TO THE MANTUA. THE SKIRT IS LOOPED UP AT THE SIDES WITH BUTTONS AND CORDS, REVEALING THE WRONG SIDE OF THE MATERIAL. THIS SEEMS AN ODD ARRANGEMENT, BUT THE JOINS ARE STITCHED WITH THE SEAMS ON THE RIGHT SIDE OF THE SILK AND IT WAS OBVIOUSLY INTENTIONAL THAT THE WRONG SIDE SHOULD SHOW, PROVIDING A CONTRAST OF SURFACE.

THE MANTUA WOULD ORIGINALLY HAVE BEEN WORN WITH A DEEPLY FLOUNCED PETTICOAT, AS MAY BE SEEN IN CONTEMPORARY ENGRAVINGS.

THIS PATTERN AND AN ARTICLE WITH FURTHER DETAILS ABOUT THE MANTUA WERE FIRST PUBLISHED IN "COSTUME", THE JOURNAL OF THE COSTUME SOCIETY IN 1970.

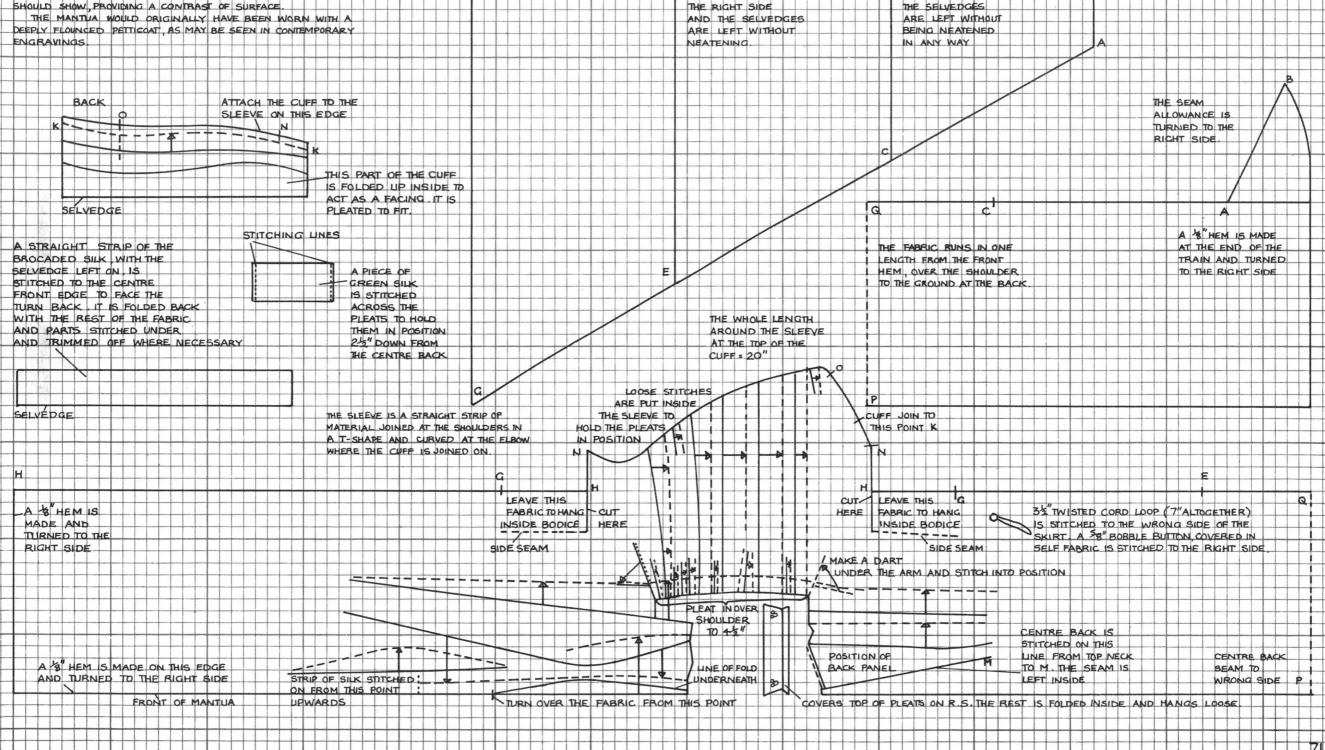

JOIN IN FABRIC, THE SEAM IS TURNED TO THE RIGHT SIDE AND THE SELVEDGES ARE LEFT WITHOUT NEATENING.

JOIN IN FABRIC, THE SEAM IS TURNED TO THE RIGHT SIDE AND THE SELVEDGES ARE LEFT WITHOUT BEING NEATENED IN ANY WAY

THE SEAM ALLOWANCE IS TURNED TO THE RIGHT SIDE.

BACK

ATTACH THE CUFF TO THE SLEEVE ON THIS EDGE

THIS PART OF THE CUFF IS FOLDED UP INSIDE TO ACT AS A FACING. IT IS PLEATED TO FIT.

SELVEDGE

A ⅛" HEM IS MADE AT THE END OF THE TRAIN AND TURNED TO THE RIGHT SIDE

A STRAIGHT STRIP OF THE BROCADED SILK, WITH THE SELVEDGE LEFT ON, IS STITCHED TO THE CENTRE FRONT EDGE TO FACE THE TURN BACK. IT IS FOLDED BACK WITH THE REST OF THE FABRIC AND PARTS STITCHED UNDER AND TRIMMED OFF WHERE NECESSARY

STITCHING LINES

A PIECE OF GREEN SILK IS STITCHED ACROSS THE PLEATS TO HOLD THEM IN POSITION 2½" DOWN FROM THE CENTRE BACK

THE FABRIC RUNS IN ONE LENGTH FROM THE FRONT HEM, OVER THE SHOULDER TO THE GROUND AT THE BACK.

SELVEDGE

THE SLEEVE IS A STRAIGHT STRIP OF MATERIAL JOINED AT THE SHOULDERS IN A T-SHAPE AND CURVED AT THE ELBOW WHERE THE CUFF IS JOINED ON.

THE WHOLE LENGTH AROUND THE SLEEVE AT THE TOP OF THE CUFF = 20"

LOOSE STITCHES ARE PUT INSIDE THE SLEEVE TO HOLD THE PLEATS IN POSITION

CUFF JOIN TO THIS POINT K

A ⅛" HEM IS MADE AND TURNED TO THE RIGHT SIDE

LEAVE THIS FABRIC TO HANG INSIDE BODICE

CUT HERE

SIDE SEAM

CUT HERE

LEAVE THIS FABRIC TO HANG INSIDE BODICE

SIDE SEAM

3½" TWISTED CORD LOOP (7" ALTOGETHER) IS STITCHED TO THE WRONG SIDE OF THE SKIRT. A ⅝" BOBBLE BUTTON, COVERED IN SELF FABRIC IS STITCHED TO THE RIGHT SIDE.

MAKE A DART UNDER THE ARM AND STITCH INTO POSITION

PLEAT IN OVER SHOULDER TO 4½"

CENTRE BACK IS STITCHED ON THIS LINE FROM TOP NECK TO M. THE SEAM IS LEFT INSIDE

A ⅛" HEM IS MADE ON THIS EDGE AND TURNED TO THE RIGHT SIDE

FRONT OF MANTUA

STRIP OF SILK STITCHED ON FROM THIS POINT UPWARDS

TURN OVER THE FABRIC FROM THIS POINT

LINE OF FOLD UNDERNEATH

POSITION OF BACK PANEL

COVERS TOP OF PLEATS ON R.S. THE REST IS FOLDED INSIDE AND HANGS LOOSE.

CENTRE BACK BEAM TO WRONG SIDE P

Metric Conversions

In 1975 the imperial system of measurement, based on the yard for length and the pound for weight, was officially replaced by the metric system devised by the French during the Revolution. The Système International d'Unités (International System of Units) is the modern form of the metric system agreed in 1960 at an international conference. The international symbol for this system is SI and the linear measurements, with which we are concerned here, are expressed in millimetres and metres, using centimetres whenever this is more convenient.

The transition from one system of measurement to another presented problems when revising this book. The patterns were based on a scale of 1/8 inch: 1 inch and printed on a grid designed to enable quick and easy enlargement, using an ordinary dressmaker's tape measure, when working from scale diagram to large sheet of pattern cutting paper. An additional problem became apparent when reducing the pattern diagrams to the scale of 1mm: 1cm for use with a metric tape measure. They became more difficult to read (see example given). The most satisfactory solution, to avoid completely redesigning the whole book, was to provide a metric/imperial unit conversion table with a scale rule which could be copied for use with the existing pattern diagrams, each unit representing 1cm. When using this, the reader should simply ignore the grid on the pattern pages, except as a guide to the straight grain of the material. Although the conversion ruler cannot give absolutely accurate results, as the paper on which both it and the pattern diagrams are printed may stretch slightly with variable humidity, the patterns should be correct to within 12·7mm ($\frac{1}{2}$ inch) when enlarged.

These conversion aids will enable the pattern diagrams on 1/8 inch: 1 inch scale in this book to continue in use for quick comparison with other patterns taken on this scale prior to 1975. They will also familiarise students accustomed to metric measurements with the imperial system of measurement which has been used in the United Kingdom for centuries. The fascinating story of its development is told in *English Linear Measures*, the Stenton Lecture given by Professor Philip Grierson in 1971, published by the University of Reading. Widths and lengths of fabrics were measured in inches, nails, feet, yards and ells and it is important for students of the history of textiles and costume to be familiar with these measurements and to understand how they evolved and were standardised. They should also be aware that there were variations between the English measures and those of other countries. F W Maitland pointed out in *Domesday Book and Beyond* that the English system of linear measures consisted of two basically independent groups of units, the large ones used for land and travelling distances contrasting with the small ones concerned primarily with cloth. The yard of 36 inches divisible into 3 feet, was created

in the twelfth century during the reign of Henry I and involved some revision of the lengths of the foot and the inch. It can be roughly calculated from the nose to the finger tips when the arm is fully extended. In clothiers' hands the yard measure was divided by repeated halving through halves, quarters and eighths to the sixteenth or 'nail' of $2\frac{1}{4}$ inches, which was still in common use during the first half of the nineteenth century. By the early twentieth century this unit was only used by old tailors and dress-makers, but an eighth of a yard ($4\frac{1}{2}$ inches) could still

be purchased in the fabric department of every large store in the country until the metric changeover was made.

The ell measure in England was at one time fixed by law at two yards, then a yard and a half; finally in 1406 a group of weavers made a protest in favour of the ell of five quarters (45 inches) and by the sixteenth century this was accepted as the clothiers' ell. This also continued in use during the nineteenth century. The width of 45 inches was shown on dress-makers' pattern layouts in the twentieth century,

although the word ell was no longer used.

The smallest unit, the inch, is a borrowed word from the Latin 'uncia'. Grierson suggests that this is probably from the same root as 'unguis', 'nail', originally referring to the breadth of the thumbnail, a carpenter's rather than a clothier's measure. The unit is called a thumb in Old Scots, Dutch and all the Scandinavian languages as well as 'pouce' in French. 'Uncia' is 'the twelfth part of a whole' and there are twelve inches in a foot. It is possible that 'uncia', or a word very similar to it, already referred to the

A WEDDING DRESS C 1827–29

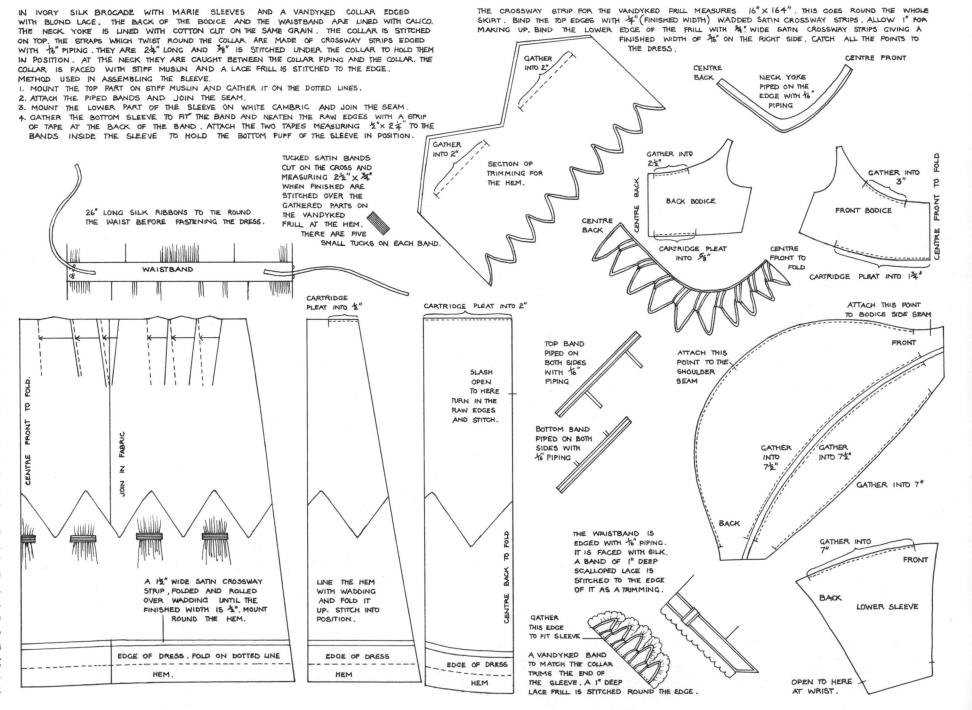

IN IVORY SILK BROCADE WITH MARIE SLEEVES AND A VANDYKED COLLAR EDGED WITH BLOND LACE. THE BACK OF THE BODICE AND THE WAISTBAND ARE LINED WITH CALICO. THE NECK YOKE IS LINED WITH COTTON CUT ON THE SAME GRAIN. THE COLLAR IS STITCHED ON TOP. THE STRAPS WHICH TWIST ROUND THE COLLAR ARE MADE OF CROSSWAY STRIPS EDGED WITH $\frac{1}{16}$" PIPING. THEY ARE $2\frac{1}{4}$" LONG AND $\frac{3}{8}$" IS STITCHED UNDER THE COLLAR TO HOLD THEM IN POSITION. AT THE NECK THEY ARE CAUGHT BETWEEN THE COLLAR PIPING AND THE COLLAR. THE COLLAR IS FACED WITH STIFF MUSLIN AND A LACE FRILL IS STITCHED TO THE EDGE.
METHOD USED IN ASSEMBLING THE SLEEVE.
1. MOUNT THE TOP PART ON STIFF MUSLIN AND GATHER IT ON THE DOTTED LINES.
2. ATTACH THE PIPED BANDS AND JOIN THE SEAM.
3. MOUNT THE LOWER PART OF THE SLEEVE ON WHITE CAMBRIC AND JOIN THE SEAM.
4. GATHER THE BOTTOM SLEEVE TO FIT THE BAND AND NEATEN THE RAW EDGES WITH A STRIP OF TAPE AT THE BACK OF THE BAND. ATTACH THE TWO TAPES MEASURING $\frac{1}{2}$" x $2\frac{1}{4}$" TO THE BANDS INSIDE THE SLEEVE TO HOLD THE BOTTOM PUFF OF THE SLEEVE IN POSITION.

THE CROSSWAY STRIP FOR THE VANDYKED FRILL MEASURES 16" x 164". THIS GOES ROUND THE WHOLE SKIRT. BIND THE TOP EDGES WITH $\frac{1}{4}$" (FINISHED WIDTH) WADDED SATIN CROSSWAY STRIPS. ALLOW 1" FOR MAKING UP. BIND THE LOWER EDGE OF THE FRILL WITH $\frac{3}{4}$" WIDE SATIN CROSSWAY STRIPS GIVING A FINISHED WIDTH OF $\frac{3}{16}$" ON THE RIGHT SIDE. CATCH ALL THE POINTS TO THE DRESS.

GATHER INTO 2"

SECTION OF TRIMMING FOR THE HEM.

CENTRE BACK

NECK YOKE PIPED ON THE EDGE WITH $\frac{1}{16}$" PIPING

CENTRE FRONT

GATHER INTO 2"

GATHER INTO $2\frac{1}{2}$"

BACK BODICE

GATHER INTO 3"

FRONT BODICE

CENTRE FRONT TO FOLD

TUCKED SATIN BANDS CUT ON THE CROSS AND MEASURING $2\frac{1}{2}$" x $\frac{3}{4}$" WHEN FINISHED ARE STITCHED OVER THE GATHERED PARTS ON THE VANDYKED FRILL AT THE HEM. THERE ARE FIVE SMALL TUCKS ON EACH BAND.

CENTRE BACK

CENTRE BACK

CARTRIDGE PLEAT INTO $5\frac{5}{8}$"

CENTRE FRONT TO FOLD

CARTRIDGE PLEAT INTO $1\frac{3}{4}$"

26" LONG SILK RIBBONS TO TIE ROUND THE WAIST BEFORE FASTENING THE DRESS.

WAISTBAND

CARTRIDGE PLEAT INTO $\frac{1}{2}$"

CARTRIDGE PLEAT INTO 2"

ATTACH THIS POINT TO BODICE SIDE SEAM

TOP BAND PIPED ON BOTH SIDES WITH $\frac{1}{16}$" PIPING

ATTACH THIS POINT TO THE SHOULDER SEAM

FRONT

SLASH OPEN TO HERE TURN IN THE RAW EDGES AND STITCH.

CENTRE FRONT TO FOLD.

JOIN IN FABRIC

BOTTOM BAND PIPED ON BOTH SIDES WITH $\frac{1}{16}$" PIPING

GATHER INTO $7\frac{1}{2}$"

GATHER INTO $7\frac{1}{2}$"

BACK

GATHER INTO 7"

THE WRISTBAND IS EDGED WITH $\frac{1}{16}$" PIPING. IT IS FACED WITH SILK. A BAND OF 1" DEEP SCALLOPED LACE IS STITCHED TO THE EDGE OF IT AS A TRIMMING.

GATHER INTO 7"

FRONT

A $1\frac{1}{2}$" WIDE SATIN CROSSWAY STRIP, FOLDED AND ROLLED OVER WADDING UNTIL THE FINISHED WIDTH IS $\frac{1}{2}$". MOUNT ROUND THE HEM.

LINE THE HEM WITH WADDING AND FOLD IT UP. STITCH INTO POSITION.

CENTRE BACK TO FOLD

GATHER THIS EDGE TO FIT SLEEVE

BACK

LOWER SLEEVE

A VANDYKED BAND TO MATCH THE COLLAR TRIMS THE END OF THE SLEEVE. A 1" DEEP LACE FRILL IS STITCHED ROUND THE EDGE.

OPEN TO HERE AT WRIST.

EDGE OF DRESS. FOLD ON DOTTED LINE
HEM.

EDGE OF DRESS
HEM

EDGE OF DRESS
HEM

small unit of a thumbnail and the length was then revised for the divisions of the foot measure. The top joint of the thumb is an approximate measure for one inch. This unit, like the yard, was eventually divided by repeated halving down to eighths of an inch, for measurements of cloth used in dressmaking and tailoring. These are the units shown on tape measures, not tenths of an inch. Anyone who has folded cloth, if only in the form of a sheet or table-cloth, will know how automatically the halving and quartering process takes place. As Professor Grierson points out, the history of both weights and measures has been governed by practical considerations rather than scientific ones.

Metric and Imperial Conversion Table

1 ell = 45 inches = 1143 millimetres = 1·143 metres
1 yard = 36 inches = 914·4 millimetres = 0·9144 metre
1 foot = 12 inches = 304·8 millimetres = 0·3048 metre
1 nail = 2¼ inches = 57·15 millimetres
1 inch = 25·4 millimetres = 2·54 centimetres

Opposite. The pattern of this wedding dress of c. 1827–9, as originally drawn on 1/8 inch: 1 inch scale, is shown on p 59 and the illustration on p 58. The scale shown here is 1mm: 1cm.
Below top. Metric conversion rule for use with the patterns in this book. This should be copied by photography for the most accurate results, as xeroxing is liable to distortion. Each unit represents 1cm and the reader should ignore the grid on the pattern pages, except as a guide to the straight grain of the material.
Below centre. Rule showing centimetres marked out in millimetres, and inches marked out in 1/64 inch. 1/32 inch and 1/16 inch divisions.
Below bottom. Rule showing inches marked out in 1/8 inch and 1/16 inch divisions.

Table of Metric Equivalents

The following tables are based on British Standards (1 inch = 25·4 millimetres exactly). Copies of the complete standards may be obtained from the British Standards Institution, 2 Park Street, London W1Y 4AA.

inches	milli-metres	inches	milli-metres	inches	milli-metres	inches	milli-metres
1/64	0.3969	31/64	12.3031	61/64	24.2094	1 27/32	46.8313
1/32	0.7938	1/2	12.7000	31/32	24.6063	1 7/8	47.6250
3/64	1.1906	33/64	13.0969	63/64	25.0031	1 29/32	48.4188
1/16	1.5875	17/32	13.4938	1	25.4000	1 15/16	49.2125
5/64	1.9844	35/64	13.8906	1 1/32	26.1938	1 31/32	50.0063
3/32	2.3813	9/16	14.2875	1 1/16	26.9875	2	50.8000
7/64	2.7781	37/64	14.6844	1 3/32	27.7813	2 1/32	51.5938
1/8	3.1750	19/32	15.0813	1 1/8	28.5750	2 1/16	52.3875
9/64	3.5719	39/64	15.4781	1 5/32	29.3688	2 3/32	53.1813
5/32	3.9688	5/8	15.8750	1 3/16	30.1625	2 1/8	53.9750
11/64	4.3656	41/64	16.2719	1 7/32	30.9563	2 5/32	54.7688
3/16	4.7625	21/32	16.6688	1 1/4	31.7500	2 3/16	55.5625
13/64	5.1594	43/64	17.0656	1 9/32	32.5438	2 7/32	56.3563
7/32	5.5563	11/16	17.4625	1 5/16	33.3375	2 1/4	57.1500
15/64	5.9531	45/64	17.8594	1 11/32	34.1313	2 9/32	57.9438
1/4	6.3500	23/32	18.2563	1 3/8	34.9250	2 5/16	58.7375
17/64	6.7469	47/64	18.6531	1 13/32	35.7188	2 11/32	59.5313
9/32	7.1438	3/4	19.0500	1 7/16	36.5125	2 3/8	60.3250
19/64	7.5406	49/64	19.4469	1 15/32	37.3063	2 13/32	61.1188
5/16	7.9375	25/32	19.8438	1 1/2	38.1000	2 7/16	61.9125
21/64	8.3344	51/64	20.2406	1 17/32	38.8938	2 15/32	62.7063
11/32	8.7313	13/16	20.6375	1 9/16	39.6875	2 1/2	63.5000
23/64	9.1281	53/64	21.0344	1 19/32	40.4813	2 17/32	64.2938
3/8	9.5250	27/32	21.4313	1 5/8	41.2750	2 9/16	65.0875
25/64	9.9219	55/64	21.8281	1 21/32	42.0688	2 19/32	65.8813
13/32	10.3188	7/8	22.2250	1 11/16	42.8625	2 5/8	66.6750
27/64	10.7156	57/64	22.6219	1 23/32	43.6563	2 21/32	67.4688
7/16	11.1125	29/32	23.0188	1 3/4	44.4500	2 11/16	68.2625
29/64	11.5094	59/64	23.4156	1 25/32	45.2438	2 23/32	69.0563
15/64	11.9063	15/16	23.8125	1 13/16	46.0375	2 3/4	69.8500

inches	milli-metres	inches	milli-metres	inches	milli-metres	inches	milli-metres
2 25/32	70.6438	4 1/32	102.394	5 9/32	134.144	7 1/16	179.388
2 13/16	71.4375	4 1/16	103.188	5 5/16	134.938	7 1/8	180.975
2 27/32	72.2313	4 3/32	103.981	5 11/32	135.731	7 3/16	182.562
2 7/8	73.0250	4 1/8	104.775	5 3/8	136.525	7 1/4	184.150
2 29/32	73.8188	4 5/32	105.569	5 13/32	137.319	7 5/16	185.738
2 15/16	74.6125	4 3/16	106.362	5 7/16	138.112	7 3/8	187.325
2 31/32	75.4063	4 7/32	107.156	5 15/32	138.906	7 7/16	188.912
3	76.2000	4 1/4	107.950	5 1/2	139.700	7 1/2	190.500
3 1/32	76.9938	4 9/32	108.744	5 17/32	140.494	7 9/16	192.088
3 1/16	77.7875	4 5/16	109.538	5 9/16	141.288	7 5/8	193.675
3 3/32	78.5813	4 11/32	110.331	5 19/32	142.081	7 11/16	195.262
3 1/8	79.3750	4 3/8	111.125	5 5/8	142.875	7 3/4	196.850
3 5/32	80.1688	4 13/32	111.919	5 21/32	143.669	7 13/16	198.438
3 3/16	80.9625	4 7/16	112.712	5 11/16	144.462	7 7/8	200.025
3 7/32	81.7563	4 15/32	113.506	5 23/32	145.256	7 15/16	201.612
3 1/4	82.5500	4 1/2	114.300	5 3/4	146.050	8	203.200
3 9/32	83.3438	4 17/32	115.094	5 25/32	146.844	8 1/16	204.788
3 5/16	84.1375	4 9/16	115.888	5 13/16	147.638	8 1/8	206.375
3 11/32	84.9313	4 19/32	116.681	5 27/32	148.431	8 3/16	207.962
3 3/8	85.7250	4 5/8	117.475	5 7/8	149.225	8 1/4	209.550
3 13/32	86.5188	4 21/32	118.269	5 29/32	150.019	8 5/16	211.138
3 7/16	87.3125	4 11/16	119.062	5 15/16	150.812	8 3/8	212.725
3 15/32	88.1063	4 23/32	119.856	5 31/32	151.606	8 7/16	214.312
3 1/2	88.9000	4 3/4	120.650	6	152.400	8 1/2	215.900
3 17/32	89.6938	4 25/32	121.444	6 1/16	153.988	8 9/16	217.488
3 9/16	90.4875	4 13/16	122.238	6 1/8	155.575	8 5/8	219.075
3 19/32	91.2813	4 27/32	123.031	6 3/16	157.162	8 11/16	220.662
3 5/8	92.0750	4 7/8	123.825	6 1/4	158.750	8 3/4	222.250
3 21/32	92.8688	4 29/32	124.619	6 5/16	160.338	8 13/16	223.838
3 11/16	93.6625	4 15/16	125.412	6 3/8	161.925	8 7/8	225.425
3 23/32	94.4563	4 31/32	126.206	6 7/16	163.512	8 15/16	227.012
3 3/4	95.2500	5	127.000	6 1/2	165.100	9	228.600
3 25/32	96.0438	5 1/32	127.794	6 9/16	166.688	9 1/16	230.188
3 13/16	96.8375	5 1/16	128.588	6 5/8	168.275	9 1/8	231.775
3 27/32	97.6313	5 3/32	129.381	6 11/16	169.862	9 3/16	233.362
3 7/8	98.4250	5 1/8	130.175	6 3/4	171.450	9 1/4	234.950
3 29/32	99.2188	5 5/32	130.969	6 13/16	173.038	9 5/16	236.538
3 15/16	100.012	5 3/16	131.762	6 7/8	174.625	9 3/8	238.125
3 31/32	100.806	5 7/32	132.556	6 15/16	176.212	9 7/16	239.712
4	101.600	5 1/4	133.350	7	177.800	9 1/2	241.300

inches	milli-metres	inches	milli-metres	feet & inches	milli-metres	feet & inches	milli-metres
9 9/16	242.888	13	330.200	4 0	1219.20	7 4	2235.20
9 5/8	244.475	14	355.600	4 1	1244.60	7 5	2260.60
9 11/16	246.062	15	381.000	4 2	1270.00	7 6	2286.00
9 3/4	247.650	16	406.400	4 3	1295.40	7 7	2311.40
9 13/16	249.238	17	431.800	4 4	1320.80	7 8	2336.80
9 7/8	250.825	18	457.200	4 5	1346.20	7 9	2362.20
9 15/16	252.412	19	482.600	4 6	1371.60	7 10	2387.60
10	254.000	20	508.000	4 7	1397.00	7 11	2413.00
10 1/16	255.588	21	533.400	4 8	1422.40	8 0	2438.40
10 1/8	257.175	22	558.800	4 9	1447.80	8 1	2463.80
10 3/16	258.762	23	584.200	4 10	1473.20	8 2	2489.20
10 1/4	260.350	24	609.600	4 11	1498.60	8 3	2514.60
10 5/16	261.938	25	635.000	5 0	1524.00	8 4	2540.00
10 3/8	263.525	26	660.400	5 1	1549.40	8 5	2565.40
10 7/16	265.112	27	685.800	5 2	1574.80	8 6	2590.80
10 1/2	266.700	28	711.200	5 3	1600.20	8 7	2616.20
10 9/16	268.288	29	736.600	5 4	1625.60	8 8	2641.60
10 5/8	269.875	30	762.000	5 5	1651.00	8 9	2667.00
10 11/16	271.462	31	787.400	5 6	1676.40	8 10	2692.40
10 3/4	273.050	32	812.800	5 7	1701.80	8 11	2717.80
10 13/16	274.638	33	838.200	5 8	1727.20	9 0	2743.20
10 7/8	276.225	34	863.600	5 9	1752.60	9 1	2768.60
10 15/16	277.812	35	889.000	5 10	1778.00	9 2	2794.00
11	279.400	36	914.400	5 11	1803.40	9 3	2819.40
11 1/16	280.988	37	939.800	6 0	1828.80	9 4	2844.80
11 1/8	282.575	38	965.200	6 1	1854.20	9 5	2870.20
11 3/16	284.162	39	990.600	6 2	1879.60	9 6	2895.60
11 1/4	285.750	40	1016.00	6 3	1905.00	9 7	2921.00
11 5/16	287.338	41	1041.40	6 4	1930.40	9 8	2946.40
11 3/8	288.925	42	1066.80	6 5	1955.80	9 9	2971.80
11 7/16	290.512			6 6	1981.20	9 10	2997.20
11 1/2	292.100			6 7	2006.60	9 11	3022.60
11 9/16	293.688			6 8	2032.00	10 0	3048.00
11 5/8	295.275	*feet & inches*	*milli-metres*	6 9	2057.40	11 0	3352.80
11 11/16	296.862			6 10	2082.80	12 0	3657.60
11 3/4	298.450	3 7	1092.20	6 11	2108.20	13 0	3962.40
11 13/16	300.038	3 8	1117.60	7 0	2133.60	14 0	4267.20
11 7/8	301.625	3 9	1143.00	7 1	2159.00	15 0	4572.00
11 15/16	303.212	3 10	1168.40	7 2	2184.40	16 0	4876.80
12	304.800	3 11	1193.80	7 3	2209.80	17 0	5181.60

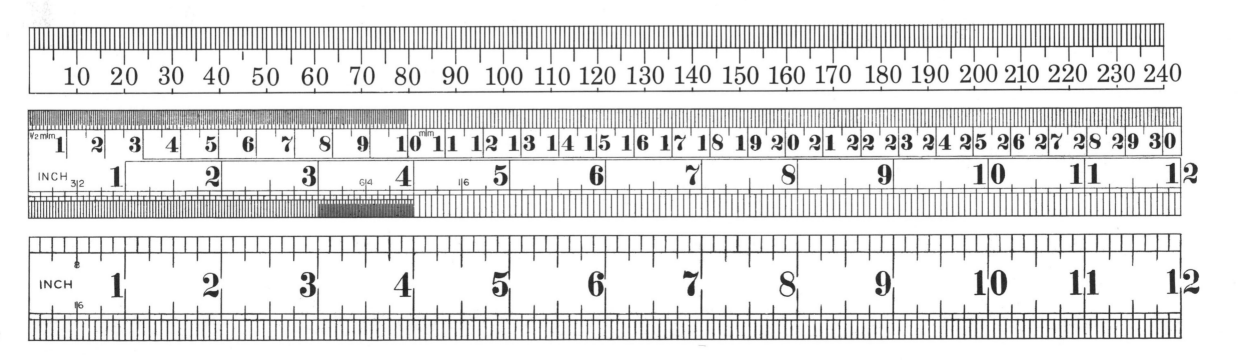

Using the patterns for full scale work

All the clothes from which the patterns were taken for both this book and *Patterns of Fashion c. 1860–1940* were made for ladies of widely differing sizes, whose figures were shaped by the corsets of the period. In the eighteenth century, for example, the shoulders were pulled right back until the shoulder blades touched, giving a narrow back and erect posture; in the 1840s and 1850s the waist was compressed, the shape of the corset allowing the shoulders to droop slightly forwards. It is important to remember how much the line of a costume can be changed by the corset, when looking at flat pattern diagrams and tracing the development of the cutting lines. Skirts were supported by petticoats of the appropriate shape, another point to bear in mind, particularly when enlarging the patterns for use today.

When a reconstruction toile is needed to try out various techniques of cut and construction, the best method is to square the pattern up to full size on a large sheet of paper marked with 1in squares, or 1cm squares if using the metric conversion tables, and cut it out. No seams are allowed; the grain lines are indicated by the grid. It is unnecessary to draw the pattern of the skirt if it is very simple. It may be drawn directly onto the cloth with white chalk. The garment should be cut out in calico, or some other firmly woven cotton, and assembled with small tacking stitches according to the instructions given on the diagram. A dress stand padded to the shape and shape of the corseted figure, with a suitable petticoat, will be needed for fittings. A stand which is smaller than the finished measurements should be used, to allow for the padding to period shape. Non-woven materials like paper cloth are often used for cheapness, quick effect and ease of handling, as they do not fray. However, for a true reflection of the problems to be encountered in cutting, a woven fabric should be used, following the grain lines of the original pattern.

The choice of fabric is most important when reproduction costumes are made for use with children

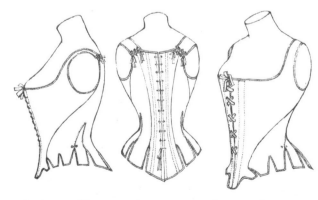

An ivory silk corset of c. 1785–90, showing the narrow back, wide front and erect posture seen during the eighteenth century. Victoria & Albert Museum.

A corset and petticoat, showing the rounded shoulder line, small waist and dome-shaped skirt typical of the late 1840s and early 1850s. An engraving from Corrière delle Dame, 28 January 1851, in the author's collection.

in schools or museum education departments. Too large a design, an inappropriate colour scheme or the wrong weight of fabric will spoil the effect. The material should resemble that of the original dress being copied, in texture, weave and pattern. Silk, fine wool, cotton lawn, poplin, velvet and taffeta are among the fabrics which are particularly suitable. It is sometimes possible to find copies of nineteenth century printed cottons, but the reproductions of eighteenth century designs in furnishing fabric are often too heavy for making costumes and will not hang well. It is usually safer to use a plain material which is closer in texture and weight to the original. In some cases the dress may be intended for a specific project, in others it may simply be an addition to a wardrobe of reproduction clothes being built up by a school or the education service in a museum for general use. Children can understand a great deal more about their predecessors, and the past begins to come alive as they realise the difficulties of managing hooped petticoats when walking upstairs or trying to run. The costume that a child sees in a museum is more interesting after wearing a similar one to discover what movements are possible in it. The ten to twelve year age group is the one where

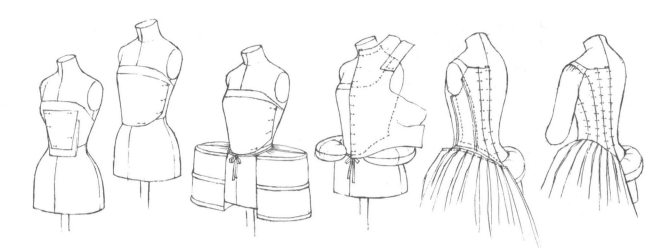

A modern dress stand, slightly smaller than the measurements required, is padded in layers to the corseted shape of the 1770s. Pocket hoops can be made from cotton stiffened with strips of plastic boning or cane. Hip pads filled with lightweight plastic foam are an alternative to pocket hoops. Calico is then draped on the stand to make a toile, in this example following the lines of the gown on pp 40, 41. The cotton is carefully pinned to shape, trimming away the surplus. The seam allowances should be turned in and pinned down on the stand to make sure that the lines are correct. The skirt pleats are pinned into position before attaching the waist to the bodice.

The portrait of Anne Dalrymple Countess of Balcarres painted in 1750 by Allan Ramsay shows a gown similar in line to that on pp 32–4. The main difference between them is the type of fabric used, here a plain silk, while the other has a brocaded design of flowers and leaves in silver thread. The pleats of the sack fall out in a characteristic way from the level of the shoulder blades in the portrait and the wide hoops are shown in a foreshortened view. The erect pose is the result of the corset pulling the shoulders back. Private collection

activities of this kind are most popular and the best way of making a costume is to start by choosing a child of average size and taking these measurements: across chest, across back, bust, waist, length front neck to waist, length back neck to waist, length of waist to ground at front and back, length of arm from shoulder to elbow and elbow to wrist when bent, round top arm and round wrist. Whatever the reason for making the dress, if a really authentic effect is wanted, the following suggestions should be followed. Choose a painting which shows a similar style of dress to the pattern selected. There are many other visual sources, among them drawings, caricatures, miniatures and engravings, where information may be found for use in conjunction with paintings (see J Arnold, *A Handbook of Costume*, pp 11–108). Make sketches to show the appropriate hairstyle, shoes and other accessories. Using the list of selected books on p 76, find a corset and petticoat of the same date. Pad the dress stand to the shape of the corseted figure, continually checking with the child's measurements. Use firmly woven cotton and pin together a toile, working on the stand, following the construction lines seen on the flat pattern diagram. Fit the toile on the child, to make sure that it is correct. Mark all the seams and any darts on both sides with a sharp pencil and put in all the balance marks. The toile can then be unpinned and laid flat. The pencilled outline is the shape of the pattern from which to cut the dress. It is possible, if strict economy has to be practised, to construct the right or left half of the toile only, but this is not so easy to fit on a child. Place all the pieces of the toile on top of a sheet of pattern cutting paper and trace off the pencil lines with a tracing wheel, marking the straight grain. The pattern should be kept in an envelope, with a note of the measurements, as it can be used again. Different

A child wearing a copy of the sack dress shown on pp 34–5, made in silk by Mrs Joan Kendall for the Schools Museum Service at the Art Gallery and Museum, Glasgow.

techniques of dressmaking were used in the past; the sleeves of eighteenth century sack gowns, for example, were stitched into the armholes from the inside of the bodice under the arms, and then laid flat on the shoulder and worked from the outside onto the linen lining. It is advisable to read the history section of this book and to visit the nearest museum with a costume collection (see J Arnold, *A Handbook of Costume*, pp 233–336) to study some surviving examples of dresses made in the appropriate period to gain first hand information. Allow turnings when cutting out the dress, and then assemble it following the directions given on the pattern diagram. Linings and interlinings should be used wherever indicated. Sometimes the toile can be used for this purpose, if it is in a firmly woven cotton, to avoid waste. Although the sewing machine was not in general use until the 1860s, much of the sewing for copies of earlier period costumes can be done by machine, but some parts will still have to be carried out by hand, often working from the outside of the dress, not from the inside as is usual today. A corset and petticoat should be constructed in the same way.

Both amateur and professional people making

period costumes for stage and television will find the patterns in this book useful for working out the quantities of material required, as well as a guide to cutting them. Films, plays and documentary programmes on television are often presented most successfully in historical settings, with costumes reconstructed very closely from contemporary evidence, paying great attention to detail. On the stage much fine detail is lost and the accurate historical representation has to be exaggerated a

Barbara Parkins as Leonie Jerome wearing a costume based on the pattern of a dress in Patterns of Fashion *c. 1860–1940 pp 52–3. The cut was followed fairly closely but the designers used a bolder trimming for the bodice than the original, with rows of braid instead of tucks at the hem and the costume is in moiré silk, while the original was in wool. This is a good example of a design using the lines of an original costume, without copying it slavishly. The costumes for Thames Television's series* Jennie: Lady Randolph Churchill *were designed by Jane Robinson and Jill Silverside.*

little and interpreted to provide extra visual interest. The patterns can be used as a base upon which to work in conjunction with the costume designer's drawings, and freely adapted.

The amateur theatre wardrobe is often short of money and if the wardrobe staff are only familiar with flat patterns, without experience of draping on the stand, they may lack the confidence to experiment with toiles. They may have no time to go to classes for help and are worried about wasting material. In this case select the costume which approximates most closely to the designer's ideas and square the pattern up to full size on a large sheet of paper. Cut out the pieces of pattern. No seams are allowed. Take the measurements of the person who will wear the costume – bust, waist, hips, length of front and back neck to waist, etc, and note the difference between these measurements and those of the pattern. Divide the increase or decrease of the width evenly between the side seams, altering the size and position of the darts where necessary and redraw the pattern. Reshape the armholes and adjust the length of the bodice. Make appropriate alterations on the sleeve to fit the new armhole shape. Cut a toile in calico for the bodice from this pattern, and fit it before cutting out the dress material. This can then be used for the lining. Alter the skirt by adjusting the length and rearranging the pleats to fit the waist when it is cut in straight widths and adding or taking out a little on the seams if it is shaped. Most people making theatrical costumes find it easier to work entirely by draping on the stand rather than from the flat pattern but either method requires practice. Information on adjusting patterns to fit different figures is given in many commercial pattern sewing books.

It is most important to keep the correct proportions and retain the position of the waist in relation to the skirt, whether high or low. The lining and the fabric may be machine basted together before

assembling all the pieces. If there is insufficient time to make corsets to shape the figure, and there are none available from stock, bones can be inserted into casings attached to the calico lining before making up the bodice, as well as placing them in casings on the seams afterwards. In professional theatre and television wardrobes stocks of corsets and petticoats are built up with each new production, and are then available for use over and over again. The amateur is advised to follow this example, where possible.

Notes on the Patterns taken from Dresses in Museums.

1. The scale of all the patterns is $\frac{1}{8}''=1''$.
2. The straight grain runs parallel to the selvedge and is indicated by the squared lines on the paper.
3. Balance marks match one section of the dress to another when put together.
4. Cartridge or organ pleating is an old method of taking in fullness (see diagrams).

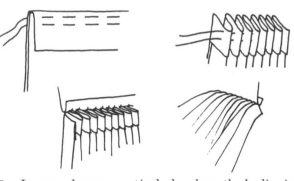

5. In some dresses, particularly where the bodice is cut on the cross, one side of a dart may be longer than the other. This fullness must be eased in gently to the short side until it is smooth. This point also applies to elbows and shoulderheads on sleeves.

NO SEAMS ARE ALLOWED. LEAVE ADEQUATE TURNINGS.

A bodice graded down to size 36″ bust and 25″ waist. It has been lengthened by $\frac{1}{4}$″ at the front and $\frac{1}{4}$″ at the back. The neckline has been raised. The dart would need to be adjusted when fitting the calico lining.

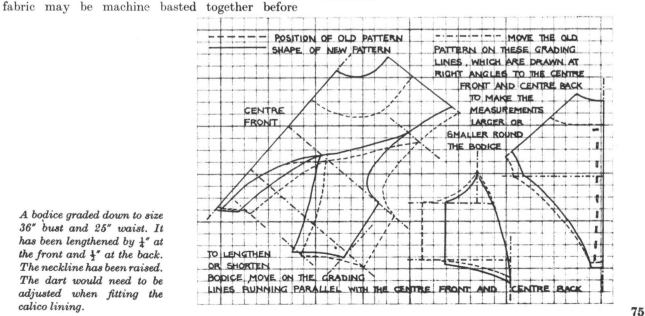

List of Selected Books

Many new books on costume have appeared since *Patterns of Fashion* was first printed in 1964. This new edition gives the opportunity of revising the list of selected books, which were chosen primarily to provide a background to the women's dresses of c. 1660–1860 described in these pages. Among the illustrations are paintings, fashion plates and photographs which show hairstyles, hats and other accessories. Information on underwear to give the correct period shape may also be found in these books. A number of technical works are now available and have been included here, together with a few books on men's costume to help those costuming plays.

ADBURGHAM, A. *A Punch history of manners and modes, 1841–1940.* Hutchinson, 1961. Illustrated with cartoons from *Punch* magazine.

ADBURGHAM, A. *Shops and shopping, 1800–1914.* George Allen & Unwin, 1964. Illustrated with 16 monochrome plates and 100 line engravings in the text, all taken from original sources.

ARNOLD, J. *A Handbook of Costume.* Macmillan, 1973. Over 240 monochrome plates. A guide to the primary sources for costume study. Brief descriptions of over 80 collections of costume in England, Scotland and Wales.

BENTIVEGNA, F. C. *Abbigliamento e costume nella pittura Italiana.* Carlo Bestetti, Edizione d'Arte, Via della Croce 77, Rome. Vol 2. *Baroco e Impero.* 1964. Covers the seventeenth and eighteenth centuries. Many monochrome and a few colour plates of Italian paintings showing costume details.

BOEHN, M. VON. *Modes and manners.* Translated by J. Joshua. Harrap, 1932–5. Numerous monochrome and a few colour plates. Vol 3 *The seventeenth century.* Vol 4 *The eighteenth century.*

BOEHN, M. VON AND FISCHEL, O. *Modes and manners of the nineteenth century.* Translated by M. Edwardes. Revised edition. Dent, 1927. Numerous monochrome and a few colour plates. Vol 1 1790–1817. Vol 2 1818–42. Vol 3 1843–78.

BOUCHER, F. *A History of Costume in the West.* Thames & Hudson, 1967. 817 monochrome and 335 colour plates. A comprehensive history of costume from prehistoric times to the world of fashion in 1964.

BRAUN-RONSDORF, M. *The Wheel of Fashion: costume since the French Revolution, 1789–1929.* Translated by O. Coburn. Thames & Hudson, 1964. 415 monochrome and 28 colour plates.

BUCK, A. *Victorian Costume and Costume Accessories.* Herbert Jenkins, 1961. 51 monochrome plates of portraits and specimens from museums. 29 line illustrations from contemporary sources.

COSTUME SOCIETY. *Costume.* The Journal of the Costume Society. Published by the Society

(1965–   ). Useful illustrated articles on various aspects of costume, bibliographies, etc.

CUNNINGTON, C. W. *English Women's Clothing in the Nineteenth Century.* Faber, 1937. 80 pages of monochrome and 6 colour plates with line drawings in the text. Descriptions of costume from contemporary sources year by year.

CUNNINGTON, C. W. and CUNNINGTON, P. *The History of Underclothes.* Michael Joseph, 1951. Monochrome plates of photographs of actual garments and some line drawings in the text.

CUNNINGTON, C. W. and CUNNINGTON, P. *Handbook of English Costume in the Seventeenth Century.* Faber, 1955. Line drawings.

CUNNINGTON, C. W. and CUNNINGTON, P. *Handbook of English Costume in the Eighteenth Century.* Faber, 1957. Line drawings.

CUNNINGTON, C. W. and CUNNINGTON, P. *A Picture History of English Costume.* Vista Books, 1960. Many monochrome plates.

DAVENPORT, M. *The Book of Costume.* Crown Publishers, New York, 1948. 3,000 monochrome plates. A comprehensive history of costume through the ages to 1860 covering dress, jewellery, ornament, coiffure and all other elements.

GERNSHEIM, A. *Fashion and Reality 1840–1914.* Faber, 1963. 235 monochrome plates from photographs of the period.

GIBBS-SMITH, C. H. *The Fashionable Lady in the Nineteenth Century.* HMSO 1960. Presents a group of fashion plates for each fifth year from 1800 to 1900.

HALLS, Z. *Women's Costumes 1600–1750.* HMSO, 1969. A catalogue of the costume collection at the Museum of London with 21 monochrome plates and 2 folding patterns of mantuas.

HOLLAND, V. *Hand-coloured Fashion Plates, 1770–1899.* Batsford, 1955. 129 monochrome and 5 colour plates of fashion plates. Contains lists of French, English and German periodicals.

HOPE, T. and MOSES, H. *Designs for Modern Costume engraved for Thomas Hope of Deepdene by Henry Moses 1812.* Introduction by J. L. Nevinson. Costume Society: Extra series No 4, 1973. 20 facsimile line engravings of Thomas Hope's neoclassical designs for ladies' dresses.

KELLY, F. M. and SCHWABE, R. *A Short History of Costume and Armour chiefly in England, 1066–1800.* Batsford, 1931, reprinted David & Charles, 1972. Monochrome and colour plates with many line drawings.

KELLY, F. M. and SCHWABE, R. *Historic costume: a chronicle of fashion in Western Europe, 1490–1790.* Batsford, 1925. Monochrome and colour plates, with many line drawings and some patterns.

KYBALOVA, L., HERBEYOVA, O., LAMAROVA, M. *Pictorial Encyclopedia of Fashion,* translated by C. Rosoux. Hamlyn, 1968. Numerous useful monochrome and colour plates, unfortunately undated in many cases.

LELOIR, M. *Histoire du Costume de l'Antiquité à*

1914. Ernst. Vol IX 1643–1678, 1934. Vol X 1678–1715, 1715–1725, 1935. Vol XI 1725–1774, 1938. Vol XII 1775–1795, 1949. Numerous plates from contemporary sources, with many drawings and diagrams of cut by the author.

LENS, B. *The Exact Dress of the Head, 1725–6.* Introduction by J. L. Nevinson. Costume Society: Extra series No 2. 1970. 30 monochrome plates reproduced from a book of drawings in the Victoria and Albert Museum.

LEVI-PISETZKY, R. *Storia del Costume in Italia.* Instituto Editoriale Italiano. Vol 3. Il Cinquecento. Il Seicento. 1966. Covers from c. 1500–1690. Vol 4. Il Settecento. 1967. Covers from c. 1720–1800. Vol 5. L'Ottocento. 1969. Covers from c. 1800–1900. Each volume contains a large number of monochrome and colour plates.

MANCHESTER CITY ART GALLERIES. *Women's Costume in the 18th Century,* 1954. *Women's Costume, 1800–35,* 1952. *Women's Costume, 1835–70,* 1951. 20 pages of monochrome plates of items in the collection in each booklet.

MOORE, D. L. *The Woman in Fashion.* Batsford, 1949. 108 plates of photographs of costume c. 1800–1927, from the author's own collection, many now at the Museum of Costume, Bath.

MOORE, D. L. *Fashion through Fashion Plates 1770–1970.* Ward, Lock, 1971. 53 pages of monochrome and 64 of colour plates.

SQUIRE, G. *Dress, Art and Society 1560–1970.* Studio Vista, 1974. Numerous monochrome and some colour plates. Dress related to concurrent stylistic developments in the major visual arts.

VICTORIA AND ALBERT MUSEUM. *Costume illustration: the nineteenth century.* Introduction by J. Laver. HMSO, 1947. Monochrome plates of items in the Department of Prints and Drawings.

VICTORIA AND ALBERT MUSEUM. *Costume illustration: seventeenth and eighteenth century.* Introduction by J. Laver. HMSO, 1951. Monochrome plates of items in the Department of Prints and Drawings.

Technical Works: pattern cutting, dressmaking and tailoring.

ARNOLD, J. *Patterns of fashion, Englishwomen's dresses and their construction c. 1860–1940.* Wace, 1965. Macmillan, 1972. Drawings of dresses showing their construction with 40 detailed patterns. 116 patterns from contemporary sources.

ARNOLD, J. Articles with patterns in *Costume,* the Journal of the Costume Society. 'A wedding dress worn by the Danish Princess Sophia Magdalena in 1766, from the Livrustkammaren, Stockholm.' No 1, 1967. 'A pink silk domino c. 1760–70 from the Victoria and Albert Museum.' No 3, 1969. 'A mantua c. 1708–9 from the Clive House Museum, Shrewsbury.' No 4, 1970. 'A study of three jerkins, c. 1600–25.' No 5, 1971. 'A silver embroidered

court mantua and petticoat of c. 1740 from the Welsh Folk Museum, Cardiff.' No 6, 1972. 'A court mantua of c. 1760–5 from the Metropolitan Museum, New York.' No 7, 1973. 'Decorative Features: pinking, snipping and slashing c. 1600.' No 9, 1975.

ARNOLD, J. 'Sir Richard Cotton's suit', in *The Burlington Magazine,* May, 1973. Article with a pattern of a suit of 1618 in the Victoria and Albert Museum.

ARNOLD, J. 'Three examples of late sixteenth and early seventeenth century neckwear' in *Waffen-und-Kostümkunde* Vol 15, 1973, pp 109–124. Article with patterns.

BURNHAM, D. K. *Cut my Cote.* Royal Ontario Museum, Toronto, 1973. Monochrome plates and diagrams showing the cut of basic T-shaped garments.

CAULFEILD, S. F. A. and SAWARD, B. C. *The Dictionary of Needlework. An encyclopaedia of artistic, plain and fancy needlework.* Hamlyn, 1972. Facsimile of the 1882 edition with over 800 engravings.

DIDEROT, D. *A Diderot pictorial encyclopaedia of trades and industry; manufacturing and the technical arts in plates selected from 'L'Encyclopédie, ou Dictionnaire Raisonné des Sciences, des Arts et des Métiers' of Denis Diderot,* [1751–65]. 2 vols. Edited by C. C. Gillespie. Dover, New York, 1959. The engravings show various aspects of fashion and the manufacturing processes involved.

EKSTRAND, G. *Karl X Gustavus Adolphus Dräkter.* Livrustkammaren Stockholm, 1959. 52 monochrome plates with 4 pages of patterns. Costumes of King Gustavus Adolphus of Sweden (1622–60). English summary.

LADY, A. *The Workwoman's Guide,* Bloomfield Books, 1975. A reprint of the second edition, 1840. Diagrams for cutting out simple garments, with dressmaking instructions.

PETRASCHECK-HEIM, I. *Figurinen nach alten Schnittbüchern,* Stadtmuseum, Linz, 1968. Catalogue of an exhibition showing tailor's patterns for men and women, c. 1500–1724.

PETRASCHECK-HEIM, I. *Die Meisterstückbücher des Schneider-handewerks in Innsbruck.* Sonderdruck ans Veröffentleichungen des Museum Ferdinandeum, Innsbruck, 1970. Text in German. An account of the master tailors of Innsbruck and their pattern books from the sixteenth to the eighteenth century, with reproductions of many of the cutting diagrams.

WAUGH, N. *Corsets and Crinolines.* Batsford, 1954. Reprinted 1972. 115 plates and 24 patterns of garments from museums and private collections.

WAUGH, N. *The Cut of Men's Clothes, 1600–1900.* Faber, 1964. 29 pages of plates, 42 cutting diagrams and 27 tailor's patterns.

WAUGH, N. *The Cut of Women's Clothes, 1600–1930.* Faber & Faber, 1968. 71 pages of plates, 75 cutting diagrams and 54 tailor's patterns.